CHARLEY GOES TO WAR

CHARLEY GOES TO WAR

A Memoir by Glen Hancock

GASPEREAU PRESS PRINTERS & PUBLISHERS 2004

To my daughters Joanne & Beau

Contents

A List of Figures

A List of Air Force Ranks

Wartime air force ranks (the navy and the army had corresponding ranks with different names) in ascending order of importance:

AC2	Aircraftman Second Class
AC1	Aircraftman First Class
LAC	Leading Aircraftman
CPL.	Corporal
SGT.	Sergeant
FLIGHT SGT. or STAFF	Flight Sergeant
WO2	Warrant Officer Second Class*
WO1	Warrant Officer First Class†
P/O	Pilot Officer
F/O	Flying Officer
F/L	Flight Lieutenant
S/L	Squadron Leader‡
W/C or WINCO	Wing Commander
G/C or GROUPIE	Group Captain
A/C	Air Commodore
AVM	Air Vice-Marshal
A/M	Air Marshal
SP	Service Police
CO	Commanding Officer

* Sometimes called "Major."
† The highest non-commissioned rank, sometimes thought to be the best rank in the air force.
‡ First of the senior ranks.

A List of Medals Awarded to Airmen

VC   Victoria Cross
GC   George Cross
DSO   Distinguished Service Order
DFC   Distinguished Flying Cross
AFC   Air Force Cross

*The DFC equivalent for non-coms was DFM,
the AFC equivalent for non-coms was AFM*

Introduction

This may well be one of the last books about the Royal Canadian Air Force in World War II written by someone who was there. It is not for those seeking new interpretations of air warfare tactics and strategies, that already having been written to death by air marshals, statesmen and professional chroniclers, who were privy to what was going on when it was happening, or who had access to classified documents not available to airmen who received reports of progress of the war only on a need-to-know basis – and there was hardly ever a need to know. Nor is it intended to bring new information to the classic stories of the air force at war as written by authors such as Derek Wood and Derek Dempster (*Battle of Britain*), Paul Brickhill (*The Dam Busters*), Max Hastings (*Bomber Command*), and Spencer Dunmore (*Bomb Run* and *Wings for Victory*).

This is only a story.

I have little hope there is anything in these recollections to steer people from organized conflict, that apparently being a normal condition of the modern world. None of the thousands of books describing the horror of war that have been written since the American Civil War – Stephen Crane's *Red Badge of Courage*, written by a man who at the time had never heard a shot fired; Erich Remarque's *All Quiet On the Western Front*; MacKinley Kantor's *Andersonville*; or the many books about the gruesomeness of Vietnam – none of these has reduced the likeliness of war in our time. I have little hope that the old war veterans marching with the Legion on Remembrance Day will do much to eliminate weapons of mass destruction. War begins in the minds of men, and it should end there. But that's not the way it works.

This book has no exalted purpose. It is simply the development of a manuscript I began 60 years ago, which now begs to be completed, even though my recollections have been filtered through three generations of social change and moral degeneration. The purpose of this book is to compress the life of a man into the experiences of six years during which the development of his character took place and his preparation for the future began.

I saw some things in those long-ago years in a way that no one else did, and some things that happened to me I venture to say happened to no one else. In fact, it is sometimes hard for me to believe that I was actually there, to participate in thousand-bomber raids, to observe the Holocaust. Did all those things really happen? Or were they a dream?

It is a strange phenomenon that veterans do not talk about the war to their children. This is unfortunate as it leaves a void in the understanding young people have of war in general and of World War II in particular. When veterans do talk about their experiences they downplay the grim side and venerate the good times, the romance, the drama, the personal landscape of men at war. And that personal landscape is an important part of the war experience, because the camaraderie of people serving together in conditions of trust strengthens their sense of dependence on and their responsibility to each other.

One of the most disquieting things about men in battle is that they cannot always identify with the reasons they are there. When I was a youth, the South African War and the Great War still reverberated in our imaginations, and they connected with our sense of empire. We missed the political significance of Canadian attitudes toward the Boer conflict – that most Canadians rallied to the cause, whatever it was, because it was the call of the motherland. We were too young and too ill-informed to be otherwise concerned that many Canadians supported the Afrikaners *against* the British. The pall of indifference still exists, and few schoolboys in Canada today can name the countries that fought against the British (and, therefore, us) in the African war, or those who fought with us in World War I. And the reason for that war – the assassination of an Austrian archduke – would hardly seem plausible in a 21st-century classroom. The reasons for World War II surpassed the usual motivations (territory, colonialism, pride, greed), and perhaps for the first time we fought a war for humanitarian reasons. Ironically, the humanitarian factor was buried under many other emotions and political machinations at the outbreak and for some time afterward. In Montreal, for instance, the czars of finance blamed the Jews for the Depression. Anti-Semitism was rife in the United States, and even Jewish refugees who sailed to the Caribbean for shelter were rejected. It is ironic that when the Holocaust was recognized it became a reason for the war to continue.

The Korean War was unconvincing to many of us, a war between those of one political ideal and those of another. And Vietnam, a conflict ostensibly against the threat of Communism to the world, was the most absurd of all the wars we remember, for it had no victory.

In this introduction I would be remiss if I neglected to establish even a superficial background to the conflict which is the subject of this book. The statistics given here are so foreign to the political mentality of the big powers who were contemplating war at the beginning of 2003, in the Middle East, that they deserve exposure, if for no other reason than to establish the enormity of human misery which was the price paid in the two great wars of the last century.

In World War I, Canada had a population of eight million. The Canadian Expeditionary Force lost more than 60,000 uniformed personnel, more than our total casualties in World War II, when our population was about 10 million. (Almost as many died, incidentally, from a widespread influenza epidemic that raged in 1918.) Sometimes obscuring the war itself, at least on the domestic scene, was the conscription issue.

French Canadians in Quebec opposed conscription, and even the war itself. Sir Robert Borden held off imposing conscription until 1918, in spite of the manpower drain at Ypres and Vimy.

In deference to young men outside of Quebec who rallied to the flag, and to encourage young men in Quebec to come forward, Borden introduced such strategies as an "anti-loafing law," and threatened to jail any able-bodied man not gainfully employed.

Again, in 1939, Prime Minister Mackenzie King was reluctant to force Canadians, and particularly the Quebecois, into the battlefields – even after Hong Kong, the Liri Valley, Dieppe and Normandy.

During the war, Canada had a peak enlistment in all forces of 780,000; of these, 43,000 were killed or went missing. Another 19,000 were wounded. By contrast, the United Kingdom, with a population of 48 million, lost 70,000 civilians alone. Germany's population (including Austria) was 79 million, and there were 10 million in the forces. Casualties amounted to four million. The U.S., with a population of 130 million, put more than 16 million men and women into uniform, and suffered a million casualties. Russia, with a population of 193 million, had 20 million in the armed forces and sustained more casualties than all the other countries combined.

The Jews, of course, did not have a country, and their loss to the criminality of the war was six million.

In World War II more lives were lost and more property damage sustained than in any other war in history. And all this without weapons of mass destruction.

This story is about the air force. During World War I, Canadians wishing to fly with the RAF took training at their own expense, but by 1917 the Royal Flying Corps had opened training schools in Canada, and by the end of that war almost a quarter of the pilots in the RAF were Canadians. Much the same situation occurred in the early stages of World War II.

Young Canadians, frustrated by the lack of flying opportunities in Canada, went to England to join the RAF, and many of them excelled in the Battle of Britain and other air operations.

It is to the British Commonwealth Air Training Plan that the air forces under British command owe their success. It became clear early in the war that both aircraft and crews to fly them had to be produced in quantity, and quickly. While in 1938 the Canadian government was allowing Canadians to enter the RAF at the rate of 120 a year, there was a plan in the offing to train Commonwealth pilots and other aircrew in Canada. While Mackenzie King was doing some fancy jockeying around the sensitive – in Quebec, that is – matter of jurisdiction in any scheme to train Commonwealth flyers in Canada, eight private flying clubs were commissioned to train pilots for both the RAF and the RCAF. Bush pilots were trained as instructors. In October 1939, the Air Training Plan had progressed to a point where a budget of $600 million was presented to the members (Britain, Australia, New Zealand and Canada), to last until March 1943, when it was expected the war would be over. Of course, in the end it would cost a great deal more than that, and the war would continue for two more years beyond 1943.

The result of all this was that 97 flying schools to train aircrew were eventually established across Canada. Twenty-four of them, like Greenwood, Nova Scotia, were operated by the RAF. In all, they produced 131,553 aircrew personnel, among them some Poles, French and Norwegians, and a few from British colonies in Central and South America. In the course of their training, more than 900 died in flying accidents.

From this essential flow of airforce manpower came 48 Royal Canadian Air Force squadrons for Overseas service. Seven RCAF squadrons served on the RAF's Coastal Command, operating over the North Atlantic. Canada further enhanced its contribution to the war effort by establishing 14 independent Canadian squadrons to operate under the aegis of No. 6 Group, Bomber Command.

As many as 232,632 men and 17,030 women served in the RCAF, and 17,101 lost their lives.

While Canada did have a kind of conscription early in WWII – young men were called up for service at home – it is important to remember that all those who served in the air force, flying Spitfires and Hurricanes, Lancasters and Liberators, Wellingtons and Halifaxes, volunteered to do so. We took a great deal of pride in this.

I suppose that everyone sometimes contemplates what would have happened to my generation had there not been a war. Would we ever have gotten out of the Depression? Would so many of those returned men and women have gone to university to learn what they would never have dreamed of before – to fly to the moon, to find cures for polio and to transplant human organs? My guess is that we would have achieved all these remarkable things because man is naturally curious about the unknown. But it would have taken much longer than it did.

This book is written not to pad the plot of a much-told story, but to describe how one man lived and grew in an environment of conflict that will never again be experienced by anyone. It is candid enough to describe the ego that often eclipsed his good sense.

CHAPTER 1

For King & Country

It was a delightful morning in Nova Scotia's Annapolis Valley on the day of 4 September 1939. There was a buzz of excitement in the air around the Palms, the hangout for students, as groups gathered in my little town of Wolfville to discuss what had happened the day before. Great Britain had declared war on Germany. We had all known that war clouds had been gathering in Europe, and in spite of Neville Chamberlain's bogus peace pact with Adolph Hitler, the feeling was that sooner or later there would be war. But Poland was a long way off, and it was hard for veterans who had returned from the Great War just 20 years before to believe that anything would come of it.

In the local cinema, Pathe News had kept us informed as Spain became embroiled in a revolution in 1936, and as the Italians invaded Ethiopia, and we had followed remotely the Russian invasion of Finland. But these war games were being played in places most people in the Valley had never heard of before.

My crowd of late-teenagers, who would form the backbone of defence when the war finally got underway, didn't know how to react. For a time, at least, we enjoyed the illusion that these events had little to do with us.

Ireland had informed the big powers that if war came it would remain neutral. Belgium was quick to follow. On September 2, Britain had begun to deploy bombers in France, and the day after Britain's declaration of war, the Royal Air Force, flexing its muscles to express determination, launched an attack on Germany's naval bases at Wilhelmshaven and Brunsbuttel. It was the first offensive in the war by the RAF. Twenty-nine Wellington and Blenheim bombers were sent on the mission; 10 of them were unable to find their targets because of the weather. They returned to their home bases without dropping their bombs. One plane bombed a town in Denmark, which at the time was neutral and 110 miles off the intended targets. Three other aircraft went after a ship in the North Sea until they discovered it was a British man-of-war, and they went home in embarrassment. Seven of the 29 aircraft were shot down by German anti-aircraft artillery.

It was a disastrous way to enter a war that would last for six more years, and understandably not much was said about it until records were made public after the war.

On the same day that Britain officially met Germany's threat, other outposts of the far-flung British Empire, which still flaunted the imperial red on the map of the world, declared war – India, New Zealand and Australia. Canada held back for a week, time enough to establish its independence and allow Prime Minister Mackenzie King to play a political game with Quebec, which had no desire to support England in any way – a traditional hostility left over from the Plains of Abraham.

King had met Hitler in 1937 and was impressed with the extent to which he had strengthened Germany's economy. Lord Beaverbrook, who didn't believe there would be a war, Henry Ford, aviator Charles Lindbergh, and even the Duke of Windsor were said to admire the German dictator.

At once, Winston Churchill, who had been out of politics for some time, was appointed First Lord of the Admiralty. This cryptic message was sent out to all British ships: "Winston is back." Thus began a career that would make Churchill the "man of the century." An evacuation to the country of people from large English cities began on the second day of the war, and the RAF dropped six million propaganda leaflets over northern Germany on the mistaken impression that the German people would censure the Führer. Britain was to drop leaflets of one kind or another many times throughout the six years that followed.

On September 1 – two days before the war officially began – the British passenger liner Athenia was torpedoed and sunk off

GLEN HANCOCK · CHARLEY GOES TO WAR

the coast of Scotland on its way to Canada; two days later the German submarine U-39 was sunk by Royal Navy destroyers. On September 5, the first air-raid warning of the war was sounded and RAF fighters took to the skies to intercept the enemy, only to discover that the warning was false. There were no enemy bombers. Nevertheless, two RAF Spitfires shot down two RAF Hurricanes.

It would be learned soon enough that Britain was ill-prepared for war.

Meanwhile, the United States had anticipated Germany's power grab and had permitted an accelerated delivery of war materials across the Canadian border, which had to be officially stopped when Canada entered the war.

As September dragged on it became apparent that Germany fully intended to dominate Europe, and particularly Britain. Some of the Valley boys, inspired not so much by all these momentous happenings as by traditional allegiance to the mother country (they had been weaned, you see, on the *Boy's Own Paper* and the heroics of Lawrence of Arabia), started to drift off to the recruiting offices. The trickle soon grew to be a flood of grocery clerks, automobile mechanics, students, bank clerks and farm workers, not wanting to be the last to go, and not unwilling to trade their static Depression jobs for a uniform and $40 a month. The majority of these men enlisted in the army, but most of them would have been called up for home service in any event. These were fellows who were lured by excitement and adventure; they wanted to be where the action was. They went off for training at places like Camp Borden and Petawawa in Ontario, and Aldershot, of course, which was located near the Kings County shire town of Kentville. Early in 1940 they left for Overseas, not just for a "tour of duty," but for the duration.

Some of the townspeople could still remember the spectacular reception given to William Regan when he returned from the South African War. Others could recall Private George Prince from Port Williams, just three miles from Wolfville, who was the last Canadian soldier to be killed in the Great

War. A monument marking the historic Battle of Grand Pré in 1747 stood three miles to the east of Wolfville. In Canning, the home of Sir Frederick Borden, former Minister of the Canadian Militia, there was a monument to his son Harold, who had been killed in the South African War. A few miles to the east at Hantsport was the grave of Petty Officer William Hall of the Royal Navy, who was the first black man to be awarded the Victoria Cross, for valour in the Sepoy Rebellion in 1857. So there was a kind of aura of gallantry and glory that pervaded the community.

Nova Scotians have a close relationship with aviation. Alexander Graham Bell lived and worked at Baddeck, not only on aids for the deaf and on telephones, but on the flying machine. Early experiments there led to J. A. D. McCurdy's making the first air flight in the British Empire at Baddeck. A junior colleague of Bell's at Baddeck, Lieut. Thomas Selfridge of the US Signal Corps, had the doubtful distinction of being the world's first airplane casualty, when a small aircraft piloted by Orville Wright crashed at Fort Myers, Virginia, in 1908.

Closer to home, Wolfville residents Karl Cleveland and Ron Kierstead had served in the Royal Flying Corps in the Great War, Kierstead having won the Distinguished Flying Cross. And Stuart Graham, a former resident of Wolfville, but now an inspector of civil aviation in Ottawa, was a bush pilot, as well as the first professional peacetime pilot in Canada, and would later be inducted into the Canadian Aviation Hall of Fame. He often made tricky landings on the tidal waters of Wolfville Harbour.

People in Wolfville had watched in awe as the British airship R-100 floated over Cape Blomidon on its successful trip in 1930, and when the German Zeppelin *Hindenburg* was seen in Halifax on its fateful flight to the United States in 1937 people were suspicious that it was taking pictures of our coastline.

When we were kids we would race over the dykeland following a low-flying biplane we hoped would land. When it did, we would go up for a couple of circuits for the price of $4.00.

All this helped urge many of us towards the air force.

In the summer of 1939, when there had been few intimations of what was happening on the world scene, I was working as a correspondent for the *Halifax Chronicle* and had covered the New York World's Fair. I returned to university in the fall. By then, many of us were struggling with the idea of suspending our studies until the war was over. (In a newspaper article I advised against it.) A few had already gone to England to sign up with the Royal Air Force. The Battle of Britain was in progress by the summer of 1940, however, and Britain was surely in need of aircraft and pilots to fly them.

I wasn't all that interested in flying as such, but the time had come to bite the bullet.

A news story had appeared in the Halifax paper announcing that the RAF was looking for 5,100 pilots. By this time Sam Kenny, Orlay Bligh and some other fellows I knew had been killed while serving in the air force. It wasn't that I had any noble feelings of replacing them, but I went to Halifax to Military District No. 6 where the RAF was recruiting, or rather, where the military was recruiting for them. I was not yet 21, and I had to have written permission from my father, which he gave more willingly than I had expected.

My documents took a while getting through the system. One of the requirements was a birth certificate. I had never had cause to get one before that time, and when I applied to the Registry of Births in Halifax for that vital piece of paper, I was told that I didn't exist. Nobody by the name of Glen Nelson Hancock was listed. After much ado in the records department it was finally discovered that there was a "Charley Nelson Hancock" registered, whose birthdate coincided with mine. It so happened that my mother had sent my grandmother to register my birth as "Glen Nelson Hancock." The old lady, being a Victorian traditionalist, believed that the new baby should bear one of the Hancock male names – Sidney, Thomas, John or Charley. Taking matters into her own hands, she arbitrarily decided my name should be Charley Nelson Hancock (not Charles or Charlie, but Charley). So my real name was Charley, though my passport noted that I was "also known as Glen." I have to explain this, if only to account for the title *Charley Goes*

to *War*. But it didn't really matter, as the moment I joined the
air force my name became "Hank," and I was never known by
any other.

With my papers in order, I waited. RCAF qualifications were
a bit more stringent than those for the other services, and that
gave air force recruits a feeling of exclusiveness, if not elitism,
that appealed to those who favoured the air force blue uniform. But as I had been making these preparations the RCAF
had expanded its recruiting programme. My application was
transferred to them, where it stalled.

All through the summer of 1940 I was on tenterhooks, waiting to be called up. I was filing a lot of copy for the Montreal
Standard and appreciated the income. More importantly, I had
fallen in love with a local girl.

In spite of the war, the morale of everyone I knew was high.
Things like sugar and butter were rationed. Silk stockings
were out and nylons were not yet in, so the girls painted their
legs. Sometimes they drew lines to imitate seams, and some
even fabricated runs.

Life wasn't all that dull in the Valley. There were lots of
dances to go to, teeming with girls released from boyfriends
who had already gone Overseas, and with soldiers who were
training at Aldershot. Admission to the dances was 35 cents.
Cigarettes were a cent apiece, and a glass of beer – if you could
get it – was 10 cents. War was fun.

Nothing seemed to change during the Depression. If you
could earn a dollar a day it wasn't going to take you anywhere.
Unless you were a professional, like a doctor or a lawyer, a
minister or a teacher, you couldn't expect a very high standard of living. Even an inexperienced young teacher couldn't
expect more than $600 a year. And those who were waiting to
be called up couldn't take jobs anyway. I was becoming embarrassed by the round of farewell parties my friends were giving
me, and it was a relief when I received from the post office an
OHMS envelope that changed my life.

CHAPTER 2

Posted to Manning Depot in Brandon, Manitoba

H alifax in September 1940 was a curious amalgam of war-time activities. The streets were thronged with uniforms, mostly naval. The Old Town Clock, snuggled under the Cita-del, looked down on the Commons, to which the citizens had fled when the disastrous explosion occurred in 1917. A carni-val was now in full swing there, despite the fog and drizzle that accentuated the drabness of the slums in the Fortress City that day. Smells of hot dogs and mustard, spun candy and popcorn clogged the nostrils.

I made my way from the train station to the recruiting centre on Barrington Street and took a seat on a bench occu-pied by several other young men who had been called in as I had. Behind a cluttered desk sat a clerk with leading aircraft-man propellers on his sleeves, and on the wall behind him was a gigantic framed picture of an airman enjoying a sumptuous meal in an airman's mess. To those who had been suffering Depression food this was an added inducement, but I won-dered if they ought to have displayed a portrait of the King instead.

The little group that moved over by one chair every time a name was called was getting used to waiting, as well it should, since waiting was a full-time occupation during RCAF famil-iarization. As I waited I thought of some of my friends who were fighting the Battle of Britain or the battle in the desert. Syd Ford had left college to join up. He would become the youngest wing commander in the RCAF, bemedalled, and beloved by his comrades. Gordon Troke had sat on this same bench only weeks earlier. He would win the Distinguished Flying Cross.

In due course I found myself seated before Flying Officer J. D. Guild, a recruiting officer, who had fought in the Great War, his tunic splashed with ribbons. My documents being in order, I was thrust through another doorway, into the inner sanctum, to greet the senior officer, Flight Lieutenant Harcourt-Vernon, also a veteran flyer of the RAF, who supervised my pledge to "Serve anywhere His Majesty saw fit to send me."

Thirteen men were sworn in that day, and we all thought we were going to be pilots. But that depended on a number of things beyond our control, including the need at the moment for any particular aircrew trade, or the availability of a training facility. It is impossible to choose a good pilot from physical appearance or educational qualifications. The key is "flying sense." You either have it, or you don't. And if you don't you are benched later, at flying school.

As we left the Halifax CPR station for the four-day trip to Manning Depot (we did not use the American term "boot camp") in Brandon, Manitoba, we had a chance to size each other up. We were all young, unsophisticated, leaving home for the first time and thrilled with expectation. We began to feel the camaraderie that would be a lasting feature of our air force service. There was six-foot-three MacLennan of New York, one of the many Americans who were impatient with US neutrality and had crossed the border into Canada. There was Charlie Dickie of Canning, Eric Hockey of Kentville, Jack Hiltz of Berwick, "Moon" O'Connell and Ron Christie of Halifax, "Buck" Mason, Dick Tapp, and "Frenchie," who joined us somewhere in Quebec. And there was Charlie Cohen of Wolfville, who had joined the merchant marine early in the war; his ship, the SS *Magee*, had been sunk by a U-boat off the coast of France. After we split in Brandon, I would only see Cohen and Hockey again.

As we click-clack-clicked along, out of Nova Scotia into New Brunswick, through the seemingly endless woodlands of Quebec, we reflected on the previous three weeks, the time spent standing stark naked while doctors stared at our finer points, asked us questions about measles and chicken pox, asthma, tonsillitis and venereal disease, and subjected us to the mercury test for lung pressure strength. And, of course, we thought of our girlfriends, wondering if we would ever see them again.

"Come on, seven!"

That and the shuffling of cards was the theme of our journey to the great Canadian west. It was a pleasure travelling by train in those days – excellent meals served by snappy waiters who hadn't lost their peacetime politeness. And a berth for everyone. But it was a luxury that wouldn't last forever.

Quebec was picturesque, with lines of snake fences, and grand churches towering above the hardy French women working in the warm autumn fields. Past the historic cities of Ontario. Honeybees and clover, peaches and apples, grapes and garden crops, wheat. Fish in every stream. On the prairies it was harvest time as well, the yellow fields passing our windows endlessly. The good earth, flat and vast, a panorama broken only by grain elevators on the horizon.

All we wanted to know was when we would start flying. But when the train reached Brandon there were no planes. Manning Depot was the hockey arena where the Brandon Winter Fair was held, now sanitarily whitewashed and capable of providing accommodations for 2,000 men. A man with two stripes – a corporal – was assigned to us, as father-confessor and friend. A group of airmen at the entrance to the depot shouted to us as we arrived: "Is there anyone from East?" Our innocent response was: "Yes, we're all from the East." Our greeters laughed and said: "To hell with the East!" – but in a week we would feel like veterans, too, and ask the same traditional question.

Manning Depot was on 11th Street. Recruits learned how to march in the arena on the ground floor. Under the bleachers were offices, dental and medical records, accounts, clothing stores and orderly rooms in which our personal files were now ensconced. Our quarters were on the first floor, called "A" Squadron, where we were assigned upper and lower cots. "B" Squadron was on the second floor, which provided more beds as well as a writing and recreations room and a mess hall.

When we marched to get our uniforms it seemed that all 2,000 men were there, and we were at the end of the line. By and by a corporal (not the one who was our father-confessor and friend, whom we never saw again) approached the noble 13 and told us to sit down on the bleachers. This was at 8:00 AM, and at 5:00 PM we were told to come back "tomorrow." Next day we were issued "housewives" (kits to hold buttons, needles and thread, airmen for the use of), suspenders and ties, shirts and underwear and hats, all too big or too small. "You can exchange them later," we were told. We traded. We were issued greatcoats, mitts with trigger fingers, balaclavas and galoshes. The underwear were doozers, with fully enough room in the seat for a bushel of potatoes besides yourself. (For the first six months I wore boots two sizes too small.) At the end of the line everything was dumped in a pile and our regimental numbers were stamped on the garments. My number was R65474.

We were confined to barracks for the first two days, getting inoculations, milling around, wondering what we were supposed to be doing, and being indoctrinated into the cardinal laws of the air force. The laws were called King's Regulations (Air) – KR (Air) for short – and they listed all the things you couldn't do. If by chance you did anything that wasn't listed, there was a clever (or sneaky) little codicil called KR (Air) Section 40, and all such offences fell into that category. Apparently there was a lot of thievery going on, and when watches, cameras and wallets were reported missing the air force establishment took a dim view of it. "We know who you are," the NCO would say, "but we want you to come forward voluntarily." If the guilty person did not come forward – and no one expected he would – everyone was confined to barracks, which I thought was grossly unfair.

In uniform (L to R): Hank, Charlie Dickie, Charlie Cohen, "Moon" O'Connell, Eric Hockey, "Frenchy," Mac MacClelland, Jack Hiltz and Ron Christie

Once, walking through the arena on my way to the recreation area, I stopped to watch an airman doing pack drill for some offence. He was wearing full webbing and carried a rifle. On his back was a pack filled with sand. As I was wondering if he had "come forward" someone bellowed from behind me. It was Sergeant Major Sullivan, the highest ranking NCO. He told me to move on and mind my own business.

In the recreation room, airmen who had nothing to do were writing letters, to girlfriends, wives and other folks at home. I wrote every day, sometimes twice. I was missing my girlfriend, Reta. Although I was left-handed and wrote slowly, I had a good hand. Chaps passing by would stop and look over my shoulder. "What do you write about?" they asked. I thought it an inane question, as there were all kinds of things to write about. But, then, most of them had never been away from home before and had never written a letter. It bothered me to see pens poised over paper in contemplation, minds blank.

With only a little persuasion, I ended up writing letters for anyone who would pay me 10 cents. They all started: "I have just finished another exciting day of flight...."

We did a lot of route marching. And I liked that, despite the pinching boots. It was quiet ("no talking") and it gave me an opportunity to think of home and Reta. Every morning at daybreak we mustered on the street outside the arena. Flight Sergeant Barney Lewis would bark us into line and call us to attention, which sounded like potatoes being dropped into empty barrels. Then Barney would turn us over to Warrant Officer (2nd class) Blundell, who would bellow at us for a few minutes and then hand us back to Barney, who in turn would hand us over to a corporal who would take us on a route march around the city for the rest of the morning.

The first night that we were let out on the town, chins up and shoulders back, we felt proud and thrilled. The streets were full of people, all airmen.

At first sight, there wasn't much to see in Brandon. Rossiter Street was dominated by the MacKenzie seed elevator. You could see restaurants, beer parlours, some cheap hotels and pawn shops. I had never seen a pawn shop before, but it was a practical way to dispose of clothing and other civilian equipment no longer needed. Locals could get a good pair of brown shoes for $2. The pawn shops were starting to display fancy riding boots, 10-gallon hats and tooled leather belts, discarded by the Americans – mostly Texans – who had come up to Canada seeking action.

Since 1880 Brandon had been the second largest city in Manitoba. Around it in every direction were bold prairies, flat as a plate – jackrabbits, gophers – with the Assiniboine River winding placidly through them to join the Red River at Winnipeg. The West was young. History in Manitoba was dominated by the Riel Rebellion and the Selkirk Settlements. There was a government experimental farm, a mental hospital, and a college affiliated with the Baptists. Brandon had been a Hudson's Bay post, and was named after an ancestor of Lord Selkirk.

Now, in 1940, Brandon's biggest industries were the air force and the war. Not everyone in Brandon was imbued with the spirit of national sacrifice, however. I overheard a man in a pub saying to a companion: "If this war goes on for another year, I'll have my house paid for."

After two weeks at Manning Depot we were becoming hard. Intakes arriving a week after we did were the greenest of recruits and we were the toughest of veterans. We had learned that there was a time to be smart and a time to be dumb. And we *never* volunteered. We never complained. Charlie once grumbled about flies in the prunes. The sergeant took his name and number and the next day he found himself in the kitchen swatting flies.

I was in Brandon for four weeks. On the last day of the fourth week there was a rumour that we were being posted. No one knew where. But, then, rumour mongers don't give out facts. Rumours were common in everyday service life, and they were classified into three categories of "gen." "Pukka gen" was unadulterated fact, the truth. "Duff gen" had the possibility of being true, and "cookhouse gen" was sheer nonsense. And there was a lot of that going around.

The gen we were getting was pukka. We were moving.

Unlike the army, where soldiers joined a regiment (usually with their hometown friends) like the Princess Patricia Fusiliers or the West Novies, and the navy, where recruits were posted to a ship, the air force would split up training groups anywhere in the alphabetical nominal roll in order to fill requirements at training schools. All during my air force career the nominal roll was split with me in the middle. I would be sent in one direction, and my buddies would go off somewhere else. After a while I would end up with no one I knew.

It was traditional that new aircrew recruits should spend two or three weeks on "guard duty," which was usually at some isolated facility under construction. They became familiar with a rifle and learned to use it, but probably never would again. After guard duty the airmen were sent to an Initial Training School where candidates were classified into one of the aircrew trades – pilots, navigators (then called observers), wireless-operator/air-gunners (known as "WAGS"), and straight air-gunners, trained only for gunnery. They finished their training at Service Flying Training School, or Astro and Gunnery schools. Ground crews were sent to schools for mechanics, clerical workers and the like.

One hundred and ten men, all dressed in No. 1 Blue, buttons shined, were lined up in threes in the arena, their hands resting by the seams of their trousers, their eyes facing front, and oh, so proud. We were on draft. All through our foot drill and orientation we had responded to the coarse commands of a dozen airmen wearing corporal's stripes (airmen endowed with the acting, unpaid authority and duties of non-com instructors). Today we were under the watchful eye of a flight sergeant we had never seen before. He paraded us around the arena as though we were his prize horses, and station Sergeant Major Sullivan paid him high compliments for having trained us so well. A squadron leader gave us a pep talk, told us to hold the torch high and wished us good luck.

We still didn't know where we were going.

New recruits were coming in to take our place. Among them I saw a Leading Aircraftman, the only one in Brandon, and he had a white flash in his cap, which meant that he had completed Initial Training School. He had failed one trade and was ready to remuster into another. But he envied us now because we had not yet had the chance to fail.

We were lined up in three ranks and numbered off to 35 – Hancock, Hanson, Herrick.... We were set aside and another 35 men (the number of men in a training course) were called off – Holmes, Inman, Lawrence, Morrison, and sent in another direction. I was the only one in my group from Halifax. I had hoped to go east, but the destination of my contingent was Prince Rupert in British Columbia, about as far as I could get from Wolfville. Prince Rupert, we were told, was lost in the northern wilderness. It rained most of the time. Houses were built on wooden piles driven into the cold ground; the inhabitants were mostly Eskimos. The wolves came down from the hills at night to steal food. Lumbago, chills, mental depression and chronic maladies were endemic.

Charlie was in Winnipeg for some sort of Jewish holiday, as was Lew Germain, another son of the Chosen, so they missed the draft. We packed our duffle bags, sold our civvy clothes to a second-hand dealer downtown, and bought money belts, although few of us had any money.

Someone noticed that we were all identified on the manifest as "navigators" instead of pilots. This was disturbing, but we were told, "Forget about it. You'll be reclassified later." I don't know why that made us feel better.

CHAPTER 3

Six Weeks in the Rain
at Prince Rupert

W e left in the night, and by morning we were click-clack-
clicking quietly over the prairies, the scenery unchanging for miles, the land stripped of its waves of oats, barley,
wheat, flax, rye and linseed, with winter coming on. Slowly
we began to realize that we were no longer individuals. We
were a social entity, a composite person, moving by numbers through the routine of the day. I thought of little communities we rolled past, from which had come the men who'd
approached my family's door for food in the early part of the
Depression, when the prairies were devastated by drought.
And I thought of the little places where we had so lately been
sitting on recruiting office benches – Kentville, Clinton, God-
erich, Aylmer, Almonte – and which were now drained of their
youth. I thought of my girlfriend, and missed her, replaying
our music in the privacy of my mind – "Stardust," "Skylark,"
"Only Forever," "My Buddy." Bit by bit the 35 airmen were getting to know each other, as they would with other groups in
other places during the next five years.

We wondered about the war. Norway and France had fallen.
London was under siege by Nazi bombers. In the United
States, 16,400,000 men were registered for the draft. Hitler
had announced 12 October 1941 as the date for his invasion
of Britain, an invasion that he would later postpone while
he tackled the Russians on the Second Front. This eased our
silent concern about being too late for the action.

The conduction officer was Sergeant Gilmore, and he had
us marching on the morning streets of Edmonton while the

train was stopped for victualling. I remember how dull it was, and how cold. There wasn't a building higher than three storeys, and not a soul in sight. It would be years before I would see Edmonton grown into a metropolis of "friendly people." If there had been no war, many of us would never have seen the prairies or the Rockies, the great, majestic Rockies, a mighty barrier of mountain peaks, reflecting on their heights the blue of the sky. Glaciers slipped unnoticed towards the valleys, a splendour told only to the speechless eye. I felt small and insignificant, and for a moment I felt ashamed that we were at war.

The click-clack-clicking continued as we climbed higher and higher, en route to the Pacific coast on the other side of the mountain range. As we reached Prince Rupert, an outgoing train of 35 inquisitive airmen passed us. We were their replacements.

Prince Rupert, halfway up to Alaska from Vancouver, reminded me of a sugar bowl with just a few grains in the bottom and one side broken away. Three miles to the west was Seal Cove, where an air force station was being constructed. On all other sides were mountains. When the sky was clear enough, the entrancing northern lights could be seen. Nestled snugly at the bottom of the bowl that was Prince Rupert were little houses built on piles driven into the swampy earth. Ten thousand people lived here, white and Oriental fishermen, woodsmen, lighthouse keepers, and families of miners. The order for dress for everyone was rubber – rubber boots, rubber hats, rubber coats.

We were the second draft to strike Rupert. Our accommodations at Seal Cove were in a single unfinished hut, the floor and rafters rough and unpainted, but no lights. There was a crude alcove for ablutions, and other accommodations were provided in a damp and sometimes icy eight-holer called the "sanitation hut," used by all the ranks, including officers, who persuaded us it wasn't necessary to stand up and salute when one of them came in.

The mess was half a dozen mudholes from the sleeping hut. It was the only other inhabited structure on the site, except for the guardhouse, and it provided sleeping quarters for the Commanding Officer, Flight Lieutenant Doyle from Halifax, and space for the orderly room and the kitchen, which lacked several essential operative necessities, including a stove and a cook. Actually, it wasn't a mess at all, as nobody ate there. We had our meals in the back room at the Commodore restaurant in Prince Rupert.

Rupert was the terminus of the Canadian National Railway – there was no place else to go. Besides the air base construction, the industries of Rupert included a government dry dock, a fisheries cold-storage plant (where a frozen shark had been on display for such as us for several years), lumber mills and, of course, the "Hump." The Hump was a great curiosity for us country boys. It was the only registered prostitution district in Canada, and was made up of a cluster of neat but small living units which were approached by a boardwalk. The girls were inspected on a regular basis by the Department of Health. Only once a week were the girls allowed in town, and not to pursue their profession. It seemed like a good arrangement. The girls enjoyed the limited freedom, and the community was assured that health standards were maintained.

On the station the busiest spot was Newcombe's, a kind of convenience store, adjacent to the guardhouse, which provided space for the post office. But it was active only about every 12 days, when the mail would come in on the ship, the *Prince George*. There was a jukebox at Newcombe's, and two attractive waitresses, who were the daughters of the proprietor and therefore off limits.

On the shoulder of a nearby hill, near the No. 1 guard post, was a cluster of little shanties, about which romped chubby Japanese children. Strangely quiet, they regarded us with considerable reserve. (Canada had treated its Japanese population poorly up to now, and would continue to do so. In 1942, at the urging of politicians in British Columbia, all Japanese within

160 kilometers of the Pacific coast would be removed on the pretext that Japanese Canadians threatened Canadian security.)

The station covered about a square mile, and this is what we were to guard. We didn't know what we were guarding it from. We were each issued a Ross rifle and bayonet. Mine was No. 722 and I hoped that one day my mention of it would encourage some old vet from the Great War to say: "Me lad, I used that rifle in the Battle of the Marne." The rifles had been packed in grease since 1918. We had to remove the grease. Then we were taken to the range to learn how to use them. This was my first experience with firearms, although when I was eight I had a cap-pistol; even so I was grossly inexperienced and unfit to be trusted with the safety of one of the King's aerodromes.

This was the general routine. Twelve of us went on duty at 8:00 AM and worked for shifts of two hours on and four hours off. Then we would sleep in the guardhouse. In the afternoon we would have the rifle drill and listen to lectures on Lewis and Vickers machine guns, both used in WWI. At 5:00 PM we would go on duty again. This time we would work only through the night and be dismissed at eight in the morning. It wasn't really so bad, except for the rain and the boredom. One morning I awoke from a wonderful dream about Reta to see a seagull the size of an albatross sitting placidly on the foot of my bunk. This was not unusual. Those of us who were in love suffered miserably. We thought of nothing else while we were slogging through the mud. First loves were hard to deal with. Letters came in bunches, and we devoured them famishedly.

We were getting along well as a group and morale was high, but it was a boring existence. We were losing our sense of our individual identity. But we were taking on a new one. It started with the loss of our names.

Essentially, surnames are used in the service, but even they take second place to regimental numbers. Christian names

are usually avoided, particularly if they have effeminate conno-
tations, like Clair, Dale, Marion. (Parents use either too much
or too little imagination when they name their children.) But
in the service the Christian names which come with the numbers are invariably abbreviated: Pete, Wally, Hal. Names are
changed without ceremony, and sometimes you just respond
naturally to a moniker that seems to fit. If your surname
is Anderson they will call you Andy. If it is Perkins you will
answer to Perky. If it is Danberger you will get Dan. Chaps with
given names like William, Andrew and David, whose mothers
had taken care to protect them from diminution, became Bill,
Andy and Dave. MacDonalds, MacLeods, anyone with a Scottish name ended up with "Mac" or "Scotty." If one had a good
old Scandinavian name like Mjolsness he would probably be
called "Joe." Woodman became "Woody." Martin became
"Marty." Brown was changed to "Brownie," and, of course,
Miller, for whatever reason I have never learned, took on the
handle of "Dusty." If the airman was older than 25, or balding,
he responded to Pop, Pappy, or Gramps. Physical attributes
were quickly conceived as "High Pockets," "Lefty," or "Tiny."
Sometimes an unflattering name like "Lard Arse" was handed
out, but, in deference to feelings, it often became just "Lard."
Racial and ethnic identities were usually left intact. There were
no Kikes or Polacks, although there were lots of "Frenchies,"
"Newfies," "Aussies" and "Newsies." My friend Charlie Cohen
picked up his nickname later in Regina, when he was required
to command a flight of airmen (the army called them platoons) to get his sergeant's stripes. He couldn't remember any
of the commands so he left-wheeled them around and around
the parade square, ending up with the indelible handle, "Left-
wheel Kelly."

Most of the Rupert gang were from the east, from Ontar-
io and Quebec. Only three of us were from Nova Scotia –
Irving, Sullivan and myself. Orest Bodner, C. W. A. Coop, W.
J. Downer, Norm Grove, Bruce Shaver, "Kit" Karson, Blackie
Wilson, Bill Hedley and Bill Woodward are names that will live

with me forever. Most of them would make the supreme sacrifice. Jack Elliott would appear on the "Missing, believed dead" list. Chuck Proctor, who snored like an Anson at Rupert, went on to win the DFC in 1943.

Don Sugrue was one of the first to be killed in action, shortly after arriving in England in 1941. Jerry Edwards appeared on my Overseas bomber station one day in 1944 as Base Wing Commander. Phil Ellison, from Regina, completed his second tour of duty with me in England. Brebner, Lucien ("Shadow") Brooks from Powell River, Hughie Langton, Tony Stevens (who would be a prisoner of war for two years), George Tait, a true gentleman of the air force who would become a navigator and win the DFC; all of these were from British Columbia. Bitsy Grant, whose father had been one of the first radio men in the air force in the Great War, was shot down over enemy territory. He was a Squadron Leader. Doug Hargrave, "Siggy" Lee, Barry Needham, Bill Smyth and Dick Tapp all served their country well, and I mention their names because it is their achievements this book commemorates.

Sometimes, on a boring Rupert night, one of us would fire his rifle. (We were given five .303 rounds, but none was supposed to be in the breach.) When this happened the whole camp was alerted, following the book, and the duty officer, Flying Officer Christie, had to hie to the location. He took a poor view of the paperwork involved. "Why did you fire your rifle?" he would ask, knowing he would get an asinine answer like: "I thought I heard something." And the airman may well have heard something, as Japanese fishermen frequented the shoreline. The airman would end up rehearsing the procedure:

"Halt. Who goes there? Friend or foe?"

"Friend."

"Advance and be recognized."

"Pass, friend."

The following morning everyone would be talking excitedly. It was all we had to talk about.

One night, Bitsy Grant, who wasn't old enough to go to the pub, fired a shot through the roof of the guardhouse and was confined to barracks for three days.

We had been at Prince Rupert a month without being paid (40 bucks a month), and morale began to sag. We had to wash our own clothes. A rough mess had opened and we started taking our meals there. Unfortunately, sittings had to be staggered. There were 35 of us, but only 30 plates.

When we had been in Rupert for a month some postings came through for a few potential observers who had been sent there while waiting for openings at Air Observer School. Bob Manners was one of them. He slept in the bunk below me. He was one of those nomadic chaps who never told definitively where his home was. He was born English, was educated in China where his parents were missionaries, and he had lived in Canada and the United States. When he left I appropriated his rubber boots. He was killed in the Battle of Britain, and I have often thought of those neat block letters of his name in the boots, which I crossed out for my own.

Rupert taught us a lot about ourselves. On civvy street you avoid people you don't like, but in the service you have to live with your companions, close to them, feeling their breath, watching them shave, lending them your soap. One of the Rupert boys seemed to be a misfit. He bragged a lot about his job in the stock exchange in Toronto. It galled us that everything he said about himself turned out to be true. Bolton was good. He was quick and intelligent, and he became one of my best friends. He would lose his life in a flying accident at Service Flying School.

Although we were often bored and frustrated at Rupert there were a lot of things we learned to do to entertain ourselves. The new cook, Tom Evans, was a former basketball coach in Vancouver and he brought together a good team which practised at the Rupert community hall. I played forward with a speedy curly-headed lad from Ottawa named Bonner, who would win the DFC for his service as an observer in a Catalina flying boat squadron in Singapore and Ceylon. We played in a league including a civilian team and one from an encampment of 2,000 Canadian soldiers in the area. The air force team was ousted by an army squad called "The Fighting Irish," captained by a man named Rubenstein. Other players on the team were Goldberg, Padlowski, Doucette, Tomashevitch, Zacharias and Pribickevitch.

Bob Brown was a fine singer, and besides holding forth at any opportunity with his repertoire of naughty ditties, starting with: "There was an old lady from Cork ..." he was just as adept at Gilbert and Sullivan light opera. We were appreciated at the two beer parlours in Rupert, and we would sing for our beer. Women were allowed in the pubs, but they had to sit by themselves on the other side of a pony wall separating them from their boyfriends. One of the beer parlours kept a long table reserved for the air force. No airman was allowed to pay for his refreshments (which was good, because we had no money). Beer cost 10 cents a glass. Every time Bill Hood would sing in his fine Irish tenor the management would serve a round of drinks. And there was a friendly old chap, who kept a light somewhere along the coast, who came once a month to Rupert to spend all his money buying rounds for servicemen in the beverage room.

Rupert people ate shrimp with their beer. A bewhiskered old gent would spread a newspaper on our table and for 25 cents he would heap a pile of jumbo shrimp, red and plump, amid the glasses. We shelled the shrimp and ate them, and at the end of the evening the floor would be awash with the sweet juices of shrimp shells.

Then there was the Knights of Columbus, an organization of the Catholic Church that would serve the recreational needs of servicemen wherever they were for the rest of the war. We went to their canteen to dance with the local belles when we had passes. It was here that Don Sugrue would play my love song "Stardust" over and over.

Food at the new mess was boring – cheese and steaks every day. Some of us would take to the woods in search for rabbits, and we acquired a boat from the marine department to go fishing.

We learned a lot at Rupert, and we were beginning to grow into men. Although at first in our gullibility we had saluted taxi drivers, hotel doormen and anyone else who wore a flat hat, that was all in the past. We were now gentlemen veterans of the air force, psychologically indoctrinated, disciplined.

We were glad to leave the rain and the isolation when we were posted to the Initial Training School (ITS) in Regina, Saskatchewan. Jubilantly, we waved at the new intake as our trains passed. We made no comment.

CHAPTER 4

Thinking of the Girl Back Home

M ost boys in uniform had a girlfriend back home, except for a few, like "Moon" O'Connell, who had a dog. Some of these were serious relationships and were intended to be consummated when the war was over. Others would wilt on the vine as time and distance overcame the ardour of conviction, and the exchange of letters became less and less frequent. Getting letters from home, and particularly from those with whom they shared a kind of pact for the future, sustained them. The service knew this and doubtless the postal department worked overtime to see that letters and parcels were delivered promptly. Sometimes letters came in bunches, and correspondents started to number them so they might be read in sequence.

As I've mentioned, for most men in uniform, writing letters was a new experience. They had never before been separated from family and friends, and it had never been necessary for them to correspond. The fact is, many of them didn't know how to write a letter. Their minds were so filled with the things they wanted to say that when they sat down to write they couldn't think of anything to say. After recounting again the fullness of their last farewell at the rail station or the bus stop, and once they had reiterated the emotions of love they were feeling in their hearts, there seemed little else to say that the censor would not expunge.

There were, however, some friendships that strengthened during wartime absences. Some people were able to say in a letter things they couldn't say face-to-face, and the more lovers explained themselves to each other the closer they became.

Even so, being separated for a long time often caused insecurity and even suspicion to arise. Mortimer Alder would say later: "There is only one situation I can think of in which men and women make an effort to read better than they usually do. When they are in love, they read for all they are worth. They read every word three ways; they read between the lines and in the margins ... they may even take the punctuation into account ...."

The war ended many romances that might have survived. A letter of condolence from a commanding officer or a chaplain would release girls at home from their vows, but they were reluctant to dispose of those love letters, which were read and reread until the pain had passed and they could get on with their lives.

The "Dear John" letter was constantly showing up in the air force mail bag. This was a massive attack on an airman's faith in people, but inevitably it was his pride that suffered most. He might write one or two letters of appeal, and when nothing was forthcoming he would accept this situation and go to the canteen to get drunk. Years later, when he went home again, he would see the man for whom he'd been rejected, and might well be amused at the man's paunch and bald head.

The Dear John letter was symbolic of the fickleness of love. There were times when servicemen were unable to accept the situation at home, when morale suffered, when they would even take their own lives. But it was unfair to expect a girl to keep a light in the window for an absent lover who had no restraints placed on his romantic pursuits, who observed a double standard. It was unfair that girls were expected by decorum to shut down their social lives when their boyfriends were enjoying the merry, carefree lifestyle that the war had created. Although the hometown boys were gone, there were plenty of good-looking men in training camps scattered all over Canada who were seeking female companionship, just as the local lads were doing wherever they were stationed. There were "Dear Jane" letters, too. So it was a two-way street. Either party could invoke the classic rule of the day – I can't dance with a letter, so I'm in love with the one I'm near. The break-up of romances, in the end, didn't have much influence on the progress of the war, and the world would still revolve as it always had when the war was over.

We often had conversations on the question of fidelity, in the guardhouse at Rupert and elsewhere during lulls in training. But most of the questions remained unresolved because they were too subjective. We agreed that our lives changed as circumstances changed.

The few among us who were married remained steadfast to their promises, but as time went on situations changed and their attitudes towards those so far away often changed as well. Those who weren't married went through the same moral scrutiny and arrived at the same attitudes, perhaps a bit sooner.

Always on the agenda for these discussions was the question of whether soulmates eventually found each other. Is there a right person for every man or woman, a made-in-heaven twosome, two souls entwined by fate? Even more pertinent was the question of whether you could love more than one person at the same time. (Harems and polygamous alliances didn't count, as they were inherent in cultures not our own.) We all looked for answers to accommodate our inclinations. It was good to have these conversations about ideas we'd never thought about before, although, in the end, each of us was left with his conscience as his guide.

Addison posed a fundamental question when he wrote, "If I were in heaven, would I look down and see only thee?" None of us was very comfortable with the answer.

I have broached the subject at this juncture because I was beginning to question my own constancy. I loved my girl back home with a painful intensity. But although I'd been away from her for only four months, I was finding it less urgent to write letters to her, and other things were intruding on the quiet moments that I'd reserved to think about her.

CHAPTER 5

We Become Leading
Aircraftmen in Regina

For a long while we sat in silence as the train puffed through the Rockies, drawn by two engines that belched smoke from their funnels. We counted telephone poles to determine the speed of the train. And we thought about the new friends we had made during the weeks we were in Rupert, friends whose names and faces we would remember forever, long after they had died and were buried. Strangely, our thoughts were not of the war which had brought us together. The war in Italy was in progress and Italian prisoners were being taken by the thousands. The British had launched the first offensive in North Africa. The English city of Sheffield had been hit hard by the Luftwaffe only days ago. Laval had been ousted from the Vichy government in France. The RAF had launched a strategic bombing raid on Mannheim, an industrial city on the Rhine river. It included 135 bombers that over a period of six hours had dropped 89 tons of high-explosive bombs and 14,000 incendiary bombs, with a loss of 13 aircraft. And on December 18, Hitler had decided to open a second front by invading Russia. It was the first big mistake he would make during the war. Yet our thoughts were not on these important events. We were thinking of home.

Just before leaving Rupert we had been paid and had received our Christmas boxes of apples, nuts, candies, cake and cookies, and cigarettes. This was my first service Christmas, and I learned that a box from home was only *addressed* to you – it belonged to everybody. Everyone looked at the photographs of girlfriends and shared in the glow of Christmas. We sang carols and passed the fudge and chocolates among other passengers who seemed a bit overwhelmed by our hilarity. A little girl beamed as she put her hand in a candy box and restless travellers were thankful for the Christmas atmosphere we created. I noticed a man with the white collar of the clergy and I offered him a sweet bread my Aunt Fannie had sent; but he refused it. I went back a second time, and on the third try he accepted. From that moment on, we had the blessing of God manifest at our railroad party.

At Jasper we made an unexpected stop due to a landslide some miles ahead, and we waited in the little community for two days until the blockage was cleared. Jasper was the divisional point on the main line of the Canadian National Railway and was named after Jasper Halls of the Northwest Company. Jasper National Park had been established in 1930, and then as now it was an oasis in the wilderness. Wild creatures lost their instinctive suspicion in that protected haven. Rabbits paused as curious visitors watched them, and then returned politely to their nibbling. Elk, with silent tread and poised antlers, picked nonchalantly at bits of food behind the houses; deer leapt through the underbrush. At a more reserved distance the majestic, albeit awkward-looking, moose looked solemnly out on the sanctuary. But little creatures, the weaker things – mice, moles, squirrels, chipmunks, snails, snakes, lizards, hopping and crawling things – lived life as the undefended must always live, dangerously.

While we were in Jasper the townspeople feted us. We were treated as though we'd already won the war. We marched to church and the good man pushed aside the sermon he had prepared and his impromptu homily made us tingle with pride.

It was Christmas Eve when the train finally arrived in Regina, and it was snowing softly. Regina was the home of the Royal Canadian Mounted Police. Last-minute shoppers moved silently. Back home, the evergreen tree in the parlour would be decorated with silver bells, tinsel and popcorn strings. Long-secreted packages would be carefully drawn from cupboards and closets, and cherished culinary delicacies envisioned for the following day. But there would be vacant chairs at the feast.

The snow snowed. We were given the first 18-hour pass since we had pledged allegiance, and the kind people of Regina helped fill the time with yuletide spirit. A few men could get home for the holiday, but most of us depended on community organizations and friendly people to provide seasonal hospitality. There were more invitations than there were airmen. On the streets people tipped their hats to us and women smiled pleasantly. Messages on the bulletin boards invited airmen to Christmas dinners. Bill Woodward, Don Irving, "Ace" Bolton and I went to a home on Montague Street and were royally entertained. Later we went to a reception at the home of Judge Bigelow and his gracious wife. We were the lowest rank in the air force, but we mingled easily with Regina's elite, and with officers, around whom we still felt uneasy.

Judge Bigelow was more than just a host. He offered a suggestion that made it possible for us to keep track of our contingent long after we left Regina. We gave him a list of the 35 in our group, with our home addresses. Every time we moved we were to send our new air force addresses to him, together with any information we had about others in the group. For months afterward Judge Bigelow would compile a "newsletter" to send back to each of us, by which we were told when promotions and medals had been awarded, and when any had been killed in action. In this way we would learn that from the original group of 35, only five survived the war.

C andidates for aircrew positions had to go through a rigorous training program – months of study, and a life expectancy of only a few weeks at the end of it. The Initial Training School, which was located in what had been Regina College, now enclosed by a high wire fence, was the academic centre through which all aircrew passed. It was here that we learned navigation, airmanship, aerodynamics, meteorology and aero-engines, and continued our study of air force law – the KR (Air) and those testy (4 to 44) inhibitors. It was at ITS that trainees were finally classified according to trades – observer, pilot and wireless-operator/air-gunner (WAG). At that time observers were also trained as bombardiers. They wore the observer's "O" and were called Navi-Bs. Later, as new navigational aids became available, observers became navigators, and a new trade, bomb-aimer, was introduced. The two trades wore "N" and "B" on their wings, respectively. Engineers for Canadian heavy bombers were all borrowed from the RAF, but when the war neared its end a surplus of pilots took over engineering positions Overseas. Straight-air-gunners, who were always in great demand on Overseas squadrons, did not go to ITS, but went straight to bombing-and-gunnery schools, where they learned about Browning guns and various kinds of turrets, and then proceeded directly Overseas and into bombers after only a few weeks of operational instruction. Some of them were not yet 18 years old when they went into action, and many of them never got any older.

As airmen we had no actual rank, but we were classified as Aircraftmen, second class (AC2). There wasn't anything lower. We would be reclassified as Leading Aircraftmen (LAC) when we left ITS, and then we would wear the coveted white flashes on our caps, to indicate aircrew status. It seemed that wherever we were there were also army establishments, and we had to become familiar with the corresponding ranks. As mentioned, airmen were classified to start, and then went on to Corporal, Sergeant, Flight Sergeant, Warrant Officer (2nd class), and Regimental Sergeant Major, the highest and most privileged non-commissioned rank. They wore a combination of stripes and crowns on their sleeves. The army had similar ranks, starting with Lance Corporal, wearing a single stripe. Commissioned ranks were the same for the army and the air force, except that air force officers wore stripes on their sleeve. The army officers wore a combination of pips, crowns and crossed swords on their shoulders.

"Up on your feet! There's work to be done!" (Air force disciplinarians did not use the foul language so often employed in current American war movies.)

After all the year-end festivities were over, this morning salutation brought us back to reality. Cpl. Kent's six-foot-three frame had held up a prison warden's uniform in pre-war days. He didn't care whether the boys liked him or not. Most NCOs were friendly towards us, and, knowing that in a few months many of us would be officers, they were perhaps a bit envious.

We got up on our feet and were soon outside the barracks, doing wake-up calisthenics in the snow.

Flight Sgt. Al Pat had written a book of poems and offered them for sale to the new intake. We were all frightened of NCOs, and he was a Flight Sgt., so we didn't refuse.

The first class was in law and discipline. Pilot Officer McKenzie was the instructor, and he wove into his lectures interesting anecdotes of his personal experience in the courtroom, engineering the acquittal of defendants whom he knew to be guilty. Many times in our future careers we would be victims of circumstances and of the rule that for every offence someone must pay. That was why whole training wings lost their passes because someone stole something or someone showed up on parade with unpolished buttons and dirty boots.

On civvy street it isn't anybody's business if you stroll down the sidewalk without a tie. Nobody cares if your mouth is stuffed with chewing gum, or if you're smoking. But in the service, restraint and discipline were key. We did not know it then, but what we learned from the officious disciplinarians would save our lives in future tight spots.

Pilot Officer McKenzie introduced us to the 1,200 pages of penalties that could be handed out to airmen who committed offences not considered delinquent in civil law. Sections of 4 to 44 of the King's Regulations were required reading every three months. I never knew anyone who read them even once. Inebriation was dealt with summarily in air force law – the first offence was on the house. The second offence cost $5, the third $10, paid in cash or deducted from one's pay. Unofficially extended leave resulted in pay stoppages for each day a man was AWOL, and for the first time spent in detention, and for the amount of expenses accrued by the service police in apprehending the absentee. These penalties weren't fines, they were "stoppages." The difference was moot.

Each man in the service is entitled to a "redress of grievance," which simply means that if he feels he has been unjustly wronged by his corporal or his sergeant, he can go to the next highest rank, right up to the officer commanding. This is all pretty tiresome (and it is meant to be), involving defaulter's parades (he is guilty until proven innocent), standing at attention, sirring, and all the while waiting in the guardroom under close-arrest. This procedure is carefully detailed to the rookie at ITS, so that he can think twice before questioning working-party details that consign him to cleaning lavatories.

There were many unusual passages in the King's Regs. In one paragraph it was stated that it is strictly forbidden to take a horse into the barracks. Someone probably did it once, and the rule is likely still on the books.

While we were digesting the rules by which we would conduct our lives in the air force, we got on with our training at ITS. The link trainer was one of our first experiences. The Link Trainer is a teaching aid, invented by a Yank called Ed Link. It is a stationary contraption resembling the cockpit of an airplane and it simulates actual manoeuvers of an aircraft in flight. My instruments told me I was 50 feet below ground. Then the instructor who monitored the training manoeuvers with instruments outside the trainer told me through intercom that I was going into a vertical spin.

Other courses were armament, parade drill and mathematics. The mathematics instructor, Flying Officer Henderson, held constantly over our heads the threat that we would be exiled to Mossbank (a desolate spot in Saskatchewan) as GDs (general duty classification) if we didn't learn our cosines, logarithms and anti-logarithms. Henderson insisted we salute when we entered his classroom. Then there was a course on signals and "health and sanitation," which was the hardest course at the school. We took up the physiology of flying, the characteristics of the middle ear, oxygen lack, bends, et cetera.

I wrote my final exam on the subject while in the station hospital, suffering from influenza.

We had now arrived at the real starting point of our air force careers, when we would actually begin training on aircraft.

At this juncture we took the "gentlemen of the air force" business more seriously. Ego and vanity urged us to embrace the image, if not the rank, of officers, if only to impress the girls we met at the Trianon dance hall.

The No. 1 Blue uniform that had been issued at Brandon was made of a sturdy material that had a surface of downy nap. We laboriously shaved off the nap with razor blades to make the fabric seem less like general issue. The shaving process also gave the impression of long use, which suggested long service, a special status in any airmen's group. To avoid daily pressing of our trousers (which had buttoned flies) we sewed the seams. We were issued regulation boots, and whenever we thought we could get away with it we would wear highly polished shoes, challenging the duty guard at the gate, who might well be one of our own, doing penance for some petty offence. But the most ingenious deception had to do with the felt-like collars we wore with a black tie. They were separate from our grey shirts and were held in place by studs. We would wear fine broadcloth shirts concealed under the grey collar, which would be removed once we had passed through the gate en route to the girls at the Trianon. Curiously, although we were often apprehended at the gate, I never knew of anyone being picked up by the service police for this shifty behaviour. In many ways we would go through our service careers trying to beat the rules.

When we had completed our courses we waited with growing excitement to learn how we would be classified and where we would be posted. Each member of the course was given a "confidential" (a meaningless word) personal history sheet to fill out. This seemed superfluous, as they already knew everything about us. We were to write down our technical and academic qualifications, and our personal problems. I don't think these diligently completed questionnaires ever got beyond the station WO's desk.

Squadron Leader Hutchison read out the names of the graduates, slowly, scrutinizing each airman as he stood up to answer his name. It took a long time to read the names and we still didn't know whether we were pilots or observers. At this school it was the custom to classify good mathematicians as observers, so many of us had made deliberate errors in this subject to assure our further classification as pilots – which, in retrospect, said little for pilots.

"You have been classified as pilots," the squadron leader said. The next time I saw him he was a Group Captain and the commanding officer of the Canadian Overseas Receiving Depot in Bournemouth, England.

Some big shot was coming to our passing-out ceremony, and a ceremonial parade had been called accordingly. We were there at two o'clock. Warrant Officer Tretize had dressed us off properly. All the non-coms were in their proper places. A throng of bewildered officers paced back and forth as though frightened they would not be able to get started again if they stopped.

At five o'clock we were still in place, and no big shot. So we were inspected by the supernumerary officers. F/O Davies inspected my flight. I was the last man in the rear rank, and I had not shined my tunic buttons. The officer sped through the ranks and took out his frustration at the long wait on long hair, shadow beards, et cetera. He walked quickly down the rear ranks and stopped in front of me. My heart sank. But he was looking at the man next to me. He remained silent, then moved past, only to turn abruptly and point his finger at me so menacingly that I could not answer his vehement: "Did you polish those buttons?" I didn't want to go on charge, and I didn't want to lie. While I was struggling with my conscience, Cpl. Mitchell said to the officer: "Pardon me, Sir" (he had been tailing the officer with notepad and pencil), "but this man has a new coat and the buttons won't shine." (The lacquer on new buttons takes some weeks to wear off. I should have thought of that myself.)

"Oh, that's different," the man with the flat hat conceded, and walked on.

Corporals are human after all. We liked ours. He was more a friend than a bully and little things like this didn't cost him anything.

Finally, the big shot arrived. He was a civilian in black coat, hat and grey spats. He carried a briefcase. Most civilians who wear black hats carry briefcases. This one was from the finance department and had come with a message from Mr. Ilsley himself. He wanted us to buy Victory Bonds. On $50 a month he wanted us to buy Victory Bonds! We resented that. While we were still living we wanted to spend our money on creature comforts, our own. Some of the guys weakened under the high-pressure salesmanship and bought bonds (the money would be taken out of their pay on the next parade) but later swore they hadn't.

We were given badges with propellers, emblematic of aircrew cadets, and we proudly had them sewn onto the sleeves of our tunics immediately. Almost immediately we were told to pack. We were going to Elementary Flying Training School in Vancouver.

CHAPTER 6

My Flying Career Ends
Before it Begins

Not many of the old Rupert gang were included in the draft for No. 8 Elementary Flying Training School in Vancouver. Some of them had been classified as observers and had gone to openings at navigation schools; others went to flying schools (as we were doing) in other parts of Canada. Eventually, there would be 97 air training schools in Canada under the Commonwealth Plan, a remarkable scheme for training aircrew from British Empire (Commonwealth) countries, as well as airmen from some allied nations. The first airmen to graduate from the plan were 37 navigators who completed their course at No.1 Air Navigation School in Trenton, Ontario, on 24 October 1940. This scattering of friends would be the norm throughout our air force careers. Our relationships were short-lived, and in many cases we would never see each other again.

We were elated as we settled down in a Canadian Pacific Railway train, and enjoyed the luxury of first-class travel – a berth, excellent CPR coffee and pea soup, a dining car with white tablecloths and silver cutlery, and the unexcelled scenery of the Rockies. This would all change eventually, as more servicemen began to travel cross-country, and first-class for everyone would become an anachronism.

The CPR route across the mountains was more entrancing than the CNR route to Prince Rupert. We could look down from our passenger car and see the front end of the train, pulled by two coal-burning engines, disappearing into a tunnel carved into the bowels of the rock. It was a remarkable engineering feat. British Columbia had joined the Canadian

Confederation in 1871 with the understanding that the CPR would complete its line to the Pacific Ocean within two years of the union. (A similar agreement had been made with the Maritimes as a condition of Confederation.) The last spike – reputed to have been golden – was driven on 7 November 1885, in Eagle Pass, BC, by Donald Smith, later Lord Strathcona. This was the prelude to the development of a tourist-oriented chain of chateau-style hotels at major stops on the line. We passed through Banff and beautiful Lake Louise and the Great Divide, where the Bow and the Kicking Horse Rivers have their beginnings – also by Moraine Lake, the Three Sisters, and Castle Mountain, which years later would become "Mount Eisenhower."

As I basked in the natural grandeur, I recalled that my history books commented on the building of the railroad and the tragic loss of lives incurred by the spectacular undertaking. Chinese immigrants bore the brunt of the sacrifice. Many of them died in landslides and blasting mishaps, the victims of unsafe working conditions. Fifteen thousand of them had worked on the railroad. The first of these immigrants had come to Canada from South China, via San Francisco in 1858, and founded the first Chinese community at a place called Barkerville, BC. The Chinese were treated poorly by Canadian society. After the railroad was completed a head tax of $100 was imposed, which virtually eliminated immigration. British Columbia did not want to encourage a Chinese population, and pressed the government to increase the tax to $500. The government declared that Asians were "unfit for full citizenship." The men lived as bachelors, separated for decades from their families in China, and surviving on low wages as labourers, laundrymen, teamsters and domestic servants. They were barred from all professions. In 1923 Chinese immigration to Canada was virtually eliminated. My thoughts dwelled on episodes in Canadian history as we travelled northwest.

We were all thinking of home and girlfriends as well, and the words of songs like "I'll Never Smile Again" monopolized

our reveries as we anticipated the excitement that
awaited us.

We arrived in Vancouver
on a foggy Sunday. The city
was beautiful to our eyes,
and seeing the great Pacific was breathtaking. We
observed the extensive lum-
beryards and mills along the
coast and remembered the
forests of great pines and
redwoods we had passed
through. There were hun-
dreds of little shacks built
along this milling coast.

Hank Hancock at Flying School in
Vancouver

They rested close to the huge circular saws, and reminded us
that Vancouver's population was dominated by Japanese. At
the time, we were not concerned about the process in motion
to isolate the Japanese into internment camps in the interior.

The flying school was not actually in Vancouver. It was located on Sea Island at a place called Eburne, about 12 miles south
of the city proper. It was close to the United States border.
There was very little on its surface except the Trans Canada
Airlines landing field, an RCAF hangar and the Joggins Flying
Club. Across the road a Boeing aircraft plant was being built.
Lulu Island was to the south, along with a stretch of bog,
which was a low flying area. An air-force station was under
construction at Boundary Bay. Still, all in all, the air force was a
curiosity to the Vancouver population, it being early in the war
and Vancouver being a long way from the hostilities.

Transportation to Vancouver on free nights (free until
10:30 PM, that is) was sometimes difficult. Some evenings
we went with one of our classmates, Bill Brooks, who lived in
Vancouver and originated the "Brooks Shave" (a quick dash of
powder). Other times we went with Mr. Jones, an aero-engine

instructor. Once we were picked up by a Mr. Martin, who got us guest memberships at the Pacific Athletic Club. (I don't recall much in the way of athletics happening there, but we appreciated the bar, especially since Mr. Martin picked up the tab.) We went to dances at the Georgia Dugout and roller skated at the Trianon. At Stanley Park we were disappointed by the old Redwood stump that been shown in our school geography books with an automobile completely garaged in the base. Now it was nothing but a rotten mound.

Getting back to camp was easy. There were always automobiles cruising the route we hitchhiked, with the purpose of driving airmen home. These motorists were often girls who were fascinated by the blue uniforms and the excitement associated with flying. They were perhaps equally interested in the Casanovas among us.

One evening a man came up to me in a drugstore and extended a hand in greeting, asking me if I knew a man named Goodacre in Melbourne, Australia. I said I didn't. (I had never been to Australia, although I had a cousin whose father was a gold miner there.) The man explained that he thought I might know his friend, as I was from Australia. "But I'm not from Australia," I said. "Oh, I'm sorry," he apologized. "I thought the white band in your hat meant that you were from Australia."

Going home, a World War I pilot had been asked by his wife if the white peaks meant that we were experienced in landing on snow. The white flashes distinguished aircrew from ground crew. The idea was probably borrowed from the Canadian Army Officer Training Corps where the white bands were used to distinguish officers from other ranks.

At any rate they were coveted, and we were proud to be wearing them.

As the war continued there was great stock placed in insignia, for practical purposes. By observing what the various services wore on their sleeves and shoulders and chests, one could determine the wearer's rank, his unit, his home, his length of service, the campaigns he had served in, any awards

Hank at Elementary Flying Training School, Vancouver

that he had won, and whether he had volunteered or was drafted. It was this pride in what he was that made the Canadian
fighting man one of the world's best.

The wonderful day had arrived. We were actually going to
learn to fly. No. 8 EFTS was a private flying school seconded by the air force to train airmen until proper facilities
could be provided under the developing Commonwealth

Tiger Moth crash at 17 EFTS, Stanley, Nova Scotia

Plan. Most of the instructors were civilians, and discipline was lax. My instructor was a man named Godfrey, who had been a bush pilot. Another instructor was Harley Goodwin, who had been a druggist in peace time. They were a courageous bunch. There was a proper RCAF detachment also, headed by a squadron leader whose name I can't remember.

The aircraft used at No. 8 were Tiger Moths. Other flying schools were using Fleets, and both crafts were well adapted to the instruction of young pilots. The deHavilland Tiger Moth is dismissed summarily in the encyclopedias of wartime aircraft, and its prominence pales beside that of the great operational aircraft, the Spitfire and Hurricane fighters, and the Halifax and Lancaster bombers. But the Moth was the mainstay of the airforce's initial training program. Almost every aircrew member of the RCAF (as well as aircrew from other Commonwealth countries) flew alone for the first time in a Tiger Moth. It was a biplane, painted yellow – partly to make it easier to locate any that force-landed – and had a wingspan approximating that of a Spitfire. It had fixed landing wheels and a double cockpit with duplicate controls. But there was no means of communication between the two seats except by the use of a funnel through which words could be faintly heard. The Moth cruised at about 70 miles per hour, and might reach 90 with effort. But it had one crowning asset. It could fly itself.

The first days at No. 8 were thrilling. This is when it all came together. We split our time between attending classes or hanging about the Dog House, and flying. Most of us had started mustaches, now presenting a shadow on the upper lip, and we were learning the slang of flying. Some even affected the silk scarf, following the example of the Red Baron, and later, "Buzz" Beurling.

Actually, learning to fly was easy. You moved the "stick" backward and forward, depending on whether you wanted to climb or dive, or from side to side for turning right or left. This was done in conjunction with the rudder. We had learned airmanship and theory of flight at ITS – how the air streamed over the curved surface of the wing, creating lift, and how this

Hangar Johnnies in Vancouver, 1941. Gordon Dunn, Hank Hancock, Larry Bolton, and Walt Cripps

force confronted the drag of the aircraft and its occupants. The trick was to coordinate all these natural aspects of flight – the aileron, the elevators and the rudder. Some students had difficulty with the balancing requirement, which was often the reason why they were "washed out" of the course and sent to other duties in the air or on the ground. Of the 159,340 air-crew students who started courses in the Commonwealth Plan, almost 28,000 didn't make it.

There were only a dozen or so in my course, and we bonded quickly. Larry Bolton wore a white silk scarf, and I was surprised when I learned later that he had been killed at Service Flying School in Dauphin, Manitoba. If you didn't know he was good, he wasn't backward about telling you. We learned to swing the propeller. The Moth didn't have a self-starter so we had to start the engines by swinging the prop ourselves, much like cranking the old Model-T back home. It was tricky.

My man Godfrey was a good pilot, and he did his best with

me. Operating aircraft on three levels instead of just one didn't come easily. There were some things we weren't supposed to do, like flying over the mountains around Vancouver, or flying over the city itself, or flying over the ocean or the US border. One day Godfrey did all these things, out of boredom, I suspect. First he did an outside loop, which was permissible but not recommended. After breaking the other taboos he invented a new one. He dropped the little aircraft to the level of a train that was moving towards Vancouver and spun his wheels on the top of a boxcar. When we landed he calmly told me those were the things I shouldn't do. Not very likely, I thought, although I confess the adrenalin soared within me as I experienced the thrill that made young men want to fly.

One day, when I had had about eight hours of instruction, we landed on the grass after having done a series of rate-one circuits around the airfield at a thousand feet. Godfrey got out of the front cockpit, dragging his parachute behind him. Like all trainees, I had looked forward to soaring among the clouds on my own, but I wasn't quite ready for it. Just one more training flight please. Godfrey said, "You're on your own."

I remember it was a Sunday and throngs of curious spectators from Vancouver were pressing against the airfield fence (as they always did on Sunday), watching the students taking off and landing, almost hoping someone would prang. Some of the Moths had taken a beating on faulty landings, but they stood up remarkably well. I taxied out to take off and wondered what I was doing there. I couldn't even drive a car. When I got the green light from the control tower (no radio, remember) I made a normal takeoff and climbed to a thousand feet, then circled the field, doing a rate-one turn to the last. The next part of the exercise was to land. On my first attempt I levelled out too high and the aircraft dropped heavily on its tortured landing gear. We bounced 20 feet and I gunned the aircraft, climbing again to a thousand feet and circling. This landing attempt met with the same result. Away I went again, and all these many years later I do not hesitate to say I circled

Both the instructor and an Australian pupil were killed in this crash

the field until I was almost out of fuel. Attention on the ground was becoming galvanized, the spectators breathless, the folk in the control tower apprehensive.

I made a perfect three-point landing.

This should have augured well for me in the skies. But quite the opposite happened, and to this day I'm not sure why. I quit.

I had staked my whole life on the prospect of shooting down Nazi bombers over London, and quitting had not been in the cards. One of our chaps had walked into a propeller and was decapitated right before our eyes. Several of the students decided at that point that flying wasn't for them, and had applied for transfer to other duties. I was deeply moved by seeing one of my friends destroyed, but I really wasn't afraid of flying. Deep down, however, I didn't think I would ever make a good pilot. Anyway, I found myself before a commanding officer with the others. What disappointed me most was that he didn't encourage us to try again. Had he done this I would

probably have continued my training. Quitting was less hon-
ourable than being "Washed Out." The latter was an indict-
ment of one's ability to do the things that a flyer had to do.
Quitting showed low moral fiber, and this bothered me for a
long time.

All this happened in 1941.

Erwin Rommel had just become commander of the Afrika
Corps, and British forces were sweeping into Banghazi. The
Italians had collapsed. Winston Churchill had asked the
Americans to "give us the tools and we will finish the job."
(Although it would be most of a year before the Yanks would
enter the war, we could see evidence of their support, as aircraft built in the United States were pulled by horse-teams
across the boundary line near our station. This procedure
apparently circumvented the international law respecting neutrality.) Five ships in a British convoy off the Azores had been
sunk on February 13 by Luftwaffe bombers. German troops
had begun landing in Tripoli. Britain had mined the waters
off Singapore. Hitler claimed the German military had sunk
215,000 tons of shipping in two days. The Battle of the Atlantic was in full swing. Several boys from my hometown had
already been killed in the air war. Some of those who were left
at No. 8 would die in flying schools. I have never been able to
explain my action.

CHAPTER 7

I Miss Wings Parade & Fall in Love

It was still winter when I arrived back in Brandon. But the place had changed. It was busier, and the exhibition barn was teeming with new recruits, for whom there were no uniforms available. Many of them were young Americans who had become frustrated by their country's hesitation to enter the war, and had hitchhiked from places like Florida and Los Angeles to the cold Canadian prairies. The drill instructor Barney Lewis had gone, but Sergeant Major Blundell had rallied around him a new roster of disciplinarians. In addition there were some 200 LACs who had washed out of flying courses in the West and were waiting in the bleachers until something could be found to do with them. We were seasoned veterans. Among the lot were familiar faces – Prince Rupert boys like Bill Hedley, Orest Bodner, "Siggy" Lee of Kildonan, Manitoba, Blackie Taylor of Toronto, Tom Mills and Jack Harrison, who joined us from Vancouver, and Jack Favelley of Regina. It was a trying situation presented to the Commonwealth Training Plan. The Plan had not anticipated so many washouts – trainees who had flunked for faulty landings, air sickness, medical reasons, or general unadaptability. Some of the washouts would have another chance.

I couldn't put myself in any of these categories because I had quit. But it was depressing, for all of us, to have failed – for whatever reason. Among the 200 there was a slump in morale. A readjustment (a nice word) board was hastily formed at the depot to determine what was to happen to this new category of airmen. An Australian wing commander presided. Each airman, still wearing the white flashes, was assigned to duties such as fire and service-police pickets. (We explained to new

personnel intakes that the "F.P." and "S.P." on our armbands
stood for Fighter Pilots and Spitfire Pilots.) We were joed for
everything: the kitchen, the clothing stores, the broom battal-
ion.

This time at Brandon we weren't green. We were old veterans. We were experts in gold-bricking and swinging the lead.
Our futures were uncertain, and we didn't care about anything.
We didn't read the "Daily Routine Orders" (DROs). We didn't
salute or make our beds; we skipped parades, and we got away
with a lot because the NCOs and the officers felt sorry for us.
If we wanted to sleep in we just put a "Fire Picket" or "Night
Guard" sign on our bunks and nobody bothered us. We put
wedges in our trousers so we could change clothes without
removing our shoes and we wore issue grey flannel collars
and tie pins over our taboo silver-grey dress shirts when we
went through the guardhouse. It appeared in the DROs that all
airmen were to wear galoshes, winter mitts and the "tea cozy"
the air force called a winter hat. But 200 LACs challenged
authority and appeared on parade with the usual field hats,
winter mitts, leather gloves, and a mixture of boots and dress
shoes. Nothing was said, and we thought we were tough.

There was a King's Regulations specialist on every station,
and there was one at Brandon, one who knew all the loop-
holes. He had previously been stationed in Alaska and had
been refused numerous requests for a posting back in Canada.
Finally he had gone to the CO and asked for permission to
marry an "Indian squaw." He'd been posted at once. On his
next posting he had decided to go AWOL to go fishing. He
signed the book at the guardhouse and disappeared for 20
days, so was considered a deserter. It was discovered on inves-
tigation that on the 19th day he had actually walked into the
guardhouse, signed the book, and disappeared again. So the
charges against him were changed again to AWOL, for which
the penalty was only 48 hours confinement to barracks. He
had been remustered to pilot, was washed out, and was now
back in Brandon with the rest of us.

"C" Squadron was just off Rossiter Avenue, and it was isolated and dirty and crowded, and later condemned as a fire hazard. But it was where they put a contingent of Royal Air Force recruits who had come from England to enter our C.W. training program. They were fascinated by the size of Canada. Most of them were about 20 and, we thought, small in stature. We were amused that they brought with them a full war-zone kit – rifles, webbing, steel helmets and gas respirators, blanket rolls, kitchen utensils, cutlery and water canteens. Their clothes were baggy and unpressed. They were a long way from the war, but they had already experienced it at home, in Lambeth, King's Cross, Coventry and Edinburgh. They could not believe the abundance of food. At home they had been rationed for two years. I spoke to one of them and asked about the bomb damage. "Yes," he said, "the bombs do a lot of damage, but everything goes on. Anyway, your weather beats ours."

While we were waiting to go before an assessment of our future we had the time of our lives, an exclusive coterie that cruised the drinking places and dance halls in Brandon every night. There was a fine ballroom under the shadow of the MacKenzie seed elevator on Rossiter Avenue that was a good place to meet girls. Of course, with so many men in the city, the girls could take their pick. In my diary there are many names of girls I met in Brandon. I've forgotten all of them, but one.

One night a Nova Scotian named Jimmy McKenna and I were looking for dancing partners in the ballroom. I spied an attractive strawberry blond sitting by herself. I presumed she was waiting for her escort because I couldn't believe she was alone. I asked her to dance, and expected her to say, "No, thank you." But instead she said, "Yes, please." And we danced. It was as though I were dancing with an angel. A full band played "Until Tomorrow," "The Nearness of You," and Hoagy Carmichael's "A Nightingale Sang in Berkley Square," and it seemed that those wonderful songs were playing just for us. When I sensed that she was not with an escort, I started the usual routine – "Are you from Brandon? What you do? What is your name?" She told me that her name was Annie Smoltz and that she was a nurse in Brandon. She smiled beautifully and her brown eyes sparkled like champagne. I knew I was in love. She didn't look like an Annie Smoltz, and it wasn't her real name, but I always called her that. I asked her if she would meet me at the dance hall on the following Wednesday. She said she would.

When Wednesday rolled around, she was there, waiting for me. I really wouldn't have been surprised if she hadn't shown up. That happened often, and it was no big thing. We danced and talked and laughed, and bonded well, and I realized that something was happening that would be an important milestone in the journey of my life. I had had the feeling before, but this time it was more intense and more devoted.

After that we saw each other whenever it was possible. We walked in the parks, had dinner together, saw movies and took pleasure in just holding hands. Touching her was electrifying, and the whole world seemed to have moved in around us, engulfing us in splendour.

The washouts in Brandon were disposed of in various ways. Some were remustered to other flying trades; some to ground duties. Others were discharged and sent home, where they would be picked up by the draft and given a choice of joining the regular army or becoming a uniformed zombie, protected from Overseas service by Mackenzie King's political maneuvering. Zombies were identified by their weird clothes, and servicemen didn't like them because they weren't on active service.

The air force was opening up a new trade, conceived to take up a personnel slack Overseas. This was called "straight air gunner," and required minimal training. Civilians did not qualify, only washouts. It was probably felt that the washouts were so desperate they would jump at any chance to get back in a plane again. The high mortality rate of air gunners was downplayed. "Happy" Perritt would take this air-gunner carrot and win the Distinguished Flying Medal. Bill Hedley remustered as a navigator, and Jack Hiltz as an air gunner. Both would die in action.

Sgt. White was our NCO. He turned us over to a corporal one day so the corporal could pass the drill test for his third hook. The corporal wasn't very good at giving commands, but the fellows liked him. We were in a precision drill squad and when the corporal gave a command on the wrong foot, we just went through the movement; we knew what he wanted us to do and we did it. He got his sergeant stripes.

A few washouts were given another chance at flying. To my surprise, I was one of them, in spite of the fact that I had quit. Eventually, I went to EFTS at Portage la Prairie, Manitoba, for refresher, and then on to Dauphin, Manitoba, for service flying instruction in North American Harvards, single-engine aircraft, more like the operational aircraft than the Moth. The Commonwealth program called for 720 of them for advanced training. A Harvard had a 600-horsepower Pratt and Whitney radial engine under a huge cowling. It was perfect for train-ing – better, I think, than the Yale, which was used in other flying schools, like Camp Borden. Flying again was a psycho-logical jump for me, but I adapted quite well to the routine at Dauphin, although I made few friends, since I was within easy bussing distance of Winnipeg, where I would meet Annie at her aunt's place when I had a long weekend leave.

The day before the Wings Parade, I wanted to have one last flight over the prairies. Without my realizing it, the roar of my low-flying plane spooked a herd of cattle and they stamped-ed through a fence. When I returned to base the Service Police were there to meet me. A farmer had taken the number of my aircraft and reported to the school. The penalty for this kind of caper was severe, and was intended to inculcate in a pilot an appreciation for discipline. Usually, the culprit was sentenced to hard labour in RCAF prison. I was put under close arrest and was summarily grounded, and later given my walking papers. I missed the Wings Parade, but a compassionate adju-tant handed me my wings at the same time as he gave me my discharge papers and a ticket back to the point of my induction in Nova Scotia. Emblazoned on the file was "Honorable Discharge for Reason of Psychological Instability."

I have not belaboured this episode in my air force career as it is not something I like to talk about. I never piloted a plane again, except on two brief occasions. I once flew a Hudson patrol bomber over the city of Halifax, and I once flew a Halifax heavy bomber returning from a bombing raid over the North Sea. On each occasion the pilot was in the rear of the aircraft relieving himself, and the navigator was furious.

CHAPTER 8

Hard Labour on a Prairie Farm

For 10 dollars I bought a suit and topcoat from a Yank who'd come across the border, and I went back home, where my odyssey had begun. I said very little about the pursuit of my aviation fantasies. The town was like a vacant house. Most of the local boys had gone into the services. I renewed my relationships with the old friends who were left, and I was glad to see Reta again. Our love affair had been illicit, but the man to whom she'd been engaged had gone to England with a Nova Scotia regiment. We had often alluded to marriage, but no specific vows had been made. Yet I found myself in an awkward position, as letters came each day from Annie, and every night I was out with Reta.

During the months I had been away, several local boys in the air force had been killed, and this made me feel even more that I had not been doing my part and had wasted a lot of the government's money. Charlie Dickie, who had joined up with me a year before, had been killed in a flying accident at the Malton airport in Ontario.

The politics of war were coming to a head. In July 1941, Churchill had sought to form a partnership with Stalin against Germany, and a pact of mutual assistance between the two nations had been signed, even as German forces pressed towards Leningrad. Reichsmarschall Goering revealed an order for the elimination of the Jews – the Final Solution. We did not then realize the full impact of this order. All Jews in the Baltic were required to wear Star of David arm bands. I could not identify with this. In my hometown there was only one family of Jews, and most of them were now in uniform. Spain averred to the Americans that the war was already lost

and that they should stay out of it. Meanwhile, the US government froze all Japanese assets in the States. (The real war for
the Americans was still months away.) Britain followed suit,
and Japan in retaliation froze all American and British assets
in Japan. In June, the Soviet news agency TASS issued a denial
that there was tension between Germany and the USSR, but
that wishful thinking died when Hitler's forces commenced
his ill-fated assault on Soviet territory, a move that probably
contributed more to the ultimate defeat of the Nazis than any
of Hitler's other directives. Moscow was bombed on July 21,
about the same time I was packing my bags again in response
to the increasing lure of Brandon.

Marj Gue was about the only friend of mine in Wolfville who
had a car, and she was planning to drive to Camp Petawawa, to
see a friend of hers who was about to go Overseas. My cousin,
Marion Millett, wanted to visit a friend at Rockcliffe in Ottawa.
So the three of us set out for points west. I was off the RCAF
payroll and hadn't saved very much (the air-force pay was
$40 a month, plus LAC pay and, when it applied, flying pay
of about a dollar a day). But our shared expenses were minimal. Gasoline cost 27 cents a gallon. A dollar a day would take
care of meals, and accommodations at B & Bs accounted for
another dollar. There wasn't much traffic, fortunately, because
although I shared in the driving, I hadn't yet learned how to do
it and didn't have a licence.

I left Marj at the camp, about 100 miles northwest of Ottawa,
and boarded a train for Brandon. I had no plan beyond a
reunion with Annie, but our relationship solidified and we
soon exchanged vows. I stayed at a Brandon hotel – I think it
was the MacLaren – where the rate was $2 a day. Annie and I
lived the life of Riley for a week or so. When my money was
gone, however, it was imperative that I do some planning
for the future. It was embarrassing to see the air force flight
parades marching about the Manning Depot, young men on
their way to fight the war. Actually, had I thought of it, I could
have stayed at the Depot – free board and lodging. There were
many men roaming around in civilian clothes. I could have

lost myself in that human complex, spent my time in the recreation room reading and writing. There could be lots of reasons why airmen were not on parade. At night I could have taken an empty bunk and no one would have known the difference.

However, to support my lifestyle a while longer, I went to Western Union to send a telegram to my father asking for more money. But it cost a dollar to do this, and I was flat broke. The man in the telegraph office paid the dollar out of pocket and when a voucher for $20 arrived a few hours later I repaid him.

When it was time to go, I left the hotel without paying the bill. (I later sent them the money and they sent my suitcase to me.) I spent the last two nights in an outbuilding at the exhibition park, shaved and washed at the railroad station, and wondered how I'd ever gotten caught in such circumstances.

Annie knew nothing about my plight, and I was too proud to tell her. With only small change in my pocket I left Brandon by train. It wasn't first class. In fact, it wasn't any class. As night fell, I made my way to the rail yard with some notion of emulating the hoboes who had called at our home during the Depression. I even crawled under one of the boxcars and climbed on the rods. "Riding the rods" was a common cliché, but I quickly determined that no one could actually ride the rods without losing a couple of legs. This was all new to me, but I had to survive. Finally, I selected a flatbed car laden with large construction timbers, their irregular ends allowing me to find a space large enough to conceal my body. The thought occurred to me that it might be days before the train would move. I rationalized that the timbers were from British Columbia and so we wouldn't be going west. But then, I couldn't be sure the train wouldn't head north. I waited uncomfortably for a couple of hours in the darkness and then heard the railway police walking along the tracks. The train began to move.

Winnipeg was about 80 miles from Brandon. But it seemed farther that night. It was still summer and it was warm, but I was afraid the load of timbers would shift and crush me. My discomfort was added to by the fact that my position under the timber left me exposed to cinders coming from the engine's smokestack, which smarted on my face and required me to keep my eyes closed. My only consolation was the thought that I might live to one day laugh about my experience.

The train stopped now and then, to take on water or shunt another car onto a coupling. But when daybreak came there was no doubt that I was in Winnipeg. Rail lines were everywhere. I had seen a picture of them in my school geography text. The Hub was the rail terminal of the west. My next move was to alight from the car without attracting attention from the police – who were in fact more interested in preventing acts of sabotage than in apprehending a hitchhiker from the Maritimes.

I checked into a hotel not far from the rail station. It was seedy, but it was cheap – a dollar a day. And I could afford to stay about two days. My first priority was to come up with a practical plan. My objective was to get back into uniform, so I couldn't take a job in the interim. At the air force recruiting centre I was confronted by Pilot Officer Glenn, who gave me little encouragement; but, both desperate and determined, I asked to see the Commanding Officer – which did not endear me to Glenn. The CO turned out to be J. D. Guild, now a Flight Lieutenant, who had first inducted me into the air force in Halifax. I told him as much of my story as he needed to know, and he was cordial, but considering my service history and the "psychologically unstable" brand, he proposed that I get a job on a prairie farm (harvest was in progress and farmers were having trouble getting help) and get myself straightened out. When the season was over I could come back and reapply. I accepted the "straightened out" reference without offence and resolved to do what had to be done in order to get back into the air force in any capacity. Again, I was broke.

Harvesters were hired first through a union, and if you didn't belong you had to go to the end of the line. Somehow, I started a conversation with an old gentleman who said he knew a farmer who was looking for help. He gave me directions to the Hanna farm in a place called Vivian, about 20 miles east of Winnipeg. He said I was to mention his name.

At this juncture I hadn't eaten for about two days. I had heard about down-and-outers wrapping themselves in newspapers and sleeping on park benches. I tried it, and slept comfortably, expecting, nevertheless, to be moved by a patrolling policeman, but I wasn't disturbed.

I had never realized how stressful it is to be an honest person, broke, in a strange environment and without friends. But what had to be done had to be done. I went back to the tracks and followed them eastward.

Later on I left the tracks, thinking I might hitch a ride on the road. The road was dirt, narrow, and there was no traffic. It was raining, as it would through most of that fall. I ate an apple I found floating in a ditch. When it was dark I looked for a place to sleep and saw a haystack a little ways off the road near a barn. I clawed my way into the base of the stack and slept snug and dry until morning. I got out of my bivouac to discover I had spent the night in a manure heap.

Somewhere along the isolated road I came upon a settler's house and, spent and bedraggled, I asked the inhabitants if I could have a drink from the pump in the yard. It was just past noon and at their invitation I sat at a heavy pioneer table and ate ravenously from a leg of lamb, still warm from the oven. The man and woman sat and watched curiously as I ate. Later, I would write to them and receive a return letter from their granddaughter, who was about my age. They gave me directions to the Hanna farm.

Vivian was hardly a town, it was more like a crossroads. I always thought that places with names had to have a presence, but Vivian was only a location, a spot in the prairies that would have been missed completely if it hadn't had a name.

The Hanna farm occupied about a section of land (640 acres, roughly a square mile). There was some woodland, but mostly the farm was seeded with oats, wheat and flax. The farmhouse sat well back from the road, and I walked down a long lane to get to it. Holly Hanna was expecting me, and I had a job, even though I had never been on a prairie farm before. The first night I slept in a bunk in what had once been a granary. I was disturbed by shadows that dashed by the open window against the light of the moon that followed the rain. Rats. Rats were everywhere, on my bed, climbing up the wall. The following night I was given a room in the house, and I ate with the family. (Holly and Mrs. Hanna; Mrs. Hanna's mother, Mrs. Grant – upon whom the gentleman in Winnipeg had a latter-day crush – and a daughter, Barbara, who was 16 and went to school in Winnipeg. When she was home, Mrs. Hanna made a point of keeping her away from me.) It was a wet season, and many days passed when the fields could not be worked. It was the rule that harvest hands (mostly what they called "breeds") had to be housed and fed, but not the usual five meals a day, and they received no pay. There were four boys (the Wickhander boys) who lived near the farm in an ancient log cabin. They harvested in season, and did odd jobs during the rest of the year. All four had served in WWI. We became friends.

Charlie, the foreman, also became my friend, and protected me from Holly's various attempts to exploit me. When we weren't working in the fields there were fences to be fixed, mash to be made for 36 pigs, and 100 white Leghorn hens to be brought down out of the trees each night. These tasks fell to me, the new boy on the block. And, of course, when there was nothing else to do there was the woodpile. Holly wanted me to learn how to milk a cow, but on Charlie's advice I declined. Enough was enough.

I do not wonder that many farm boys made good pilots, especially if they had operated a binder, which required the coordination one might use in a Link Trainer. There was a lever on the binder to elevate and depress the spool, which rotated like a windmill and brought the upright grain into the cutter. There was also a lever to adjust the tying place, which should be in about the middle of the sheaf. And there was a foot pedal to trip the carrier, which ejected about four sheaves every 10 yards. All these movements had to be synchronized, the operator's eyes darting from the spool to the string, to the canvas table, and to the carrier and the rows of sheaves. These farm boys would already have learned good eye-hand-foot coordination before trying to fly a plane.

Charlie was a part of the great west which had died. He had in his time upturned many acres of the earth, watched the seed scattered, watched the first green sprouts appear, watched the crop grow and ripen. He had cut whole fields with a hand-scythe. He had seen the grasshoppers and the locusts corrupt whole sections of fine grain, and strip a family's wealth to the horizon in 24 hours. He had watched the west grow, had himself cleared uplands and irrigated parched earth. He had seen fortunes made and lost. His knowledge of bush, field and pasture, and most of all his mechanical skills, made him indispensable to any farm he served. He knew every corner of the Hanna farm, every place where the fence was weak. Now that he'd been made foreman, however, he'd lost his ambition; he did no more than was required of him as regular farm help.

Charlie took a liking to me, however. He taught me how to harness horses quickly, how to field-pitch and spike-pitch. He never scolded me for the mistakes I made, as long as I corrected them. Most of all, he encouraged me to finish every job I started.

Charlie and Holly hated each other. Charlie stayed on because he was alone, his family grown and gone, and he was too old to move about. Holly would have fired him, but there was nobody to replace him. And no farm that size can run properly without a foreman. So Charlie and the boss endured one another because of their mutual need.

I have never regretted my farming experience. The Hannas got the idea that I was in the air force and on their farm for some sort of therapeutic reason, which, of course, was true to a point.

The first job in the harvest was to cut the grain using the binder, which tied the grain stalks into bundles with twine. Then came stooking, a back-breaking task of bringing four of the sheaves together in such a way as to protect the crop from the rain. I think my tender fingers were permanently damaged by the string on the sheaves. I had no gloves, but one of the Wickhanders gave me a pair, which was doubly welcome when it came to stooking an oat field that was mostly thistles. Next came the task of field-pitching the dried stooks onto a stake wagon, drawn by a team of horses. The stooks were carted to the threshing machine somewhere in the field and spike-pitched onto a belt on the thresher. (The threshing machine was shared according to a cooperative arrangement, in which several farms used the equipment in turn, which I thought very sensible.) Then the threshed grain was carried away to the granaries in a box wagon. Because this was a wet season the grain in the granaries was hot, on the brink of exploding. Turning the grain over with a huge scoop shovel was another job to which I was assigned.

I'd never worked so hard in my life, and vowed never to do so again. I was awakened at dawn by Charlie, in the room next to mine, as he scratched a match to light his pipe. (There was no smoking in the fields, but most of the men had snooze, which differed from snuff in that it was a tobacco paste, which was placed inside the lips to dissolve – the teeth as well as the lips.) We worked until dusk. On Sundays I rode a horse, given to me for recreation, and I raced elated over the harvested fields and far away, a thrill that only a rider knows. The only footwear I had was a pair of dress shoes I bought in a Winnipeg used-goods shop for $2. But they were soon ruined in the stubble. I took them off when feeding the pigs, and I went barefoot as I walked through the sty checking to see that the runts were given enough to eat. Their sharp hooves cut my feet.

One day I decided I'd had enough, and I walked back up the long lane, pondering my future and realizing that I was doing all this more for love than for King and Country. Before I reached the road I made a pact with myself. I would go back and finish the harvest, lest I should go on quitting when the going got tough.

The harvest crew got restless when it was wet. They bunked in the old granaries where the wheat had dropped through the cracks in the floors, there to be met by rainwater, forming a concoction that must have been close to pure alcohol. I saw them lacing it with Gillette's lye – "to give it bite," they said.

During one of these rainy periods, Holly gave me $10 and I went into Winnipeg for a day. I ate at a downtown diner where you could buy a full-course meal – soup, main course of roast beef or chops, with all the fixings, plus cream pie and coffee – for 20 cents.

I had been at the farm for 45 days when the harvest finally ended. I concluded that I'd been exploited, but that it had been for a good cause.

CHAPTER 9

Cloak-and-Dagger
Caper in Winnipeg

I took the bus into Winnipeg. Holly had paid me off with $20 for my work on the farm, and when I reached the Hub I checked into a cheap hotel and discovered a horseshoe-style restaurant where meals cost 20 cents. There were flophouses in Winnipeg where you could get a bed for 25 cents, but you couldn't stay there during the day, and I wanted to establish an address for contact with Annie and the air force. Mrs. Hanna had washed my shirt at Vivian and I washed my own socks. But I looked shabby, so I had my suit dry cleaned for 50 cents, while I waited in my underwear. I bought a pair of socks at the Five and Dime for 15 cents, and I spent another dollar and a half for a pair of shoes and a small carpetbag at a pawn shop.

First thing the following day I appeared at the RCAF recruiting centre. Flight Lieutenant Guild was surprised to see me – had forgotten about me, in fact. But I had taken his advice, and I was tanned and healthy, and I think he felt saddled with some responsibility to support my agenda. It was clear that I wasn't going to return to an aircrew trade, but I was prepared to do anything if I could just get back into a blue uniform. I think Guild was embarrassed, and I have no doubt he ignored my service record file in order to expedite my departure from his jurisdiction as soon as possible. I was remustered as a radar technician, which was a fast-growing ground trade, keeping pace with the development of radar as a war weapon. I took the oath, swore again to serve King and Country. Then I went back to my hotel address and waited to be called up. I had no idea how long this would take – days, even weeks. Meanwhile my $20 was dwindling.

I went back to the recruiting centre every day. Nothing. I had checked in with Annie and she made plans to see me off in Winnipeg. She was delighted that I was no longer going to fly. I did not share her delight, and already there was a plan beginning to form in my mind.

The autumn season moved rapidly into cold weather, and I despaired that the air force would not beckon before I starved to death. Finally, pressed by my critical situation, I made a bizarre move. I joined the army. I could not have done anything less rational, but I had come to making snap decisions just to solve the predicament of the moment. This was the beginning of a cloak-and-dagger operation I can hardly believe actually happened.

Young American boys were coming from Montana and Minnesota and Illinois. I joined the flow and checked in as Gregory Strand, with a cock-and-bull story about my father's being a medical officer in the British Army at Hong Kong. I gave a bogus Illinois address. I had no documents, claiming all my belongings had been stolen at a train station. It didn't matter. The army wanted young men like me, and I was sent at once for a medical examination. In those days the army did the medical and dental work for both army and air force, and I stood naked with a few army recruits and several air force candidates while an orderly administered shots, a doctor checked blood pressure and reflexes, and a collection of idle staff personnel enjoyed the display of male sexual organs.

I was given a uniform, two blankets and other paraphernalia, and was directed to a barracks by a corporal. I was in the army. Although I had no plan, I was cautious enough not to do anything that would jeopardize my changing horses again, if it came to that. I kept pretty well to myself, avoiding long conversations with other recruits which usually revolved around questions about who you were and where you were from. I joined a platoon for basic training in marching, and I was concerned when the instructor observed that I had both a right and a left foot, and asked me if I had been in the army before. (Shades of Prince Rupert drill.) I knew nothing about the army, never had any inclination to be in it, and didn't know what was to become of me. The food wasn't as good as in the air force, but it was adequate.

The government was launching a mammoth bond drive, and the recreation and entertainment people were staging a radio blitz from the Winnipeg army base. Because of my big mouth and because I was an American who could march better than the other recruits, I was commandeered to participate. The event took place in a large drill hall filled with military personnel, and I was led to the stage before a radio microphone. For a few moments I was stunned speechless, not because of the mike but because I had just seen the captain who was in charge, and recognized him as a man from my hometown, one who was managing editor of a newspaper I used to work for. If he recognized me I would be done for. I then realized the enormity of the risk I was taking with my cloak-and-dagger routine, and of the consequences if I were found out. Fortunately, the captain was occupied with other things when I went through my spiel about hating the Germans and wanting to avenge what they were doing to my father. I kept telling myself to play it cool and not overdo it, and I gave them what they wanted to hear.

The next day I talked with Annie, and she said she was sure she'd heard me on the radio.

Thanksgiving was coming up, and the whole barracks was going on a 48-hour pass. That night when I checked into my hotel there was a letter from the air force, asking me to report at once to the recruiting office. This was on Thursday. My appointment was confirmed, and I was given a file of documents, a rail ticket and meal vouchers to Toronto. I was to leave on Saturday, the first day of my 48-hour pass. While I was sorting out this schedule a telegram came from Annie saying that Charlie "Left-wheel Kelly" Cohen had just graduated from navigation school at Rivers, Manitoba, and would be passing through Winnipeg, en route east.

After duty on Friday, I exited the guardroom with my pass and all of my personal possessions, and went to the station to meet Charlie's train. I didn't want him to know about the army thing, so I changed into civilian clothes, which was taboo for army privates. As I waited, the corporal of my platoon walked onto the platform with a sergeant major. Had I been in uniform nothing would have happened even if they'd seen me. (I would surely be recognized if they did see me, given my "expertise" at marching and my radio appearance.) I hid behind a pillar and waited. Luckily they moved on before Charlie's train arrived.

It was only a whistle stop, but Charlie and I had a good reunion, most of it centred around Annie, whom he had just seen in Brandon.

That night I packed my meagre belongings into the carpet bag, except for the khaki uniform, still smelling of the clothing stores, which I had wrapped in brown paper and addressed to my father.

The following day I paid my hotel bill with the last of my money (I did not want to leave anything contentious behind me), and I went to the rail station to join with several other recruits who were also heading for No. 1 Manning Depot in Toronto the Good. (Ironically, I had been delegated to carry the personal files for the group.) As the train moved slowly from the station and gained speed, I breathed easy again, satisfied that Gregory Strand had been laid to rest and that I had my own identity back again. Then one of my companions said, "You look like that Gregory fellow I saw at the medical examination." But the subject was dropped, and it never came up again. I thought of Scott's aphorism: "Oh, what a tangled web we weave when first we practise to deceive."

As the wheels of the train click-clacked under me, I mused over the deception I had just perpetrated and wondered if I might be considered a deserter. No, I couldn't be. I was still a loyal member of the King's Brigade. I still honoured the oath I had taken. If I was guilty of anything it was that I had taken too many oaths. It was the perfect betrayal. I wasn't even "Away Without Official Leave," and I had a pass to prove it. I also had an air force identification card. On Monday, of course, when the army called in all those passes, Gregory Strand would be in trouble, and the military police would be out with their guard dogs to look for him. But, then, perhaps, they wouldn't care too much about another Yank absentee.

CHAPTER 10

Charley Searches for
His Identity

The legacy of the war, for those Canadians who fought in it, is not entirely negative. The good memories from that period are often associated with the people that we met – fellow service people, crew members, entertainment celebrities, residents of foreign countries, girls. Often, our war stories of adventure, intrigue and horror, pale beside this human experience. Apart from the friends I made on the train trip from Winnipeg – Sid Fein, Bill Thomas, and Joey Stone, brother of the ballet dancer Paddy Stone – I met several old friends I had known in Wolfville and at college, like Malcolm Dennison, Count Waleski-Lachinski – a Pole who, like myself, was taking more than a reasonable amount of time to orient himself – Roy Cook and Vernon MacCausland, both from Prince Edward Island, and Dick Caldwell from Boston. They were all waiting for the next phase of their careers, postings to training schools or remustering. I saw Jim Beveridge, from Wolfville, who was taking his doctorate at the University of Toronto with Sir Frederick Banting, and would later become President of Acadia University. It was interesting to see, and sometimes meet, famous NHL hockey players, and Foster Hewett, who as a hockey broadcaster was more famous than the players. And movie and radio stars like Al Jolson, Ronald Coleman, Gracie Fields, Woodhouse and Hawkins, Nancy Carroll, actor Harry Carey, and band leaders Cab Calloway, Mart Kent and Glen Gray. Gray's band was playing at Sir Henry Pellatt's Casa Loma in Toronto. I met members of the "Happy Gang," a popular Canadian radio show at the time.

No. 1 Manning Depot was located on the site of the Canadian National Exhibition. Almost every night at the 'parade square' in the cow barn, a spectacular entertainment was showcased, for "the morale of the troops." Of course, we met a lot of girls, to dance with, to go to the movies with, to talk with. It was not difficult to meet girls. There were organizations in the city – the YMCA, the Knights of Columbus and others – that did their best to ensure that servicemen were not lonely away from home. The best place to meet girls was at dances. If a boy was going to offer to take a girl home after a dance, he was careful to first ask where she lived. Toronto was a big city (still smaller than Montreal, though) and if a girl lived too far away she was on her own. Eileen Westgate was an artist, and sister of Murray Westgate, the Imperial Oil advertising personality. She invited me to her apartment on Bloor Street and entertained me royally with sweet biscuits and tomato juice, cans of it, in lieu of alcohol. I met a family named Carroll, who lived in Roxborough and were my friends all through the war and after.

Soon after I arrived at Manning Depot, I volunteered to join the station's precision drill squad. This was a bond-raising gimmick. A "flight" consisted of about 30 airmen who trained to do all the maneuvers (some of them brilliantly complicated) by silent count instead of vocal commands, probably the same way the Radio City Rockettes learn to do their synchronized high-kicking maneuvers. We were good. I went with the flight to New York to perform, and we were a great hit.

Eventually, I was posted to the detachment at the University of Toronto to begin training as a radar technician. Roy Cook, Goosey MacCausland and Ken Griffin went with me. I had no real interest in radar and wasn't sure I had the ability to handle the technology. It was heavy material, and candidates for the course needed special qualifications. I couldn't imagine anything I had done in the air force to date that qualified me for anything. However, the course was the only reason I was in the airforce, and it was the only way in which I could effectively pursue my agenda and get back into aircrew.

Acadia University grads meet in Toronto (L to R): Dick Caldwell, Vernon MacCausland, Hank Hancock and Roy Cook

We were billeted at East House, a brick and stone U. of T. dormitory in which thousands of students had lived during their university years. It had been commandeered by the government for military use. This was no hardship for the university as its student population had decreased considerably since the outbreak of war, and East House may well have been surplus. Many of the colleges in Canada were providing housing for the services – like Regina College, where I had taken ITS; Brandon College; and King's College in Halifax, where the Navy trained.

The course was more practical than most air force courses, in that radar was a field in which one would be able to make a living after the war was over. Radar could locate objects at a distance and under obscure conditions. It was of special use in the measurement of speed and target range, although these applications were not yet perfected. Radar could discern aircraft in flight and project the image on a screen. Radar could detect ships at sea. It could screen islands and coastlines, and its usefulness in war was obvious. Once the theory was understood the student tackled the technical aspects – the cathode tube, scanners and antennae. Aircraft warning, identification of friend and foe, prediction and bombing systems all developed from this basis.

Most of the candidates had been to college and found that the course was just like being back in the classroom. We were free to move about when not in classes, and discipline was minimal. Sergeant Wood informed us that we couldn't smoke in corridors (though it was all right in bedrooms). We couldn't drink in the dormitory, and we couldn't have female visitors. Toronto the Good in those days had no lounges, and the taverns closed down completely on Sundays, leaving the Blind Pigs free to take up the slack. They sold beer in large quart bottles.

The commanding officer was Flying Officer Kinney, whom we rarely saw. Our instructors were members of the university staff, Dr. Ireton, Prof. Heywood, et al.

I was appointed Flight Commander at once, which meant only that I would lead the detachment to Hart House for our meals and salute the cenotaph en route. Occasionally we would go to the Casino, the Old Howard of Toronto, to see burlesque strippers like Gypsy Rose Lee and Lily St. Cyr, and a gaggle of American comedians and singers who were stars in their own right, but who had to take their gigs on the circuit.

We had not been long ensconced at the U. of T. when the direction of the war changed drastically. It was snowing in Toronto on the morning of 8 December 1941, when news came that the Japanese had bombed Pearl Harbor the day before. British positions in the Pacific area had also been attacked, but this was overshadowed then, as it is now, by Pearl Harbor. Fortunately, the bulk of the US Pacific Fleet was not in port, but four battleships were destroyed. One hundred and eighty-eight airplanes were lost, 2,334 American servicemen were killed and many more were wounded. The Japanese had fewer than 100 casualties.

Rear Admiral Isaac Kidd was aboard the *Arizona* when the Japanese attacked and he manned a machine gun on the

Radar mechanics at the University of Toronto, 1941

ship's deck. The *Arizona's* magazine blew up and the ship sank. Kidd's body was entombed in the hull together with 1,103 others. The sunken vessel would remain their tomb, and it would be left in the harbour as a revered memorial.

The adrenalin flowed in our veins as we heard the news of the Pearl Harbor attack. We realized that the emphasis of the war would now be in two global areas. For the time being at least, Britain would still be supported by the Commonwealth in the German war, and the US would concentrate on the war in the Pacific, where Commonwealth countries (like Australia and New Zealand) were already involved.

At this juncture the time came for me to change horses again. We were approaching "the bar" in the course at U. of T. that would separate the sheep from the goats. Some of the class of about 30 had felt the strain of the concentrated instruction, and had opted out. I did the only thing I could do to get back into aircrew; I failed the bar. When I was posted again, Flying Officer Mullen said apparently I was going back to flying. I could hardly believe this, and any false hope was despoiled when I arrived at No. 1 Service Training School in Camp Borden. There was no one to meet me at the rail station and when I arrived at the base no one knew why I was there. The following day I learned that I had been remustered arbitrarily to the broadest and most obscure trade in the air force – General Duties (GD). This was in effect a personnel pool which supplied bods to do everything outside the regular trades. I looked upon this as the beginning of the six months wait required before an aircrew remuster could be made. But the people at Camp Borden weren't interested in that.

This time I was alone. None of my old buddies were with me; they had gone on, hopefully, to better things. The only familiar name in the camp was that of Major Drake-Brockman. He had been a British Brigadier, and had been stripped of his rank – down to private – for striking an ordinary soldier. (General G. S. Patton would do the same thing, but suffer a lesser punishment.) Drake-Brockman had offered himself to various armies, and had ended up as a major in the Canadian Army. (The air force had a flying school on part of what was more familiarly known as an "army camp.")

I was attached to the station service police detachment. Being a service policeman looked like a cushy job. And it was. Some of the men wearing the arm band looked upon the job as a perpetual vacation. It was a perfect niche for someone with no ambition. Except for Sgt. Ptolemy, D. E., Corporal Baxter and LAC Lord, all the men in the detachment were acting corporals – Hannay, Moran, Jorgensen, Williams, Skrypnychuk, and Frank Smart. The acting rank gave the men on patrol duty a bit of authority, but I think their rank was without pay. Flight Lieutenant W. E. Johnson, former chief of police for the city of Windsor, was in charge. He had been a pilot in the Great War, and I admired him. I used to go with other SPS to keep order in Barrie, Penetanguishene and Orillia, Simcoe county towns where airmen went for recreation. Everything was gratis; rail passes, coffee in restaurants, and even at the brothels. Everyone wanted to be on the good side of the SPS. Back at the office they learned that I could type, so I was seconded to administrative work. I was happy about this, as I had started to write a column called *An Airman's Diary* for the hometown newspaper, and my new routine accommodated this. Occasionally, I would serve at the gatehouse.

On the world scene at this juncture (mid-January 1942) Clark Gable's wife, Carole Lombard, had been killed in a flying accident. Joe Louis had enlisted in the US Army. Jack Dempsey, at 48, had been turned down, but Man Mountain Dean, the wrestler, at 50, was accepted. More importantly, it was revealed that since the war began Canada had sailed in convoy some 8,000 ships carrying more than 50 million tons of food and war materials. News items like these only amplified the fact that people like me hadn't made any contribution to the war effort. This urged me to take some positive action. I went to see the chaplain and I realized that in him I had an ally, someone who thought the six-month waiting period was a waste of time, considering the shortage of aircrew overseas. He said he would take my case up with the Re-selection Board. I did not expect much to come of it. About this time some new regulations had come into effect. Men over 26 were too old for aircrew duty (pilots and observers). The educational requirement had been lowered to Grade 10, which would qualify several thousand young men previously ineligible. Also, in view of the Japanese war, a grand muster parade was held at Borden to see if anyone could speak German or Japanese, presumably for intelligence work. Of course, there were no computers to check personnel files for this information.

One morning, after having spent the night in the guardhouse, I was told to report to the adjutant's office. I had no idea what this was for. I reported as ordered and the adjutant tore a strip off me for not having shaved. Apparently the chaplain had approached the Re-selection Board after all, as I was being posted to RCAF Headquarters in Ottawa. The adjutant did not seem distressed that I was leaving, although

I am sure he didn't like my having gone over his head. I was convinced at last that the squeaky wheel does get the grease. I wasn't quite sure what was happening to me, but at least Ottawa was where the decisions were made, and I might as well be there as anywhere else.

My posting to Ottawa was not strictly intended to be of service to me. They were apparently short of GDs at Air Force Headquarters.

Ottawa, in the spring of 1942, was bustling with the activity of wartime bureaucracy. A fairly small city as national capitals go, it was now bursting at the seams with the second line of defence, thousands of men and women drafted from small towns across the nation to handle the administration of the war. Bank Street was a charivari: foreign languages on the street and in the shops, trolley-booms sparking as the archaic cars clanked along the streets; restaurants and movie houses filled with people for whom the war was an exciting adventure. The city was fluttering with girls. It also had two first-rate newspapers, *The Citizen* and *The Journal*. And, in his office in the spectacular parliament buildings, which cast their Gothic shadows on the Ottawa River and the Eddy Match Company, William Lyon Mackenzie King, prime minister extraordinaire, brooded over the conscription issue. Princess Juliana and her family, of the Netherlands, were ensconced in Ottawa for the duration of the war.

Lloyd Robert Shaw (the father of Alexa McDonough, former leader of the New Democratic Party) was general secretary of the YMCA, but his preoccupation at the time was with Carleton College. The college was in the process of becoming founded by Henry Marshall Tory, a Nova Scotian who had already participated in the founding of the University of Alberta and the University of British Columbia. Lloyd was secretary (unpaid) of the founding group, and I occasionally sat in on informal meetings as his guest. I had the honour of having my suggested name for the college – Durham – vetoed.

One was always running into familiar faces in the capital city. On one occasion I was riding the trolley during rush hour when the Hon. J. L. Ilsley appeared and fumbled his way to the motorman. Ilsley was from Nova Scotia and I had cast my first vote for him. At the time, he was the minister of finance, responsible for all the money Canada was paying for the war, but – probably to his embarrassment – he didn't have a nickel for tram fare. I was standing nearby and offered him a five-cent piece, which he accepted graciously and said: "I'll see that you get it back." But it didn't matter, as I was somewhat in debt to the Department of Finance anyway.

The day I arrived in Ottawa I was given an address on Bronson Avenue, where I rented a room for $6 a week. I shared it with Darrell Larlee from New Brunswick, who was in much the same situation as I was. We were both GDs. The following day I was posted at the entrance to the Jackson Building, where I opened the door for ranking officers and saluted them. Once in a while I would see the great Air Marshal Billy Bishop, who had shot down 72 enemy aircraft and won the Victoria Cross in WWI. I reported each morning for roll call and was assigned my job for the day. When I was on the fire-warden shift I spent the night punching clocks in various areas of a building. At other times I would empty wastebaskets.

It was time for the squeaky wheel again, so I got permission from my sergeant to talk with Flying Officer Wilcox. My brief was simple. Just get me back into aircrew again. He pawned me off on his superior, S/L Campbell, who said my case had been pushed as far as it could be pushed. "Nothing can be done." It was an attitude that challenged me.

At that time my job was changed and I was employed in the Printing Division, where I spent the day collating mimeographed pages of training booklets. I did so well that my superior, a civilian, asked to have me located there permanently – another "achievement" that I didn't appreciate. I was not anxious to be doing anything "permanent," as that would make it more difficult for me to be on my way.

I had leave coming up, and I thought it would help my morale if I went west to see Annie. It would have been more convenient to meet her in Winnipeg, but I couldn't take a chance on being recognized by some clerk in the army adjutant's office, so I asked her to meet me in Brandon.

Although correspondence from Reta had almost ceased, Annie had maintained the kind of contact a lover could accept as promising. It was great to see the love of my life again. I had kept her only on a need-to-know basis concerning the stratagems of my career progress. In fact, she would have been happy enough if I continued dumping Billy Bishop's wastebasket. At least I would be safe. She was terrified at the prospect of becoming a war widow.

Annie and I became fully engaged during this visit. I wasn't sure I wanted to get married, but it was what she wanted, and I knew if I didn't commit legally, I'd lose her. Yet I couldn't afford to live in a hotel and buy a ring at the same time.

Being in love is terribly wonderful. We didn't talk about politics or religion, or literature or dogs. I didn't even know whether she was Protestant or Catholic, although I did know she wasn't Jewish, despite the name she'd given me when we'd first introduced ourselves. We talked about ourselves and our future together. I knew I would be a journalist, and she seemed happy about that. Young people in love spend a lot of time doing nothing, in complete silence, satisfied with the moment, the touch.

I can't understand why psychiatrists and psychologists don't regard love as a neurosis, like anger and fear. It certainly isn't rational, any more than is hate, jealousy or anxiety. I knew very little about the anatomy of love, having been raised in a family entirely of males. And I didn't know how to respond sensibly. The commitment we make to love is one of the most important things that happen in this life, yet we seem to know less about it than we know about fishing. To me, love was always an experiment in contrasts. It was a source of happiness and enjoyment. Yet it was also a source of pain and misery and disquietude. I couldn't say my love for Annie was resolute and unchanging. It changed constantly, influenced by what I read in her letters and by what I wrote in mine. I knew love was fickle. When I was with Annie I thought of Reta. When I was with Reta I thought of Annie. I could only conclude that I loved them both. Parting at the rail station was an emotional experience that I will never forget. The last caress, the last lingering hand clasp was sheer poetry.

Back in Ottawa, the atmosphere was alive with rumours of postings. And they were true. I was going to Sydney, Nova Scotia. That would be the end of my grand plan. As a last resort I went to see Wing Commander John McNab, who was chief Protestant padre of the air force and who had been one of the founders of the chaplaincy service. But he was on vacation, so I saw his second-in-command, Squadron Leader W. S. Cochram, who had been pastor of the Sherbourne Street United Church in Toronto until he'd been drafted in 1940 to go Overseas as chaplain of 401 Squadron. He had been a pilot in the Royal Flying Corps in WWI and had exercised vision and energy in the creation of an Overseas chaplaincy that moved ahead much faster then the services had intended. This was my man. To him I related my story.

Cochram directed me to the "morale survey," but before I had a chance to meet with them, I was told to pay my landlady and pack my duffle bag, as I was off to Nova Scotia. I hastened back to S/L Cochram (I was in a great state of excitement and all my activities in the Jackson paled beside my elation). I apprised him of the urgency of my predicament, and in 24 hours my Sydney post was cancelled. I was summarily remustered and I was off to No. 1 Wireless School in Montreal to become a wireless air gunner. Goodbye Venus Restaurant. Goodbye Jackson Building, Goodbye Air Marshal's wastebasket. Goodbye girls.

The Chaplaincy seemed to have an authority of its own, as well as a sensitivity and compassion that went beyond KR (Air). I never lost my respect for air force padres, and I would have a constant, though arm's length, relationship with "Cockles" Cochram for the rest of the war. I was a test case; I couldn't let him down.

CHAPTER 11

Montreal

The universe was unfolding as it should. I put the white flash back in my cap. I wouldn't be landing on snow, and I wouldn't be a fighter pilot ace, but I would be where I wanted to be in about six months. I felt great. I was sorry to learn that one of the Rupert gang, F/S Shadow Brooks of Powell River, had been killed. Just before I left Ottawa I met another Rupert man, Gerry Edwards, who was an instructor at St. Hubert's. I wouldn't see him again for many months, and by that time he would be a wing commander in charge of the Snowy Owl Squadron.

It was June 1942. A few days before, Reinhard Heydrich, deputy chief of the German SS, had been assassinated near Prague. In reprisal, the village of Lidice had been razed and every man living there murdered. The US declared war on Bulgaria, Hungary and Romania. Hitler said the Japanese were using poison gas in China; "... if Japan persists," he said, "in this inhuman form of warfare, retaliation in kind will be meted out." Japan invaded the Aleutian Islands unopposed. German submarines were mining US waters off Boston Harbour. Canada and Russia resumed diplomatic relations. Rommel defeated the British Eighth Army on his way to El Alamein. The FBI arrested eight German saboteurs who had landed by submarine on Long Island and on the coast of Florida. British civilian air-raid casualties for June were 300 killed and 337 injured. News coverage of the war was severely restricted, and much of what was happening in war zones missed us entirely – not that we were particularly interested in "geopolitics." It appeared, however, that the war was far from over.

The No. 1 Wireless School was located in what had been

St. Mary's Hospital. It stood in view of Brother André's shrine
of St. Joseph, and was surrounded by one of the most colourful cities in North America. Montreal was then the largest city
in Canada (population one million) and the second-largest
French-speaking city in the world. Montreal was not as old
as Quebec, but since the first permanent settlement in 1642
it had been the financial centre for the province, and perhaps
for Canada. It was also the centre of a rich cultural heritage.
We wouldn't participate in the culture except that which we
gained through osmosis from the physical structure of the
city – the bridges, historic streets and monuments, Mount
Royal, and the great St. Lawrence River, stretching easterly
towards the sea. We knew about Camillien Houde, who had
dominated Montreal politics as mayor of the city until he was
incarcerated in an Ontario internment camp for defiance of
registration for military service. But for most of us, who had
never been in Montreal before, the city was an extravaganza in
which we planned to revel for six months.

I knew none of the members of my class, but quickly made
up with a few like Dutch Shaw, Gint Ginter, Giddy Gedelian,
and Sgts. Mark O'Hara and Pete Arnaldi. Arnaldi wore a navigator's badge and had retained his rank, but we never asked
and were never told why he had been remustered to WAG.
For eight hours a day we were immersed in the technicalities
of radio transmission, Morse code and operating procedure,
with no mention at all of flying.

Discipline was lax, and in the evenings and on days off we
were out on the town. The hospital was some distance from
downtown, but hitchhiking was easy. In spite of their lack of
support for the war, the people in Montreal were friendly and
helpful.

One day, two or three of us were picked up by a pleasant
man who was interested in what we were doing and expressed
appreciation. It was during rush hour and a car cut across our
path without notice. Gint poked his head out of the window
and shouted, "Why don't you learn to drive, you dirty Jew?"
A short while after that our car pulled over to the curb and

we were asked to get out. Our driver said, "I am a Jew." I felt ashamed, and have never forgotten it.

Then we heard a rumour that the entire class was going to be moved to No. 4 Wireless School at Guelph, in order to free up St. Mary's Hospital for the Women's Auxiliary Air Force, which was recruiting by the hundreds. Rumours always came first, and this one was right. The whole caboodle entrained for Guelph, the centre of a prosperous agricultural district located about 40 miles from Toronto. The government had taken over Guelph Agricultural College for the use of the air force. I would now have been stationed on four college campuses.

CHAPTER 12

Posted to Guelph

The new members of the 47th Entry at the wireless school in Guelph rode overnight from Montreal, sleeping on the floor of the train. The travelling luxuries of 1940 had long since disappeared.

Seen in the daylight, Guelph was pleasantly pastoral. It was less than a hundred miles from Toronto. The Speed River, somewhat misnamed, ran through the town, adding a charm remindful of the English Stratford-on-Avon. The English author and land agent John Galt had founded Guelph in 1827. He had planned the settlement before the arrival of its population, designing impressive buildings made of limestone quarried locally. The town was eventually known for the manufacture of organs and sewing machines. Two famous sons, the economist John Kenneth Galbraith and Edward Johnson, one-time manager of the New York Metropolitan Opera, were born there. The town was also an educational centre, the home of the MacDonald Institute, built in 1903 to teach household science, and the Ontario Veterinary College. It was at the animal college that we would spend the next six months.

The wireless school was flanked by trees and completely enclosed by a high wire fence, an early reminder that we were there to study and not to gallivant in the town's recreational centres. We were quick to notice the cleanliness of the grounds and the buildings, and we would soon learn how this standard was maintained. Guelph was a stickler for discipline. A gum wrapper carelessly dropped on the path would net the culprit 48 hours of house arrest, kitchen patrol (KP), or guard duty. Coming in after hours (if it was not possible to climb over the fence) was good for seven days of lost privileges, with lots of time to clean porridge pots or swab floors.

The school's curriculum included Morse code and the equipment used to transmit it, procedure to follow for communication in the presence of the enemy, aircraft recognition, and armament, although most of the training with guns and aircraft turrets would be given in another place. I was more or less familiar with the theory of radio transmission from my University of Toronto days, but I found the course interesting and applied myself from the beginning.

Many of the enemy (Italian, Japanese and German) aircraft we were required to recognize were old models of some of the planes no longer being used in combat, but skill in recognizing black silhouettes flashed on a screen was attained, nevertheless. Using proper operating procedures on the air would enable us to send and receive messages quickly and accurately. And even such skills as first aid were important as they might well save the life of a fellow crew member.

For those who had no technical training in radio, or who had trouble understanding the instructions that came with new washing machines and lawn mowers, learning what went on inside a radio transmitter was a problem. For instance, this bit of advice was provided, just to get the radio equipment started:

> Operating a crystal controlled T1154, switch normal Xtal switch to normal and tune transmitter in customary manner. To use, switch "Normal Xtal" switch to Xtal with crystal inserted in "Left Hand" socket above the Master Switch. Plug "E.M." Plug into mike socket on "Right Hand" of Master Switch. Amplifier 1134 must be on, and "A.B.C." switch on "C" position for operating. To tune the transmitter, set "M.O. Control" at the approximate crystal frequency with "Plate Tap" in "Position One"; tune P.A. tuning control to the maximum dip.

It was all academic because every time you moved to another school or squadron they would be using different equipment. It wasn't any different for pilots to learn the theory of air cooling systems, and no more difficult than it was for navigators to open the meteorological manual for the first time and be confronted with the names of cloud formations – cirrus, cirrocumulus, altostratus, cumulus and cumulonimbus.

We made friends quickly, and, because we would be together for longer, these were often faster friends than those I had made at Prince Rupert. Again, these are names I shall never forget: Frank O'Hara, Tex Lytton, Jack Byrne, Lyle Faulkner, Dutch Shaw, Slim Maloney, Clyde Sherwood, Pritchard, Bumstead, Dubowski and Voyce. There were also several French Canadians, including Contant and Bellemare, who didn't speak English very well and stayed mostly to themselves. There were among us (in "A" Flight) several NCOs, including Sgts. Jackson and Todd, who had remustered from administrative trades; Cpl. Dawson, Sgt. Pete Arnaldi, who wore an observer's wing; and a sergeant from British Honduras, who already wore an air gunner's wing.

Again, I was the Class Senior. I don't remember whether I was elected or appointed, but they didn't do me any favour. As in most classes, there were a few who couldn't handle the Morse key and were washed out. But it was right up my alley. I was soon able to receive a "solid," 20 words a minute without a mistake. Some instructors were kind enough to say that my key touch was like "Creed," which was a method of sending signals automatically, using a punctured tape. (Fred Creed, who was born beside a salmon stream at Mill Village, Nova Scotia, invented the first keyboard perforator.)

I had been too busy to write to Annie, but I thought of her a lot. I received nothing from her for three weeks, and then on June 11 I got three letters all at once, forwarded from Montreal. So uncertain was I of our relationship that I carried them around unopened for two days. When finally I did open them,

I was relieved to see that they exuded love and affection. For the first time I noticed that her stationery had a scent. I wrote to her at once, and again there was a long, agonizing silence. On July 8, I received a brief letter from her, and this is what it said: "What I have to tell you is not easy. Believe me. Our romance has suddenly come to an end. I wish it could have been different – but that's just the way it is. I don't, or should I say I'd rather not know where you are, but pray that God will look after you – always."

I had often wondered what a "Dear John" letter was like, but it shocked me to the core. I was confused and hurt, my heart broken and my pride shattered. It seemed that half of me had been cut away and swept into oblivion. I told my friend Jack Byrne about it (he who received a letter every day from his girl-friend in Almonte) and he laughed hilariously. He laughed, when acid was slowly eating away at my entrails.

I couldn't believe that Annie was doing this to me, just because I was training to be a WAG. She had told me she would "divorce" me if I got back into aircrew, but I didn't think she meant it. I wrote her an impassioned letter, but I never heard from her again.

Our romance may have been over, but the pieces lay in shreds within me. Jack finally tried to console me, from the strength of his own romance. He convinced me that Dear John letters were not uncommon and that you had to get on with your life. He was right, of course, but my grades were failing. I tried to rationalize what had happened. I really wasn't much of a catch. I had no money, and I was going to war, perhaps not to return. Annie was 31 years old, and it was reasonable that she wanted a more secure future than I had offered her.

As I always did when I was depressed, I wrote some poetry to express my perspective:

> Oh, lost love,
> Had you the will
> To mold my future to your wants
> What would my future be?

And I remembered something Swinburne had written:

> And the best and the worst of this is,
> That neither is more to blame,
> If she has forgotten my kisses,
> And I have forgotten her name.

That, of course, was just rhetoric; I would never forget her name.

There were lots of things in Guelph to divert one from an aborted love affair, however. There were movies and entertainment programs, and there were girls. Like all service training centres, Guelph did its best to make its airmen happy. Whenever we were at liberty we would storm the dance palaces – the K. of C. was a favourite – and enjoy a sober evening with the town's prettiest girls. At home, we used to dance with the girls we went to school with, but there would always be one with whom you would dance more often. At these camp-related dance halls, however, all the damsels were free – if not easy – targets. Had the circumstances been different, I might have fallen in love with one of them – Marguerite, Betty, Helen, Ruth. There was a lot of unrequited love in those relationships, girls falling in love with airmen they saw once or twice a week, airmen who played the field and then moved on to another training station where there were other girls. Relationships for airmen tended to be fun, but superficial. A letter coming from the last stand would be signed "Kay" or "Marion," or whoever she was.

All that skylarking had its price. The dance halls usually packed it up at 10 or 11 o'clock, and the pass had to be redeemed at 2200 hours. A lot of airmen missed the curfew and climbed over the fence, hoping there hadn't been a bunk check. If there had, they would be put on charge next day and paraded before Flying Officer Rice, our Flight CO, who would award them two or three or four days of kitchen duty, depending on how he felt.

There was a Cpl. Penlington who, for some reason I can't

remember, was (by his own admission) out "to get me." We were not allowed in our rooms during the day, but I went to mine to get a book I needed for class and Penlington caught me. Flying Officer Rice awarded me three days, with extra fatigues, which meant burnt porridge pots. I never knew why they called these sentences "awards."

Being confined to barracks (CB) and awarded KP for those three days didn't interfere with classes or other training procedures. The penalty had to be worked out on one's own time.

I wrote in my diary that Faulkner, Lyntton and Myers, the flight's bad boys, were all in detention (that meant in a cell) because they had gone on a binge and taken a tombstone from a Guelph cemetery and carried it to Toronto, without a thought for the consequences.

There was a flight of Australians on the station, and they discovered a tunnel that ran under the administration building of the college. They escaped through it one night, then stole a local bus and drove it to Toronto on a spree.

Someone stole $585 from the accounts office, and we were all confined to barracks while an air force squadron leader from Toronto investigated. It turned out to be an inside job involving a civilian employee, but the detention angered us, and there followed a rash of offences requiring Rice to earn his pay.

I reread Annie's letters often, but, as Jack Byrne had advised, I was getting on with my life, and I gradually recovered from my morale slump. But I never seemed to have any money. Smitty's girlfriend came to see him but he was broke, so I loaned him some cash. Clyde wanted to go AWOL to see his girlfriend. I financed the caper, for which he got 14 days, and I never got my money back. I stayed away from the canteen, especially on pay night, and in so doing I became the mark for all the guys who couldn't live on $40 a month. O'Hara lived nearby and he wanted to go home and see his wife, so I loaned him a few bucks. I had no money to shoot craps in the washroom (against KR [Air]), because I loaned my money to the losers. I loaned $31.75 in August and I got back $6.50. I didn't charge interest, but there was a chap who was a usurer, which was probably against KR (Air) as well. Jack Gerrard was married, and he always needed money. He used to go to the firing range and sift through the sand for lead pellets to sell.

August 1942 was a month of happenings. My nemesis, Cpl. Penlington, got the sack for not being able to maintain discipline in his flight, and he was replaced by Sgt. Munro, a big, six-foot-three, washed-out pilot turned disciplinarian. And he did maintain discipline. Entry 37 graduated, making us aware that we would be the next to do so. Guinter, Brown and Sherwood got seven days for missing bunk check. The BBC banned the popular sentimental song "Miss You," because it made servicemen homesick. I wrote another chapter of the book *An Airman's Diary*, which had the same title as my newspaper column. A few of us went to Toronto on a 48-hour pass and we were refused admittance to the Carlright Ballroom *because we were in uniform!* Flight Lieutenant Wakefield, an RAF wireless operator with a Distinguished Flying Cross, came to give us a pep talk. Murray Brown, a Prince Rupert type, had been taken prisoner-of-war. Pete Arnaldi and I drove to Detroit's watering holes – the Tropics, Vic's, Club Casanova, the Whittier, the Cascade, and the Brass Rail, a cocktail lounge that stretched through an entire city block. I thought I'd end up spending the $40 that I had saved, but the Yanks wouldn't let us pay for anything. We had the reflected glory of the RAF fighter pilots who had fought the Battle of Britain.

One day when I was practising in the station – the station simulated the wireless operator's position in a bomber aircraft, just as the Link Trainer simulated the pilot's cockpit – a corporal came to tell me that the Royal Canadian Mounted Police wanted to see me in the Orderly Room. I was stunned. I hadn't thought of the Winnipeg incident for months, and I couldn't imagine how they had finally traced me to Guelph. This meant the end of everything: my air force career, my good name, perhaps even my freedom. I shook with foreboding, and my hands were sweating as I entered the Orderly Room.

Sure enough, there were two Mounties, all spit and polish,

and with them was Frank Smart's wife. Frank was the only person from the Camp Borden military constabulary with whom I had maintained contact, and I had even eaten dinner in Toronto once with him and his wife. It seemed that Mrs. Smart was suing Frank for divorce, and her purpose in seeking me out, flanked by the law, was to gain information about Frank's infidelities that would condemn him. I knew nothing, and even if I had I would have kept my mouth shut. They asked me a lot of questions and then the interview was over. I started to breathe again.

Although Guelph was anything but boring, we were becoming impatient to get Overseas where the action was. Around this time, I received a letter from a girl named Georgena, who was already in England. She wrote:

> ... Somehow, I don't think you'll get to England. You'll most probably be sent out East or somewhere like that. We don't seem to be wanting so many troops and airmen over here now. I can't help feeling a wee bit glad you are out of it, though I'd like to see you very much. You are so safe and secure over there and can enjoy yourselves all the better, whilst over here we have so many responsibilities on our shoulders. Living where there are a lot of troops, I most certainly feel right in the midst and thick of it all. I see soldiers that I've been friendly with, sometimes much younger than you, laughingly go away singing, and the next we hear of them they are in a prison camp, or have been torpedoed at sea, or killed in battle, and you'll realize that you'll never see them again. The little habits they had, the way they smiled, the kind of music they liked, it leaves a sort of empty feeling, even though you know that if they came back from the war you'd never see them again – but it's something to know that they are alive. My girl friend's brother was machine gunned and drowned, and you don't get over that so easily. It's then that you start remembering what fun you had with them in school, and all the silly little petty quarrels, how you've grown up with them, and how you won't ever see them again. Yes, on the whole, old man, I'm jolly glad you're out of it.

I'm writing to a lot of the troops who have been stationed here. Some of them have wives who are on munitions and cannot find time to write them long letters, and you know how much soldiers look forward to the mail. One I write to is an older man with no relations at all left, owing to the London blitz, and whilst he was out in Africa he wrote to my kid brother because he wanted to have letters from someone. Another youngster I write to was a jolly kid, 19, though I'm sure the authorities didn't know that. He was absolutely bubbling over to get to the Germans, now I have reason to believe he is one of the sad prisoners at Tobruk, or else he's gone West with a lot of the others on that convoy.

Now please don't think I'm morbid or depressing, or don't even think I'm trying to give you a lecture, but you just don't realize what it's like over here, and you've got to hand it over to our boys that they've been absolutely wonderful, when you see them laughing and joking it's hard to believe that some of them have been through hell – like Dunkirk – and still they come up smiling. I wouldn't miss it for the world now.

I think I'm some sort of a troop mascot. But it is all so entertaining, such great fun to live in the midst of a street with soldiers pouring from every house. So it isn't all one miserable existence. We make up a party for picnics, probably half a dozen soldiers, married, single, or engaged, it doesn't matter, and then, perhaps, my kid sister and I, and the girls next door, and the lady who lives opposite with her husband – we'll all go in crowds to have such fun. Sometimes we go boating and have races. Sometimes we go off swimming and all the neighbours and everybody joins in, even the married women and men – it's really grand to be in a crowd.

The food problem would really be laughable (if you hadn't to eat it). The new wheatmeal bread we have now is really quite nice, but it brings some people out in strange little pimples, and it affects all kinds of people in all kinds of ways. We have had some kind of strange dried eggs, too, and they are really not bad at all. The milk turns sour if you look at it, and, alas, ice cream just tastes like flour and water now. An orange and an apple just don't belong to this world at all, and I wonder what chocolates taste like. You consider it a tremendous favour if the grocer sends you three tiny tomatoes, so we mainly exist on potatoes and bread, bread and potatoes, and potatoes alone. Actually, it's not bad at all, so please don't take me seriously, but somehow you never feel really satisfied with a meal nowadays, and I admit I always feel hungry. Lucky you in Canada. Not that I'm grumbling – please understand I'm not grumbling. I wouldn't miss it. And my Red Cross penny-a-week fund and my savings group are all very entertaining, and after the war I shall be lost without them.

There are folks in this district, always go to church, very good and kind, supposed to be, and they never open their doors to soldiers or show any hospitality at all, never make one cup of tea when they've been travelling all night on a long journey without much to eat. They just live their narrow little good lives, couldn't dream of doing any war work. Dear me, no. I loathe good people – because you generally find they aren't as good as the bad ones, really.

But there I go. Talking about the war again. I think the jolly old censor will be fed up, if there is any censor to Canada.

I really didn't remember Georgena, but her sober impressions of the environment in Britain in the summer of 1942 moved me considerably. I was particularly concerned about the view that I would probably never get Overseas, and that the war might be coming to an end. It depressed me to think that I had spent so much time training for Overseas duty only to learn that I wouldn't be needed. However, it would turn out that her prediction was about three years premature.

At about this time, Jack Byrne's girlfriend in Almonte sent him a Dear John letter. It simply proved that nothing was forever, and I didn't have the heart to laugh.

I was re-establishing my relationship with Reta, and we were exchanging letters on a regular basis, trying to rekindle the ardour we had once known. I was nearing graduation at Guelph, and I hoped that this time I would be posted to a bombing and gunnery school somewhere in Eastern Canada, although the only one that might have taken me near enough to go home on a 48-hour pass – No. 10, on Prince Edward Island – had not yet been opened.

The 47th had spent a week or so at Burch, an auxiliary flying school near Brampton, where we flew in the Flying Class-room, the Avro Anson, a twin-engine general-duty aircraft that was well suited to the kind of work wireless air gunners were training for. We were getting closer to war in the air.

Six general-duty bods did not fare so well. They had left Guelph in late October for Labrador, but they were all killed when their Liberator crashed en route from Montreal. It was believed to be the result of sabotage. I shuddered at the thought that, were it not for Squadron Leader Cochram, I might have been one of them.

My test marks had risen to 90 percent, however, my deport-ments were beginning to add up. Pete Arnaldi and I had gone to Detroit again for a weekend and didn't get back to Guelph on time. F/O Rice "awarded" me seven days CB, but Pete, being a sergeant, got off scot-free.

I also ran into my Ottawa roommate, Darrell Larlee. He had remustered, and was training at Jarvis air gunnery school. And I learned that Syd Ford, with whom I'd gone to college, had won a bar to his DFC.

An Airman's Story was getting nowhere, with so many other things to do, but a prominent New York literary agent, A. L. Fierst, wrote to me saying he was interested in a book about an airman's life and wanted to see my manuscript. Unfortunately, I procrastinated right out of that opportunity.

Other aspects of my life as an airman were getting attention as well, and the *Toronto Telegram* ran this item:

> One squadron of airmen studying at No. 4 Wireless School, RCAF, Guelph Agricultural College, is setting a style which is threatening to spread throughout the entire school. It all started a few weeks ago when members of

the squadron decided to see who could grow the best mustache. The "handlebars" are in the best style made famous by the Royal Air Force, with long, waxed ends protruding well out. And according to the NCOs at the school, the airmen are putting as much time and attention on their mustaches as they are on their tunics and buttons.

Sporting the best of the handlebars, I spent Christmas 1942 with the Carrolls in Toronto, listening to Beethoven's 7th Symphony in A Major. It would be the last time I would see them, although we kept in touch even after the war.

Inspector General (later Air Marshal) George Croil came to Guelph to pin Sparks Badges on our sleeves. How proud we were. The promotion also meant a small boost in pay. Right after the graduation party (where copious quantities of Burke's Jamaican rum – Annie's special potion – were consumed) various segments of the entry were dispatched in the blackness of the night for bombing and gunnery schools where they would receive the last part of their training.

Twenty-four of the 47th entrained for Dafoe, Saskatchewan. Again, I was joed as Class Senior. After Dafoe, I would never see most of them again: Stanley Boudreau, Worcester, Mass.; Edward Began, Parry Sound; Marc Contant, Montreal; H. J. Graham, Stratford; J. P. R. Bellemare, Cap-de-la-Madeleine; R. G. Hanson, Milwaukee, Wisconsin; J. C. Olivier, Sudbury; Joe D'angelo, Brampton; Jack McCulloch, Portage la Prairie; Mons Duke, Huntington, Ont.; Brian Lea, Point Dalhousie; Al Braunstein, Winnipeg; Jack Byrne, Almonte, Ontario; F. S. Russell, Toronto; Fraser Hendrick, Port Credit; Jack Chamberlain, Toronto; Bob Fitzpatrick, Hamilton; John Enright, Renfrew; Doug King, Winnipeg; Louis Gonzalez, Thorold, Ontario. There were also Meyers (of Forest Hills, NY), Corbett (of Kenora) and Micklestone (of Toronto), whose Christian names I never knew.

Remembering them now, all these years later, their appearance and characteristics are as clear to me as when we parted.

CHAPTER 13

Getting to Know the
Browning Machine Gun

T he air force knew what it was doing when it selected Dafoe, Saskatchewan, as the site of its No. 5 Bombing and Gunnery School. It was flat prairie, with no dangerous elevations for low flying aircraft to run into. It was isolated – the horizon was uninterrupted for 360 degrees – and offered little to distract trainees from the serious business of learning how to use aircraft guns. But it was cold – always below zero in the winter time. We thought Dafoe was the most godforsaken, forlorn spot on the face of the earth, but we would be there for only the last four weeks of our training. Our course was essentially the same as that taken by "straight air gunners," who were in great demand at the time to do nothing but operate guns. Some of them who had joined up at the age of 17 1/2 would have completed their training and be in operations Overseas by the time they were 18. In fact, when there was a shortage of gunners Overseas their course was sometimes shortened so they could get into action sooner.

In the Royal Air Force, ground crew armourers were employed as air gunners when extra gunners were needed, but they got only a few pence extra for this and were not even considered aircrew. When they weren't in the air they returned to their regular duties. Incredibly, early on in the RAF it was believed that educational qualifications need not be considered when selecting air gunners. Anyone who could use a gun and had guts could be a successful air gunner – if he lived long enough. Eventually, the RAF recognized the value of air gunners and awarded them the rank of sergeant.

At Dafoe, the RCAF bods who were taking gunnery training would be sergeants on graduation, and some of them would be given commissions.

We concentrated on aircraft recognition and had to know, on site, all enemy aircraft. We would sit in a darkened room for hours, learning the shapes of German and Italian aircraft – the Fiat G55, Macchi and Folgore, and Nazi Dorniers, Junkers, Heinkels and Focke-Wulfs in their various marks – from silhouettes flashed on a screen. It was necessary to memorize their wingspans and the lengths of their fuselages, so that when placed in the ring-sight of a Browning machine gun we could tell how far away the approaching aircraft was. For instance, at about 200 yards an Me. 109 coming head on would just about fill the ring-sight. There would be no point in firing the guns when the enemy aircraft was out of range, but as soon as it came into range, one had to act.

We weren't expected to recognize Japanese aircraft.

Some of the German fighters carried 20-mm cannons, with a greater firing range than the .303 Browning guns with which most of the RCAF bombers were equipped, giving them the advantage of being able to fire on our aircraft before our guns would be effective against them. This situation demanded quick evaluations and decisions from the gunner and manoeuvrability from the pilot.

Ground training on guns and in turrets was intensified at Dafoe, and we began to understand the true role of the air force gunner. We learned everything about gun turrets. We practised getting in and out of them in simulated emergencies. We learned how to remove a faulty breechblock and clear jammed shell-belts; how to repair, improvise and inspect. Seconds of indecision could mean the death of an air gunner and perhaps all members of the crew. So we began to feel important, although in effect wireless operators were only auxiliary gunners when they were in action.

We practised in turrets on the ground and in the air. We were using Bolingbrokes, and, I think, some Bristol Beaufighters, and Beauforts, British two-engine fighter-bombers.

These last may have already received their baptism of fire, and been downgraded for training in Canada.

The Bolingbroke was a sturdy aircraft, and the leading edges of its wings could mow down trees in a forced landing, like scythes cutting a stand of wheat. I did all my flying at Dafoe in Bolingbrokes, operating a mid-upper turret and firing on drogues (a canvas air sack the shape of a cigar, towed by another aircraft). I remember thinking how fortunate it was that there were no cattle or built-up areas below us. We did a lot of flying, but I never knew whether I hit the target or not. I guess they expected the gunner to act on instinct when he got into action. In addition to the Browning gun, which was made in Toronto and was used by the RCAF until the end of the war, we used the Vickers Gas Operated (VGO) gun. This water-cooled machine gun had been designed in 1894 and fired only 60 rounds a minute. It was now obsolete for operational use. In fact, much of the equipment we trained on – the radio sets at Guelph, the turrets and guns at Dafoe – was already obsolete. The only thing that hadn't changed was the ammunition. Point .303 bullets lasted until after 1945.

We had one 48-hour pass during the course, and most of us went to Saskatoon for a Valentine's ball. The whole station shut down for it. Although the dance was at the Bessborough Hotel, one of the elegant railroad inns, Jack Byrne and I stayed at the YMCA.

It is entered in my logbook that on 22 February 1943, I qualified as an air gunner, and some big shot – I have forgotten who – pinned the wings on my chest. At that time, all aircrew except the pilots received a half-wing. The original design had called for 13 feathers, but in deference to the superstitious one of the feathers had been eliminated. Later, a crown was added to the half-wing, and still later the air force gave full wings to all members of aircrew.

I led the class, which pushed my ego up a notch or two. Doug King came second and Jack Byrne was third. It wasn't just that I'd done everything in the précis. I'd done more than

Class No. 47 at Gunnery School in Dafoe, Saskatchewan. (Back Row, L to R) Edward Beagan, Perry Sound, ON; Marc Contant, Montreal; J.C. Olivier, Sudbury, ON; J.P.R. Bellemare, Cap de-la Madeleine, QC; R.C. Hanson, Milwaukee, USA; H.T. Graham, Stratford, ON; Joe D'Angelo, Brampton, ON; Jack McCulloch, Portage la Prairie, MB; (Front Row, L to R) Stanley Boudreau, Wocester, Mass.; Hank Hancock, Wolfville, NS; Bob Meyer, Forest Hills, NY; H. Corbertt, Kenora, ON; R. Mucklestone, Toronto, ON

that: tearing the guns apart – Brownings and VGOs – stirring them up and putting them back together, even with my eyes closed. I studied aircraft silhouettes in my mind before I went to sleep. I was determined that I would do better than good, be better than best. All three of us were given commissions, but we were given sergeant's stripes and white arm bands to wear until our promotions were officially gazetted.

Oh, how proud we were. I could not help thinking of F/O Glenn, F/L Christie, the farm at Vivian and S/L Cochram, and all the things I had done in order to be there at that moment. And I thought of Annie.

It was now clear that the Overseas posting, towards which I'd been striving for so long, was imminent. I looked out the train window as we sped over the frozen prairies, leaving Dafoe, and reviewed the larger picture of the air-war I was about to enter.

Early on, there had been the Battle of Britain, at its fiercest between August and October of 1940. On the eve of the Battle, the RAF had 609 Hurricanes, Spitfires and Defiants, while the Luftwaffe had 1,089 Me. fighters and more than 1,500 bombers. By the end of the battle, the RAF would have lost 915 aircraft to Germany's 1,733.

In May 1942, the first major contingent of the American air force had arrived in England. The famous thousand-plane bomber raids had commenced at the end of May, when the RAF bombed the cathedral city of Cologne. The aircraft used had been mainly Wellingtons, Manchesters, Hampdens and Halifaxes. Forty-two British planes were shot down on the Colgne sortie. Canadian-built Mosquito aircraft had flown their first mission over Cologne. In reprisal, the Germans bombed the English cathedral city of Canterbury.

In addition to the battles in the air, the Battle of the Atlantic was raging. The Germans had mined the area off Newfoundland, and, on 13 October 1942, the ferry *Caribou* had been torpedoed by a German U-boat during its regular run between Sydney and Port-aux-Basques, Newfoundland. One hundred and thirty-four lives had been lost. This may appear insignificant beside other historic marine disasters in the North Atlantic, like the wrecks of the *Titanic* and the SS *Atlantic*, but Canadians were deeply shaken by it, and by the fact that the war had come so near to their shoreline. The sinking of the *Caribou* had precipitated Prime Minister Mackenzie King's decision to invoke the politically ominous act of conscription. The event had affected me on a personal level, as well, to a degree that I had trouble understanding. I'd recorded the disaster in my diary when it had happened. More than any of the horrors of the Overseas war, it had instilled in me a persistent feeling of foreboding.

S ome of us had planned to rendezvous in Winnipeg, on our way east, with Doug King and Al Braunstein. I had asked Jack Byrne if he would accompany me to Brandon, en route to Winnipeg. I wanted to see Annie. I had no illusions about reconciliation, of course. I guess I wanted to show her that I had promise, even as an air gunner, or a wireless operator. I think, also, that I wanted her to know that I had received a commission. This would be like saying to her, "I have promise; you should have given me a chance."

I did not know what to expect as Jack and I climbed the stairs to Annie's parents' apartment on Rossiter Avenue. I didn't know how I would explain my presence there. As the door opened and I saw Annie's mother and the look on her face, my heart stopped beating. For some reason I knew the next minutes would be wretched and painful. When Annie's father appeared out of the gloom, my feeling of impending disaster intensified.

Annie had married a ground crew NCO just after she'd sent me the Dear John letter. It was strange that it had never occurred to me that the real reason she'd left me was for another man. I'd just thought she wanted a more secure future. I was ashamed of my naivety.

Annie had been on her way to Newfoundland to be with her new husband in October 1942, and was among the casualties when the *Caribou* was torpedoed in the Cabot Strait. When I heard this, my whole body felt numb. The visceral ache was still to appear, but for the moment I just fought the shock that reverberated through my being. Even in my grief, I remembered the ghastly feeling of dread that had possessed me when I'd first heard about the disaster back in Guelph.

When next I was alone a tear left the corner of my eye and dribbled down my face, and I thought of something someone had said about crying: "Tears are something you lose from the inside when you've lost something from the outside."

Seeing how much my presence was distressing Annie's grieving parents, I expressed my sorrow, bade them farewell, and left.

CHAPTER 14

No. 31 (RAF)
Operational Training at Debert, NS

We did rendezvous in Winnipeg. Lea, Braunstein, Byrne, King and Duke. We stood on the corner of Portage and Main and confirmed the city's reputation as the "Windy City." Doug King and Al Braunstein lived in Winnipeg and they put us up while we were there. We went dancing at the Cave, a simulated cavern with stalactites made of fireproofed material. (There had previously been a fire there.) It was a gala occasion. Our hosts had rounded up a bevy of girls for us to escort, and I enjoyed the company of King's sister. I never saw any of these people again.

I thought only obliquely of the morning I had arrived in Winnipeg "on the rails."

The long train trip to Nova Scotia gave me time to get my thoughts in order. Jack Byrne was right. I had to get on with my life, and I was determined to let the universe evolve as it was meant to.

I had been away from home for 18 months, and I thought of all the things that had happened in that time. The Dominion Atlantic Railway coach I had boarded at Windsor Junction swayed and clacked noisily as familiar scenes came into view. There were thousands – millions – of men and women pursuing wartime duties in foreign fields who were thinking of home as I stepped down from the train, and I felt the privilege of at last returning to my roots.

News of my old friends came to me quickly. LAC Charlie Dickey had been killed in a flying accident at a service flying school in Ontario. Syd Ford of Liverpool had received the bar

Gunnery graduation party at the Cave in Winnipeg: Hank Hancock, Jack Byrne, Al Braunstein and girls

to his DFC, and Sub-lieutenant Keith Forbes had won the Distinguished Service Cross as a submariner. F/L Red Chisholm of Kentville had won a bar to his DFC in the fight in North Africa. Moon O'Connell had won the DFC and was killed while instructing in a Mosquito at RAF Greenwood. He had been a member of the famous Demon Squadron. In January 1942 he flew so close to a German warship he was attacking that one of his bomb doors was torn off by the ship's mast. Two boys from nearby Port Williams, Grant Graves and George Lantz, had been killed as air gunners. Charlie Cook, another WAG, of Waterville, was dead. Sgt. John Armstrong, an observer from Port Williams, was also dead. F/L Brownie Trask, of Yarmouth, had been taken prisoner.

Meanwhile, I had reunited with Reta, and all was right with the world again. Charlie Cohen had innocently told her about Annie, but she never mentioned it, and neither did I. All of my four brothers were now in uniform, too.

A telegram came from Air Force Headquarters in Ottawa, where lately I had disposed of the trash from Billy Bishop's wastebasket, advising me that I had been commissioned pilot officer, with a new regimental number – J24072. I removed the arm band and got measured for a uniform. I recall that the air force bought my first officer's uniform, but after that I was on my own.

I had no idea where my next posting would be. There were several possibilities: I could remain in Canada as an instructor; I could be sent directly overseas; or I could go to an operational training unit in the Commonwealth group, and then be posted to a Coastal Command squadron operating in the North Atlantic or the Caribbean area.

It was destined that I would go to the Operational Training Unit (OTU) at Debert, Nova Scotia.

Debert was a mud hole. It was a flat expanse of desolation near Truro, the Hub of the province, shared by the army and the air force. This was the first OTU to be completed by the Commonwealth Air Training Plan. It had been designated No. 31, and was operated by the Royal Air Force. It was intended for the training of Coastal Command crews, which flew new aircraft from the United States to Britain, aircraft without armaments – no guns, no armour plate – but rigged with extra fuel tanks for the trans-Atlantic flights that were still a rarity.

The Lockheed Hudson was the aircraft in service at Debert. Auxiliary aircraft were Lysanders and Ansons. It was a Hudson in which Norman MacLeod Rogers, Minister of Defence, had been killed when it crashed at Bowmanville, Ontario, in June 1940, nevertheless, the Hudson was a good maritime patrol bomber. It had a good range (2,800 miles) for a twin-engine aircraft, a speed of 253 mph, and could fly close to the surface of the sea when looking for subs. The RAF had used the Hudson first on 10 December 1938. Armament consisted of two fixed .303 Brownings in the nose and two in the mid-upper turret. The operational crew numbered five, but at Debert there was only a crew of four – the pilot, the navigator, and two WAGs, alternating on the guns.

Some of the Guelph gang were at Debert. I teamed up with Sgt. Dutch Shaw and we went looking for a pilot and navigator.

Dutch had met Mickey McKee, a navigator a bit older than we were, who had been a schoolteacher in Ontario. We thought he would be a good teammate. I picked out a pilot named Bill Ames, whom I remembered seeing at Brandon when he was a Warrant Officer (sergeant major, second class). He was now commissioned, and with 2,000 flying hours to his credit. We made an amicable foursome and we enjoyed each other's company. We did a lot of flying, a good deal of it actual surveillance and convoy work. Once, we were involved in an exciting hush-hush strategy conference inside a submarine in Halifax harbour. It was thrilling to make mock bombing runs over pleasure boats and fishing vessels in places like Chester and Lunenburg. Bill was a good pilot.

The old "Geep" radio equipment we had used at wireless school was now, as I have mentioned, obsolete, and we were checked out on Bendix. It was easy to operate, and we used a trailing aerial (necessary for picking up distant signals) which had to be rolled in manually. Forgetting that the aerial was out was fatal when flying low and when landing. Most of our training was in the air, learning to coordinate flying, navigating and communication. Flight times were usually from four to five hours, but could be as long as 10 hours, night or day. There was one air crash at Debert while I was there. I was on the burial detail.

I shared a room with Murray Souter, a super Australian navigator, who told me about Ned Kelly, the Australian Jesse James, and about A. B. Peterson, who wrote "Waltzing Matilda."

I also met an Englishman at Debert, an RAF chap, who was still an AC2, the equivalent of an army private, after serving for 22 years – almost as long as I had been alive.

I first experienced the privilege of rank when a batman was assigned to me. He was a civilian employed at the base and was responsible for polishing my shoes and tunic buttons, and sometimes for pressing my trousers. One time I asked him if he could get me a bottle of booze, as my crew had planned a gala in Truro to greet Reta, who was coming for the weekend. Liquor was rationed (one 12-ounce bottle a month, by permit) but there was always a way to get it if you knew the right people – or wrong people as it turned out. I made a deal with the batman, who knew someone who knew someone, and I ended up with a bottle of bourbon, an American drink which had probably been "imported." I put the bottle on the table in my room, and when I returned from a flight I noticed that the bourbon had turned blue. Someone, and I always suspected it was the batman, had taken the top off (the usual trick was to pour off a part of the liquor and fill the bottle up with water) and, having lost it, replaced the top with the one from my ink bottle – which would have been acceptable but for the fact that the top had been partially filled with blue ink, which was now floating conspicuously in the potion. In any event, I had to conceal my displeasure, since having liquor in the rooms was strictly taboo, especially for a novice pilot officer such as I.

Reta and I were married on 1 May 1942. The union would last for almost 56 years, until she died from Alzheimer's disease at the age of 83.

It was a typical wartime wedding, fairly private, at the home of long-time friends in Wolfville. My training squadron shut down for the ceremony and my crew attended the event. When we were on the train en route to Wolfville, I noticed Reta's father. He did not know me, but I approached and sat down beside him. He said he was on his way to attend his daughter's wedding. I said, "I know. She is marrying me."

That night Reta and I went to Halifax, where friends of ours who knew Mart Kenny, the band leader, took us to dance at the Nova Scotian Hotel. The band played "Stardust" for us, and it remained ever after "our song."

I returned to Debert the following day, and Reta went back to Wolfville, and to her job at the Royal Bank. The OTU course ended just after that and we were all given 10 days leave before going to Newfoundland to join a Coastal Command squadron.

CHAPTER 15

Fighting the Battle
of the Atlantic

Torbay wasn't exactly what I'd had my heart set on. It was
clear early on that I was not going to be a fighter pilot, but
I had hoped for a posting to a bomber squadron. However,
there was a war on in the Atlantic, and Newfoundland, not yet
part of Canada, was considered "Overseas." The address was
Canadian Army Post Office (CAPO no. 5), and this satisfied a
psychological need we had to be in the war.

There were two squadrons on the station, commanded by
a legendary bush pilot, Group Captain Grandy. One of these
squadrons was No. 145 Squadron, flying Venturas, and the
other was No. 5 Bomber Reconnaissance (BR) Squadron,
flying Cansos, which were amphibious Catalinas. The Ventura
was originally produced to meet British requirements for a suc-
cessor to the Hudson. It entered Bomber Command in 1942,
but switched to Coastal Command in 1943, with various armament and equipment changes. The aircraft was powered by
two 2,000-horsepower Pratt & Whitney Double Wasp engines.
The bomb bay carried bombs, depth charges and a single tor-
pedo. The range had been increased to 1,100 miles, and the
aircraft had a speed of 315 miles per hour at 15,000 feet. The
Americans used .50 calibre machine guns, but I think we had
installed .303 calibre Browning guns in an upper turret.

My squadron – 5 (BR) – was using the Canso aircraft, which
was essentially the Consolidated PBY Catalina, with the added
ability to land on water – a convenient faculty given the area
in which my squadron operated. It was a distinguished aircraft, tough and dependable. The first of these aircraft was

produced in 1935, and from then until the end of the war the Canso saw service in every war zone. The Canso was built in Canada by Boeing. It had two Pratt & Whitney radial engines. It wasn't much for speed, but it was range rather than speed that was required for the job it was doing. It cruised at about 180 mph and its range was 3,100 miles. The wingspan was 104 feet, two feet more than that of the great Lancaster bomber. The Canso had an observation blister on each side, where two Browning guns were fixed. It had a crew of eight – a pilot and co-pilot, a navigator, three engineers, and two WAGs, who did double duty in shifts on the radio and guns.

We liked the Canso.

There was also a Hurricane fighter squadron on the station, but I never knew exactly what they did. From time to time we would also see Bostons, Lysanders and Digbys resting from whatever job they'd been assigned to do.

Gander air station was located on Gander Lake in east-central Newfoundland. It was an important and strategic air base, shared by the Americans and the RCAF. Most of the aircraft arriving from Overseas (often carrying foreign dignitaries) landed at Gander for refuelling, since aircraft at that time were not able to make it all the way to Canada or the United States without taking on more petrol. The RCAF there operated four-engine Liberators. Group Captain Claire Annis was the station commander, and we were all under the direction of Eastern Air Command (EAC), centred in Halifax, where Rear Admiral L. W. Murray of VE day notoriety was in command. On one occasion six entire crews from Torbay and other EAC bases were seconded to Gander for a panic operation. It was an interesting experience flying in the 10 (BR) Squadron Liberators.

Another part of the defence mechanism of Newfoundland was a U.S.-operated landing field at Stephenville, on the west coast. The Americans had also leased the Argentia peninsula in the southeast in 1940, and the army and navy had used it as an aerial base and military training ground ever since.

Few members of my squadron had ever been to Newfoundland before, and it was an unforgettable experience in our young lives. The island (affiliated with Labrador) was primitive, if that term can be used with decorum, when the air force arrived there early in the war. In 1945, Newfoundland was a British colony. It had been granted both representative and responsible government in the 19th century, but by 1929, in the midst of the Great Depression, things had become so bad that the colony asked the British to resume responsibility for its affairs. At the outbreak of the war, the colony was being administered by a Commission Government headed by a British governor. It was not until 1949 that Newfoundland would become a province of Canada.

In 1943, the island occupied a strategic position in the war against the Germans, standing as a bulwark for North America against aggression from the east. It was in the role of landlord that the continuing war brought prosperity to Newfoundland.

The capital, St. John's, had often been destroyed by fire in its history, and each time it was rebuilt in a haphazard fashion, almost as though people expected that fire would consume it again. The Americans settled at Fort Pepperel in the city in 1941, and would stay until long after the war was over. When Dutch Shaw, Mickey McKee, Bill Ames and I arrived at Torbay, just 10 miles from St. John's, we found the capital city – and Newfoundland generally – quaint, friendly and unsophisticated, with a fascinating language and a delightful sense of humour.

Curiously, education in Newfoundland was denominational. The Catholics, Anglicans, Presbyterians, Baptists and even the members of the Salvation Army operated schools for their own flocks.

The interior of the island, as we would see it from the air, was desolate and forbidding, although it was dotted by lakes, which teemed with trout and salmon. Moose and caribou roamed freely at the outskirts of landlocked harbours where we could see the saltbox houses, painted all the brightest colours in the spectrum. Newfoundland was once the home of the Beothuk Indians, now long extinct. It was the world of Sir

William Grenfell, the medical missionary, as well as the inspiration for Art Scammel's "The Squid-Jiggin' Ground," and many other Irish-flavoured folk songs. Newfoundland was an accumulation of isolated fishing communities with picturesque names like Goobies, Come-by-Chance, Joe Batt's Arm, Conception Bay and Dildo.

At the mouth of St. John's excellent harbour there was a huge iceberg left over from the spring floe. It remained there all through the summer.

The St. John's landscape was dominated by the Roman Catholic Basilica, of Romanesque design, and the Gothic Anglican Cathedral. A winding road led up to Signal Hill where, in Cabot Tower in 1901, Marconi received the first transAtlantic wireless message. The Newfoundland Hotel (the only proper hostel in the city, and one of the few brick buildings) stood near the harbour, where a variety of vessels, maimed by torpedoes and gunfire, assembled to lick their wounds and await repairs.

One of the privileges of being an officer was that you could bring your wife to Newfoundland, as long as there were no children. Reta came over to join me in the early spring of 1943. She had been born in Scotland, but for the trip she was required to get a Canadian passport, which identified her as "a British Subject!" (Of course, air force personnel did not need passports.) She took the S.S. *Burgeo* to Port aux Basques, the *Burgeo* having replaced the *Caribou*, and then the famous narrow-gauge "Bullet" across the territory to St. John's, where I met her, complete with side arm (a service revolver issued to all aircrew personnel) to create a sense of bravado. Actually, the only airmen who typically wore side arms were accountants when they picked up the payroll from the bank, and even then it was seen as ostentation. But it was good to see Reta. Living accommodations in St. John's were practically nonexistent, and it was, perhaps, foolhardy for me to challenge the inconveniences that faced airmen living off the base. We did find a room on a temporary basis, however, and I left Reta to fend for herself until my crew were off the flight order. She entered the only restaurant she could find, but left soon after when she saw a customer drinking out of the ketchup bottle. Eventually, we would discover Stirling's Restaurant, the only acceptable one in the city.

I had befriended Gibby Love, a pilot with No. 145 Squadron, from Vancouver, and Alf Edwards, from Ontario, a station accountant who had been seconded by His Majesty's Constabulary to secure the currency found on the bodies of 99 casualties of a disastrous fire in the Knights of Columbus hostel in St. John's. Both Gibby and Alf's wives were on the island, and they had rooms at a place on Forest Road. Reta and I went to the house and were fortunate in obtaining a large furnished room. The landlord was Alain Frecker, who had come from St. Pierre and was Superintendent of Education in St. John's. We established a friendship that would last for many years. He was eventually Minister of Education in the Joey Smallwood government and then Chancellor of what would become Memorial University.

Those days in Newfoundland were probably the best times of our lives, carefree and loving. We went to dances at the Navy Club and to parties held in the officers' mess at Torbay. Although the three girls cooked many of their meals together at the Freckers' – they were able to get fresh food at subsidized prices at the United States commissary – Stirling's became a popular eating place, and there were also frequent dinners held expressly for the wives at Torbay.

In between patrols of duty, we explored St. John's, went to movies in a made-over cinema where the seats were higher at the front than in the rear. We visited Petty Harbour to see codfish drying on the flakes in the sun, and we had picnics at Bannerman and Bowring parks.

The St. John's Regatta was a classic annual event held in August, and the townspeople didn't allow the war to interfere with it. Reta and I wanted to see it, so we followed the crowds, only to end up in a Catholic cemetery where a burial was taking place.

Shopping was hilarious. The clothing stores had stocked

out-of-style shirts and sweaters for so long that the hangers were coming through the shoulders. "Git yourself here!" the clerk would say, when she had moved herself along the counter. Or, "Stay where you're to and I'll come where you're at." The Irish Newfoundland humour permeated every gathering.

In the mess, officers took turns censoring the station's outgoing mail. (No postage was required for letters from servicemen, but letters mailed in St. John's cost three cents.) The airmen got used to information restraints eventually, but often the censoring chore provided many laughs. A correspondent writing to a wife or girlfriend would say: "I can't tell you anything about the weather. It's about the same as it was last year this time, but I wasn't here then. But it's pretty gruesome, anyway." Another letter: "... I haven't heard from you. Wonder why. Don't want to be assuming too much. Perhaps you don't care for me any more. I guess I'd better start looking for a little blonde to help me pass the time. Am writing this letter, but will not write again until I hear from you. I love you." Letters were important. "Sorry I'm slow in writing. But you know how it is." And, "There was a dance in the mess last night, but I didn't go." Another letter ended with: "... thinking of you always. I was going to send you some money, but didn't think of it until I had the letter sealed." Then there was the man who wrote two letters, one to his wife and one to his girlfriend, but put them in the wrong envelopes. The censor didn't know what to do. On one occasion I censored a letter from a warrant officer I knew, to a girl I had been madly in love with when I was in high school. After that I would pass his letters on to someone else. While it was not the intention that the censor should be entertained by the correspondence, it was interesting to see how relationships developed over time. Generally, the letters were left intact unless there was some reference to ships in the harbour undergoing repairs, manpower postings, that sort of thing. (We were warned about writing comments in the margins, but we were often tempted.) Letter writers often included a joke "for the censor." "The AOC was inspecting the squadron," one letter read. "And he approached the aircraft on the tarmac and said to one of the crew: 'If you were in flight and the captain at the controls was suddenly wounded, what would you do?' The man replied, 'Nothing, Sir.' 'Come on,' urged the senior officer, 'This is a crisis situation. Your captain is dead. What would you do?' 'Nothing, Sir,' was again the reply. 'How dare you say such a thing?' the officer shouted. 'Sir,' replied the airman, 'I am the captain of the crew.'"

A lot of poems were included. One of them read:

> I had a date with you last night,
> We had a lovely time.
> The wine and food were perfect,
> The music was divine.
> We danced 'till after 3 AM,
> Went home the longest way;
> And when we finally said goodnight
> T'was almost break of day.
> What's more, you wore no uniform,
> The war was fought and won.
> The fears and hate and misery
> Were over with and done –
> Oh, yes, was only dreaming,
> A lot of which I do.
> But, then, I always add a prayer
> And hope it may come true.

We heard our first Newfie jokes in those days, and I read this one in a censored letter: "I saw a car parked, going uphill, with a rock in front of its front wheels." Another: A Newfoundlander crossing the strait aboard the *Burgeo* was asked if he knew which lifeboat he was assigned to. He said, "Yes," and was then asked which one. "The one that leaves first," he replied.

Life on coastal operations was casual. We spent a great deal of time, when the weather was bad, training for emergency situations we hoped would never arise – water-landing on the sea and dinghy drill. The weather was always a problem. We were plagued by high seas, strong winds and fog, all typical of the North Atlantic. We had good radar equipment and it came in handy when we couldn't see the water. Our job was to patrol and sweep, following a pattern that kept the navigator busy. Anti-U-boat, anti-shipping and meteorological flights, and air/sea rescue were our job, as was hovering over convoys and searching for enemy submarines and enemy surface vessels. Usually, we were airborne from six to 10 hours before being relieved by another squadron operating out of another base. On one run, however – on the triangle between Newfoundland, Reykjavik in Iceland, and the Azores, a group of islands off the northwest coast of Africa – my aircraft was out for 22 hours. Most of the time we were bored and tired. Peering constantly down at the grey sea, sometimes from only a hundred feet above it: it was stressful, yet we could not relax surveillance for a minute. That was why there were three engineers, two pilots and two WAGs (only one navigator, though). The third engineer served as the cook, and fortunately he was usually pretty good in the galley. When crews were out for a long time it helped morale to eat well. Steaks and salmon were always on the menu. We took turns resting in the two canvas bunks.

Curiously, although Bill Ames, Lloyd McKee, Dutch Shaw and I trained together as a crew at OTU, I don't think we ever flew together on operations. It seemed that everyone was a spare. Most of the WAGs were non-commissioned officers, and some were warrant officers, which meant they had been on the job for a long while and were not easily excited. Because I was the only commissioned officer among them, and a greenhorn, I never really fitted into their coterie. I flew as a "second WAG" until I gained some experience.

The Royal Air Force was traditionally reluctant to commission certain trades, and even pilots sometimes waited long periods before becoming officers. However, there were exceptions. Ivor Broom was one of them. He learned to fly in the RAF in 1940 and as a sergeant gained experience in flying Blenheims on low-level daylight operations over the English Channel. He was eventually commissioned "in the field" and rose to become Air Marshall Sir Ivor Broom, CBE, DSO, AFC and DFC with three bars. Actually, the officer commanding my squadron, W/C F. J. Ewart, born in Clinton, Ontario, joined the RCAF in 1924 as an aircraftman 2nd class (the lowest rank) aero-engine mechanic. He earned his wings in 1929.

My first operational flight on 5 (BR) Squadron was with S/L Krug, who soon after fell into an excavation and broke his ankle. I then flew with Flying Officer Stober for a number of long patrols. I went on several trips with Pilot Officer Zeke Taylor, who pranged an aircraft and was sent away for "psychological adjustment." I never saw him again. I was the radio operator for Wing Commander Ewart, who wanted to practise water landings. A pilot was never allowed to fly without a WAG, so that left WAGs in demand for duties that were not always exciting.

I was with Stober on a long flight of 15 hours on 21 June 1943. We were escorting a hundred merchant ships. We passed over some icebergs and a few pods of whales, and then we sighted an enemy sub that had apparently come to the surface to charge its batteries. This is where it all came together – all the training and discipline and purpose. This was the moment of truth. Adrenalin surged through our bodies with absorbing force as the aircraft was manoeuvred for the attack. But the thrill was short-lived, as the U-boat quickly disappeared below the surface of the sea and low clouds prevented us from attacking. However, we dropped the two 250-pound depth charges attached to each of the wings, with no obvious effect. Although it was a highly disappointing exercise, we were consoled by the knowledge that even when patrol aircraft failed to make a kill they were able to alert the convoy that the enemy was in the area.

There were other satisfying activities performed by coastal squadrons, including searching for lost aircraft and ships in distress. And we knew the feeling of security we gave to troops and crews of ships when they knew we were near.

In spite of the long hours of dull routine endured by the aircrews, their labours were not without moments of high excitement and glory. In August 1942, RCAF Sunderlands were ranging from Reykjavik to Gibraltar, with not much happening (most of the action at the time was in the Bay of Biscay, off the coast of France). But an aircraft piloted by Flying Officer Al Bishop (who had received a Distinguished Flying Medal in a previous mission) set out on a routine flight only to encounter a U-boat on the surface. Bishop prepared for a frontal attack and the sub began to weave. Several shots were fired from the nose gun before it jammed, leaving the big Sunderland vulnerable to fire from the sub. Although the sub made a hit and fire broke out on the aircraft, the crew were able to drop the plane's depth charges before the Sunderland crashed into the sea. The surfaced sub moved in to attack, but before it could do so there was an unexplained explosion (probably as a result of the depth charges) and the sub sank. An Allied destroyer appeared in minutes and picked up the wounded members of the aircrew (five others were presumed dead) as well as 23 survivors of the sub, who were taken prisoner.

RCAF squadrons fought on both sides of the Atlantic and would be responsible for destroying 19 submarines; they shared in the destruction of four others. Canadian coastal crews also served in the Japanese war in the Pacific. No. 162 Squadron would achieve six confirmed kills in the spring of 1944. No. 423 Squadron destroyed five U-boats during the war, and No. 407 destroyed four. Squadron No. 10, which was based in Gander, had three German subs on its kill list, and Nos. 145 and 5 on the Torbay base had also scored.

Six RCAF crew members received the highest British decorations, the Victoria Bronze Cross and the silver George Cross. Two of these were awarded to coastal command personnel on anti-submarine operations. The RCAF's first VC winner was F/L David Ernest Hornell, of Lucknow, Ontario, who was flying with No. 162 Squadron when his aircraft destroyed a German U-boat while under heavy fire. Blinded and exhausted, Hornell displayed great courage in trying to save members of his crew when the aircraft crashed into the sea; this heroism contributed to his death.

By mid-1943, most of the bods from Prince Rupert and Guelph had completed first tours of duty or had died in the attempt. Jack Jackson wrote me from Bermuda to say that Todd, Guinter and Gedelian had taken off from the Bahamas on May 31, but had not returned. Unlike aircraft that crashed on land, flying boats could disappear forever in the ocean depths.

Judge Bigelow sent out a newsletter in which he said that DFCs had been awarded to Chuck Procter, George Tait, Bill Adams and Gerry Edwards. Someone from home wrote to say that Kentville-area native Don Keith had been captured by the Germans in Egypt and put in one of the Stalags. He'd tried to escape in a junk, but it sank.

In July, F/L Hastie was killed in a Hudson takeoff in Charlottetown, and in October, S/L Lee was killed in a flying accident in Torbay. Dying in action was one thing. But dying as the result of an accident, sometimes preventable, was a humiliating way to check out. I was a pallbearer at Lee's funeral. It would be repeated often in the days to come, but hearing the bugle playing the last post was an emotional devastation and has remained so ever since.

I flew often with F/O Fletcher. His crew was made up of Warrant Officer Croskery (2nd pilot), F/O Emmons (navigator), W/O Thackery (WAG), and Sgts. Mills and McBeth. We flew close to the icebergs and the vibration of our engines caused huge boulders of salty ice to break away and slip into the sea. Often we would fly so close to the water that the trailing aerial would drag in the swell. We were too low for long range reception anyway. We would test our guns by firing at whales. Sometimes our flight plan would take us over Sable Island, the graveyard of ships, and we would see the Sable Island ponies herding in tribes on the sand.

Once, while flying with Leo Murray, we encountered a Blohm & Voss far out of its range – as we were – southeast of Iceland. We decided it was a Blohm & Voss 138, which had a tail assembly like an American Lightning. It was a reconnaissance plane with three engines and a maximum speed of 170 mph. We couldn't fly much faster. By definition we knew it was armed with machine cannon and carried up to six 110-pound bombs and an assortment of depth charges and sea mines. We didn't know whether the 138 had seen us, but we made a cautious decision not to attack it. It had probably made the same decision about us.

I flew a number of times with Leo Murray. When he went missing I thought how easily I might have been one of his WAGS on that patrol. I remember Cpl. Zacharias, Murray's first engineer, who would have made a superb barbecue chef. His steaks were delicious. Other members of Murray's crew included his co-pilot F/O Woodie, Sgt. Thompson, and Sgts. McLeod, Robin and Paise.

There were some curious happenings in Coastal Command; one of them involved a Hudson bomber circling in an area south of Ireland. To its surprise – and ultimate delight – the Nazi U-boat 570 surfaced directly under it. The sub was so surprised that it succumbed to the challenge of the Hudson and surrendered. The U-boat itself was commandeered into the British Navy and served as the H.M.S. *Graph*.

One of the difficulties of living off the station was getting to work in the mornings. We usually knew the night before whether we would be flying the following day, unless there was a flap of some kind. The onus was on the airman to know about that. One morning I missed a patrol because the bus broke down and I couldn't get a taxi in time to take off. A spare WAG flew in my place, which didn't really present a problem, but w/c Ewart tore a strip off me. And he was right.

I was beginning to feel like a veteran. Standing in the blister of a Canso, flashing signals with an Aldis lamp to the Senior Naval Officer (SNO) in the flagship below made me feel important.

There was a kind of camaraderie developing on the station, as well as a laxity in the usual discipline found on an operational station. One rainy day, a group of officers, including the president of the mess committee (PMC), was shooting craps on a pool table (playing dice was a favourite pastime, probably because it was a game that could be stopped with little ceremony) when CO Grandy came in. He had previously given strict instructions (King's Regulations) that there should be no gambling in the mess. One of the players had just received the dice when CO slipped into an empty space at the table. There was a brief silence. No one knew what to say, until the man holding the dice said, "They're your dice, Sir, and I'm playing $2 with you." Grandy was so surprised by the joviality that he just picked up the game pieces and walked away.

Canada was putting on a blockbuster war-bond drive, and VIPs from the air force were making the rounds of air stations to encourage airmen to support the war effort. This seemed a bit ridiculous, but most of us bought bonds. We were having a big bash in the mess this night and a lot of brass would be in attendance. I had written a propaganda story for *Wings Overseas*, and when the adjutant called for me to meet him in the mess, I thought it was about the article. When I arrived, however, I was surprised to see "Cockles" Cochram, now director of the RCAF Chaplaincy Service and a group captain, waiting to see me. I could hardly believe that he had gone to the trouble of finding me. But I would never again be surprised to see him, as he was obviously intent on being assured that the faith he had placed in me in Ottawa was justified. We had a pleasant chat, and that was that.

Squadron wives were bussed in from St. John's for the festivities (as well as some young women to date single officers and, I presumed, men of other ranks, who were partying in their own messes). There was a magnificent formal dinner, offering delicious fresh foods transported by plane from the mainland, as Newfoundland did not then produce much in the way of delectables. Reta and I were assigned a table which included Honorary Flight Lieutenant C. V. Tompkins, the Protestant padre, whose Sunday chapel services were attended mostly by his drinking pals. Also in attendance was a senior intelligence officer, Neil Price, who had been on the station for several days, en route to somewhere else. I knew him from university, where he had been a star hockey player for the college team.

He would go back to college after the war to study law and later to train for the ministry, after which he would become pastor of my hometown church for many years.

When I had first arrived in Torbay there was a young navigator just finishing his tour of duty. He had been ordained as a clergyman but was too young to join the chaplaincy so he'd joined aircrew, served his time on a Torbay squadron, and was now returning to Canada to become a chaplain. The night before his departure was a regal send-off. Someone even put a white clerical collar around the water jug at the bar.

I lost my hat the night of the bond-drive party. All flat hats look pretty much alike in the cloakroom, and although I had put my name inside the band someone whose head was the same size – but not, perhaps, so clear – as mine, took my hat instead of his own. I waited until all the hats save one had been claimed, then took that one and left.

As 1943 wore on, I became restless and thought it was time I moved on, closer to my destiny. I went to W/C Ewart and asked for a transfer to Bomber Command, which would ensure that I would go to England (or some other theatre of war) and join one of the squadrons there. To my surprise it was only a day or so before my request was granted. Some other personnel at Torbay were being transferred to Bomber Command, while others were being transferred to Coastal Command squadrons in the Maritimes, or elsewhere Overseas. There seemed to be a readjustment of emphasis taking place in the war against the Axis.

Almost at once, Reta returned to the mainland, where she would live with her sister in Ste.-Anne-de-Bellevue, Quebec, until our future could be clarified. Alf Edwards, who had just had an abscessed tooth removed and was augmenting the effectiveness of the anaesthetic with overdoses of Newfoundland screech, stood with me in the November chill and waved to Reta as she peered through a small window in a trans-Canada Lodestar, and was gone.

My last flight out of Newfoundland was as a passenger on

Canso "A" No. 9774, piloted by F/L Langmuir. Air Vice-marshal Heakes was aboard as we circled St. John's. We could see the vintage automobiles driving along the left side of the cobbled streets and between the rows of frame houses leaning from the wind. There was Cape Spear, the most easterly headland on the North American continent. And there, too, was Mt. Cashel Orphanage on the road to Torbay, which would one day become infamous in a sexual abuse inquiry and be closed down. Our flight plan took us over Corner Brook and Port aux Basques, and I looked down at the black restless water where Annie had gone down with the *Caribou*, two years before. For a moment I felt my senses shrouded in that icy wet, the numbness of hypothermia. I felt the struggle to live usurped by death's paralyzing apathy – the capitulation to fate – as though I were she. I imagined my body slipping into oblivion, the future lost forever, and my heart was tormented by pain and regret.

CHAPTER 16

Crossing the Atlantic
on the Queen Mary

My arrival at the "Y" Depot in Lachine, Quebec, was the culmination of three years of intrigue, scheming, manipulation and training. Now it was happening. I was on my way to the war. Apart from that, information was in short supply – on a need-to-know basis, and I guess I didn't need to know. By coincidence, I was not far from Ste.-Anne-de-Bellevue, and so I had a chance to see Reta one more time. There were no histrionics when we parted, no emotional collapse. Women seem to understand better than men that the parting kiss may be the last, and they live with it. I stood on the train step and waved in the night as Reta's figure disappeared in the steam of the engine.

I presumed that since there was a "Y" Depot in Halifax that I would have departed from Pier 21 if that had been the intention, but it was obvious that the next boat Overseas was leaving from New York, and that's where we went. We were a small contingent – 100 RCAF officers. Some of them I knew, like F/L Irving Kennedy, one of the Regina gang, who wore a DFC ribbon on his chest and was returning to England for a second tour; but most of them were strangers to me. We were escorted at night to a train waiting on a siding. The train had been thoroughly blacked out, which seemed theatrical, but it was not: it was difficult to conceal the dispatch of troops, but important that the attempt be made to do so. The train arrived in New York in the morning and we were transported at once to the docks, where we walked for miles, it seemed, to a gaping entrance in the side of a great ship – the Queen Mary. Carrying all of our possessions in metal suitcases (almost the size of trunks), we boarded.

It was a thrill to be aboard the famous Cunard liner, now converted into a troop transport. I don't know how it happened so efficiently, but the air force contingent was dispatched without delay to staterooms, converted from their previous spacious glamour to utilitarian compactness. There were about a dozen bunks in each compartment. But we were better accommodated than most other men on board. The 17,000 American troops, most of whom were black, slept on the decks. I could hardly believe that so many soldiers could crowd together in such a small space.

The Queen Mary was no ordinary boat. She was built in Swansea and sailed on her maiden voyage from Southampton to New York in 1936. What a magnificent, stately, plush ship she was then. She was more than a thousand feet long, could carry 1,939 passengers and had a speed of 31 knots. Originally, she had sported the "largest propeller in the world" (35 tons), but it had had to be scrapped because of the vibration. She was the Titanic all over again. The Queen Mary's accoutrements, her carpets and chandeliers, her silver dinnerware, her dance floors and swimming pools were enchanting. Bellboys were subjected to fingernail inspections before they were released to serve the elitist passengers, to deliver hot tea on trays at the morning door, to deliver the ship's own newspaper and to promenade high-society dogs on at least six of the 12 decks.

The building of the Queen Mary had been plagued by strikes and financial difficulties, but the government had bailed out the Cunard line for purposes of national pride. The intention was to name the liner the "Victoria." The director of the company, who was a friend of King George V, approached him to discuss the name. At the time the ship's only name was "Hull 524." The director asked the king, "Would His Majesty consent to the great liner's being named after the most illustrious and remarkable woman who has ever been Queen of England?" (meaning Queen Victoria), and King George, thinking it was his wife that was meant, said, "That is the greatest compliment that has ever been made to me and my wife. I will ask her permission when I get home." So the ship was named *Queen Mary*.

Queen Mary herself christened the vessel with a bottle of Australian wine.

All the menus on the initial voyage were autographed by Sir Edgar Britten, the Cunard commodore. And the new King, Edward VIII, inspected the *Queen* before she sailed.

The *Queen Mary* seemed quite a different vessel now. We were issued life preservers and given cursory instructions on how to use them. We were then given meal tickets and told the times they were to be used in designated dining rooms. Some of us, the RCAF officers, were arbitrarily seconded for fire-picket duty, which meant we were to patrol the various decks. It was not an onerous task. The American soldiers spent most of their time – when they weren't vomiting in the scuppers – shooting dice, the international mobile game. From time to time I would join them, and on the voyage I won $250 Canadian. The English pound sterling was worth $4.47 Canadian throughout the war. It may have been worth more in American currency, but the players accepted the pound note as equivalent to $5 U.S.

There was no fanfare as the great ship pulled away from the New York dock. In fact, most of us were unaware that we had departed until we were out to sea, where the ship began to roll slightly. In the morning everyone was summoned to the decks for lifeboat drill, which was rudimentary despite the fact that we were sailing in dangerous waters; dangerous not only because of the presence of the enemy but because we were running into a storm, a gale that worsened as we sailed eastward. It would take us four days to cross the ocean, and almost from the beginning regular meals in the dining rooms were suspended. The troops had been receiving their meals in paper containers, and eventually we would do the same.

We tried the dining room in the beginning. Although it had been stripped of its glamour, tablecloths were still in use. Cutlery and china, however, were strictly utilitarian. The ship would rise at the bow and then dip precipitously; then it would roll from side to side before dipping again. Everything slipped from the tables. Further, it was dangerous even to walk, as the angle was so steep one could hardly be prevented from running with the roll. The resultant injuries were putting excessive strain on the sick bays.

In the staterooms people were constantly rolling out of their bunks onto the deck, and it was a miracle that no one in my cabin was seriously hurt.

When the *Queen Mary* first went into service as a troop carrier she was escorted by a naval vessel. On one occasion, in October 1942, while carrying 10,000 US troops to Britain, she knifed right through the escort ship, *Curacao*. The sea was calm and visibility perfect. Sailing at the rate of 28 knots, the 81,235-ton liner was on a zigzag course to avoid subs. She made a turn without communicating with the escort, and sliced clear through the *Curacao*. It hardly made a bump, and the passengers on the *Queen Mary* were unaware that anything had happened as the great liner went on her way. A total of 338 men lost their lives in the incident. It was not until 1947 that a court decision held that the fault was with the escort vessel as it was supposed to stay clear of the ship overtaking it.

After that the *Queen Mary* sailed without an escort, counting on the zigzagging procedure and her tremendous speed to protect her from the U-boats. These assurances were not entirely convincing to those on board in December 1943, and we constantly imagined U-boats tracking our course.

Perhaps the highlight of my cruise to Britain was meeting Wing Commander Guy Gibson, who had led the elite bomber squadron No. 617 when it attacked the dams in the Mohne and Eder Rivers, just a few months earlier. He had won the Victoria Cross for his courage. He was coming from one of those pep-talk tours in the United States where he had been idolized as the greatest hero of the war – as he was, of course, in Britain and Canada. I met him by chance as he was strolling on the deck with Winston Churchill's daughter Sarah. He was particularly interested in the fact that I was a Canadian. Several of the Dambusters were Canadians, among them Flight Sgt. Ken Brown, who lived in British Columbia after the war until he died in 2003, one of the last of No. 617 Squadron. My conversation with Gibson was brief and casual, but I was impressed by his bearing (although he was small in stature) and boyish informality. I had never met a Victoria Cross winner before, Billy Bishop notwithstanding.

Gibson had been given command of No. 617 in May 1943, and 18 Lancaster bomber crews were selected to undergo a tightly secured training program, expressly for the purpose of destroying the dams which supplied power to the Ruhr. Sir Barnes Wallis had made a "bomb" and devised a procedure for using it, requiring the aircraft to approach at low levels. During the attack the Mohne dam held until Gibson's fifth run at it, and then he went on to the Eder, which was also breached. The Canadian Ken Brown was directed to participate in a diversionary flight to the Sorpe dam. He had to make 10 runs on the target because of poor visibility, under heavy fire from ground artillery, before the bomb load was dropped accurately.

Eight of the aircraft involved failed to return, and there was some question as to the importance of the raid, in view of its losses.

There is an interesting story told about the dam raids that bears telling, whether or not it is spurious. When news of the dams being breached reached Grantham, where Sir Arthur Harris and other Bomber Command VIPs were waiting for results, there was a rush to inform Sir Charles Portal, chief of the RAF, who was in Washington at the time. Harris grabbed the nearest phone he could find and said: "Give me the White House." The Women's Auxiliary switchboard operator, assuming the excited voice was that of one of the Australians on the station who tried to make calls to Adelaide and Sydney when they were in their cups, politely suggested that the caller get his batman to see him to his quarters. When Harris insisted, the girl connected him with a pub down the road called the White House.

No. 617 Squadron went on to even greater triumphs, and would continue to do so. Guy Gibson would inherit a desk job after his return from the United States, but he harangued his superiors to let him return to operations until they finally gave in. One day in July 1944, he would take off in a Mosquito to act as master bomber of 5 Group on a target near the Ruhr Valley. After the bombing he would say on the intercom, "OK, chaps, that's fine. Now beat it home." Apparently he did not heed his own advice. No one would ever know what happened. Perhaps he was hit by flak. But he crashed in Holland, Britain's greatest air hero. He was 26.

The *Queen Mary* docked at Greenock, Scotland, and General George Patton, his two pearl-handled pistols holstered by his side, like the hero of a bad Western, was on the dock to greet his 17,000 countrymen. He stood on the dock holding a microphone. "Welcome to Scotland," he said. He looked at a few of the Canadians standing near the gangway, and at Wing Commander Guy Gibson, VC, DSO, DFC and bar, who had flown 273 operations against the enemy, and said, "Welcome, also, to you young air force officers from Canada. We're glad to have you here to help us finish the job."

Major General Sir Eric Gerwin welcomed the Yanks on behalf of the British Army, and an RAF Air-commodore welcomed the RCAF officers (calling us "Australian airmen"). Probably met the wrong boat.

CHAPTER 17

Charley Joins the RCAF
Contingent in Britain

E n route to Bournemouth by train, we were impressed by
the cordial welcome we were given by the Scots people.
The Salvation Army distributed tea and cakes, and children,
waving Canadian and American flags, ran along beside the
tracks. We were warmed by this introduction to a country we
would come to love.

The journey to Bournemouth was a good introduction to
wartime Britain. Although it was wintertime, much milder
than our winter at home, the fields were green, and they
became greener still as we left the land of the heather behind
and passed through little English villages and towns, whose
names had been removed from the stations so that prowling
enemy aircraft couldn't identify the locations. The effect of
the war was more pronounced in larger communities, where
bomb damage to buildings and industrial areas could be seen.
Some of this damage was probably haphazard, poor sight-
ing by the Nazi bombers. Where the fields were more expan-
sive we could see posts, like telephone poles, driven into the
ground to discourage the landing of enemy planes. (Rudolf
Hess, deputy leader of the Nazi party, had parachuted from his
plane when he flew to Scotland on his "peace mission" in May
1941.) Cattle and sheep – we had never seen so many sheep –
grazed between the poles without concern.

As the train passed through London, we could see the still
greater damage to buildings and factories resulting from the
Blitz. We were impressed by the dozens of barrage balloons

hovering over the city, their metal chains dangling beneath them, the bane of strafing enemy aircraft.

The Commonwealth Air Training Plan was still pumping hundreds of aircrew into manpower channels, and they came first to Bournemouth. (In fact, Bournemouth was the repatriation centre for all airmen going home as well.) Bournemouth shared with other cities along the south coast of England – Brighton, Plymouth, Portsmouth – a reputation as an elitist vacation centre. Plymouth and Portsmouth were great naval centres, also, and both were heavily bombed in 1941.

Bournemouth was not quite what I expected. In fact, I hadn't known what to expect. I suppose I thought the atmosphere would be tense, one of fear and depression. It was quite the opposite. Airmen were out on the town, visiting the dancing palaces and cinemas, and pubbing, laughing and frolicking. You could not tell those who were coming from war from those who were going to it, except, perhaps, for the ribbons on the tunics of those who had been there. Everyone was in uniform – soldiers, airmen, sailors. Shoulder badges identified Canadians, Australians, New Zealanders, Norwegians and French.

The insignia on servicemen's uniforms were intriguing. They gave newcomers an appreciation of how much of the free world was involved in defending Britain against the Hun. Although air force personnel displayed nothing to reveal their squadrons, army types could be identified as members of Scottish regiments by their hats, for instance. And cap badges were the logos of the various regiments. Then there were the gongs. The Yanks came Overseas already possessing medals – medals for making their beds and for target practice (well, almost) – but the British and their Commonwealth partners were reserved when it came to medals. Those of us who came over on the *Queen Mary* were impressed by the number of fliers waiting for "repatriation" at Bournemouth who had DFMs and DFCs on their breasts. There was only one service medal Canadians were allowed to wear. Originally, it had been called the "1940-43 Star," which meant simply that the wearer had been in war operations between those dates. It separated the veterans from the greenhorns. (Unfortunately, some face-less bureaucrat later changed it to the "1940–45 Star," which stripped the award of its meaning by giving it to everyone.) The American attitude reminded me of a line from Gilbert and Sullivan: "When everybody is somebody, nobody is any-body." When campaign medals were eventually struck, for ser-vice in Italy, France-Germany, the battles of the Atlantic and the Pacific, ct cctera, one's entire service career could he seen at a glance.

There were other groups that were identified by the badges they wore on their uniforms, like the VLA (Volunteer Land Army), ATS (Auxiliary Territorial Service), ENSA (Entertain-ment Service Auxiliary) and NAAFI (Navy, Army and Air Force Institute). Air raid wardens, firefighters and the like could also be identified by their shoulder flashes.

At night the city was blacked out. The atmosphere of extrav-agance had been toned down in the grand hotels where the airmen were billeted, but it was not difficult to imagine what they had been like when the rooms were occupied by the crowned heads of Europe and the nouveau riche of America, enjoying the spas in the good old days.

I was billeted at Bathhill Court, and I was there only one day when I was seconded to the roof. There I was shown an anti-aircraft gun and told to keep a sharp lookout. There were bullet marks in the walls of the hotel and I didn't even know where the trigger was.

New RCAF personnel like myself were assigned to the "Dis-patching Wing." I never knew what that meant. On our first day in Bournemouth there was a heating crisis (there would always be heating crises) and there was no hot water for shav-ing. There were great screams of complaint. I thought after-wards how inconsiderate it was for us to complain when the British people had worked so hard to make things seem normal for us. Of course, there was a shortage of everything. We hardly ever had meat – only ersatz, mostly grain or soy-bean – and the British overcooked their vegetables horribly. Brussels sprouts, which we Canadians had never had before, were mush. We would have horsemeat occasionally. We inundated the watering places at night (we had to take our own mug or glass), and then we would go to a dance at the Pavilion, from 7:00 to 9:45 PM. The admission price was three shillings. The dance hall had a circular stage which revolved periodically and a different orchestra would appear from the other side. There were many cultural treats in Bournemouth, among them a fine symphony orchestra, an art gallery and a museum. Not all uniformed men took advantage of them, but the British patronized their entertainments. Bournemouth had a literary heritage as well. Mary Shelley (the wife of poet Percy Bysshe Shelley) who wrote the novel *Frankenstein*, was buried at St. Peter's Church, and there were houses in town once occupied by John Keble and Robert Louis Stevenson. There were several playhouses, and I attended one play in which Toronto-born Beatrice Lillie (Lady Peel) starred. It was all very exciting for someone who had never seen a real live play before.

The war came a bit closer one day when we were all issued gas masks and steel helmets. We were instructed to carry them wherever we went. And most of us did, at least for a while. The gas mask (called a "respirator") came in a canvas case which also came in handy for carrying shaving supplies and other items while on leave, and the helmets made utilitarian pillows when travelling on trains overnight. Most of the chaps – the air force fellows, anyway – just stowed the respirators wherever they were billeted. We all had a chance to use them, however, when we were run through a gas chamber in a training exercise, and were exposed to gas long enough to appreciate our masks.

While it was clear from news reports that the pressure in the war zones was lessening, there was still a lot of war to be fought. Bournemouth is on the English Channel, and the Allied bombers often went over us at night, and sometimes in the daytime, their engines droning loudly.

On February 8, this report appeared in the London *Times*:

> The Allied offensive against enemy objectives across
> the Channel was resumed today. Soon after nine o'clock

formations of bombers flew over a south coast town and headed toward France. The drone of their engines filled the sky for a considerable time, and, flying at only a few thousand feet, they were clearly visible as they headed over the sea. Targets in the Pas de Calais area are believed to have received another hammering by bombers.

Before 10 o'clock, waves of bombers were observed between Folkstone and Dover, returning across the straits. The bombers had an escort of fighters.

Security was never breached by such reports. They never said very much that those on the ground couldn't see for themselves.

One day my name was heard over the tannoy, with instructions for me to report to the commandant's office. "Cockles" Cochram was there to greet me. He was now an air commodore, and I was thrilled that he would seek me out amongst those thousands of men. How had he known I was there? "Just wanted to say 'hello'," he said. The following day was Sunday and there was a command church parade at which Cochram preached the sermon. That was the last time I saw him.

The wait at Bournemouth provided time to get brought up to date on what was happening in the war. It was amazing that so many things were going on in so many places. Apart from the drama of war events close to home, it was difficult to identify with any of them.

In Russia the tables were beginning to turn against the Germans, whose misadventure there was becoming as devastating as Napoleon's campaign against the Russians had been 130 years before. Consolidating their efforts, the Russians were recapturing oil and rail centres, and taking thousands of prisoners, mostly Hungarians. On January 27, United States bombers, previously employed in the bombing of targets in France, made their first all-American raid on Germany. The target was Wilhelmshaven, an important Nazi naval station. It was a frequent target, and well defended. The attack included

55 aircraft, of which three were lost, although the Americans had downed 22 German planes themselves. Three days later the RAF launched its first daylight assault against Berlin, flying Mosquitoes. The RAF had begun using a radar device called "H2S," which involved a screen displaying a picture of the ground over which the aircraft was passing. It was an all-weather bombing aid and was useful as a position locater, but it was unreliable.

On January 14, Churchill and Roosevelt commenced a conference with their chiefs of staff at Casablanca. There had been some criticism that the British were doing little in the fight with the Japanese, and this was true, as the war in Europe was occupying their attention. The British charged that the United States was gradually abandoning its commitment to the Germany-first policy. It was agreed at this meeting that strategic, rather than area, bombing would be used on Germany henceforth.

On the night of February 15, we heard a thundering noise over Bournemouth as Allied bombers headed in waves towards the continent. A surge of euphoria swept over me as I realized how close I was to being there with them. Hundreds of aircraft, probably all heavy four-engine bombers, had gathered from various aerodromes in Britain and were rendezvousing in the sky above us. It must have taken an hour for the sounds of engines to cease. Next day the newspapers announced that 806 RAF bombers had dropped 2,642 tons of explosives over Berlin in 39 minutes. Forty-two of our planes had been shot down. While I appreciated the damage that must have been done to the German war effort, my heart was with all the WAGs and pilots and gunners who would not be sleeping in their beds that night, and who would write no more letters home.

On the 16th, I was informed that I had been promoted to Flying Officer, although I still felt very much like a P/O Prune. I was also given food-ration coupons and a week's leave, following which I was to report to an Advanced Flying School in Wigtownshire, Scotland. Accompanying me on my leave would be an RAF sergeant and five Canadian P/Os – Coombs, Geddes, Hopper, Miller and Reid. Most of us made a reservation at No. 5 Canadian Officers Club in London. The sergeant was going to stay with friends. We would stay in London for two days, and then go on to Edinburgh and environs for the remainder of the week.

Shortly before I left Bournemouth, one last happening of interest occurred, at a Bathhill court party. The officers deposited their flat hats in the cloakroom, and it was not easy to get your own back. You could tell much about the owners of the pile of head-coverings by their hats. They were all alike, but they were all different. Field hats were tucked under tunic belts and carried with the owner. But a bright blue flat-top with the fuzz still on the fabric and a shiny brass hat badge identified a sprog pilot officer just off the boat. Hats with tarnished insignia – and faded green hats, like mine (from my saltwater days) – usually signified longer service, unless the owner had run it through the washer to achieve a worn look. Almost every air force officer removed the stiffener from his hat, whereupon the hat soon lost its shape and looked like it might belong to a veteran of the Battle of London. The floppy hat remained the mark of experience until the owner moved up in rank to wing commander, when the stiffener would be replaced, there being no reason to pretend operational savvy. And, of course, no one ever saw an air marshal wearing a hat without a stiffener.

I went to the cloakroom on this occasion to get my hat, turning them over to see the identification. I pulled a hat out of the pile and saw my initials on the sweat band. Just to be sure, I looked under the band and saw my full name exactly where I'd put it the year before. Only then did I realize that this faded hat was the one someone had taken by mistake at Torbay. The someone – with a name like George Harkness or Gregory Holmes – had checked the initials at Torbay and failed to look under the band. Men become attached to their hats, and I cheerfully retrieved mine, for old time's sake.

CHAPTER 18

Waging the War in London

M y companions and I – all in London for the first time – emerged from the tube in the area of the officers club only to find that the club had been bombed the night before, and we would not be able to stay there. The club looked like it would be uninhabitable for the duration, but, miraculously, it would be back in operation in a couple of weeks. London was teeming with people in uniform, but it was not usually difficult to acquire a billet. There were other Canadian Clubs (for "other ranks" the Maple Leaf Clubs were available, though they were out of bounds to officers), and literally thousands of London houses and flats were sharing their space (if the Blitz had spared them). Finally, one could, with a little patience, find a bed in a hotel. We managed to get into the Royal Commonwealth Institute hostel on Northumberland Street. The food was passable and the accommodation quite comfortable, if Spartan. There was a fine library and writing room. Located near Nelson's Monument and St. Martin's-in-the-Field, it was only a short walk to Piccadilly Circus, which was an attraction for most servicemen, especially on their first visit to the city.

I was frustrated by the lack of time I had available to see the many London attractions. This was the heart of the British Empire, the home of the Mother of Parliaments. This was where the Magna Carta was signed, where the Great Fire drove out the Black Death, where the little princes were murdered in the Tower; this was the home of Greenwich time; where the YMCA was founded, and the Salvation Army; where Claxton introduced England's first printing press; where Pepys kept his diary and Milton wrote *Paradise Lost*. I could walk for 10 minutes and see the swans in St. James Park, and the British

Museum, many of its priceless items having been "put away for the duration," and the Parliament Buildings, No. 10 Downing Street, St. Paul's Cathedral and the statue of Eros in Piccadilly Circus, now cocooned against damage by bombs. This was the home of the Tate Gallery and Big Ben. It was a city of palaces and private clubs. This is where Carlyle and Dickens, Boswell, Beau Brummell and Shakespeare made their homes. London was also the home of Jack the Ripper – whoever he was – and the infamous Dr. Crippen.

It was mind-boggling.

For the two days I spent in London I followed familiar directions to Scotland Yard, Madame Tussaud's wax museum, and Hyde Park, where an orator on a box was spieling his views to a solitary listener, symbolic of the British tradition of free speech. I went to Berkeley Square looking for nightingales. I strolled along the Thames, watching the Mudlarks. The Mudlarks were urchins who scavenged along the waterline at low tide. I walked down the Mall to Buckingham Palace, which had been hit by bombs.

This all had to be done in daylight, as it was difficult just to walk in the pea-soup fogs of London nights. Every building had as many fireplaces as it had rooms, there being no central heating; the resultant smog, mixed with river fog, reduced visibility to almost zero.

I took in a show at the Windmill, which was the equivalent of the Casino vaudeville house in Toronto. And I went to Whitehall to see Phyllis Dixie do her string routine. A meander around the Circus, which was dimly lit in low candle-power lighting, introduced me to the "Piccadilly Commandos," London's infamous prostitutes, who cruised the area in platoons, unmolested by the police, and apparently with considerable success, as scurrilous vendors of prophylactics hissed in the dark, "Get your rubbers here!"

What I saw around me as I walked around London's "green and pleasant town" was at once devastating and inspiring; devastating because of the damage sustained from bombs, and inspiring because of the steadfast manner in which the British people were bearing up. In the mornings, young women could be seen emerging from the underground rail-way, where they had spent the night, fresh lipstick contrasting with the greyness of the rubble above, or taking a moment to straighten the seams of their stockings before going to work, in a shop, a factory, or a stenographer's pool. The London Underground had opened in 1865. It was then four miles long, running from Paddington in the West End to Farrington Street in the east-central part of London.

What I could see needed no explanation. There were roped-off areas inside which the wardens considered the condition of the buildings to be hazardous. And behind these barricades of ribbon could be seen that courageous band of men, the bomb disposal squad, defusing a dud. Where the bricks and frames were blackened by fire, an expert would know that the Jerries had dropped incendiary bombs. Anti-personnel bombs had also wreaked their special form of destruction.

London had eight deep shelters, located throughout the city, each of which was more than a hundred feet from the surface and could accommodate 8,000 people. People generally ran to the nearest shelter when the air-raid siren sounded, and would wait there, reading, knitting, sleeping, until the all-clear siren. (One got used to the difference in the sounds.) There were other shelters as well. Anderson and Morrison shelters were installed in many homes, funded partly by the govern-ment. The Anderson Shelter was installed in the garden and could accommodate a small family. The Morrison Shelter was a heavy metal box less than three-feet high that sat on the floor in the parlour or dining room and could hold two or three chil-dren. The tube, of course, was available to Londoners who had no shelters of their own. They could retreat there for the price of the cheapest transportation ticket. It was humbling to step over and around these proud people, who accepted this utili-tarian way to stay alive in good humour.

Here and there throughout the city were large wooden cis-terns, open at the top and used to collect and hold water for the firefighters when the mains were damaged. From time to time, missing persons would turn up in one of these recepta-cles. On many buildings, particularly in the East End, where the Luftwaffe had bombed industrial plants, wide strips of adhesive paper were crossed over windowpanes to reduce the likelihood of injury from flying glass. Here, also, one could see families still occupying their bombed homes, under roofs of canvas. (Plastic was not then available, although artificial glass was used as Perspex in our aircraft.) I could hardly believe it when I saw housewives, properly attired in aprons and dust caps, on their knees scouring doorsteps, the only solid part left of a bombed flat. Children could be seen playing among the fallen bricks of their homes, as though the war was irrelevant.

There were plenty of taxis in London, but few private cars, due to the shortage of petrol, and, of course, to the fact that private automobiles simply were not being produced. But London's police, the bobbies, were always available to assist people looking for directions, et cetera. Little food shops still offered fish and chips, wrapped in newspaper for take-away, near signs saying "Business as usual." This became a symbol of London's remarkable resistance to oppression. Typically, Londoners rebuked der Führer by staging street parties as they had never done before. One could go to Lambeth Street and do the Lambeth Waltz, and to the next street, which had been similarly blocked off to traffic, to celebrate survival. Servicemen were always welcomed to these outdoor merrymakings. The roof of Holland House had been bombed, and people could still see book-lovers browsing among the shelves left intact in the rubble, as though nothing had happened.

London was in those dark days an emporium of entertainments. The theatre queues were made less tedious, in rain and shine, by the buskers. A variety of amusements was offered by this memorable clique of performers – some with considerable skills, which made me wonder why they were performing for pennies thrown into a hat, and others with no such skills, who simply gathered handouts for twirling a coloured rag on a stick. One had to make a living somehow.

And there was always the theatre itself, and the crowded market in Petticoat Lane on Sunday mornings.

There can be no doubt that the Battle of Britain was the beginning of the end for Germany in World War II, although the war went on for another five years. Officially, the Nazi aerial campaign took place between August and October 1940, but the Battle of Britain extended well beyond that date. The London Blitz, which was the focal point for the Germans, occurred in its most destructive form between 7 September and 2 November 1940. For 57 nights in a row the Germans bombed London in an attempt to knock out the RAF, in preparation for an invasion of the British Isles. Paradoxically, one effect of the London Blitz was the reinforcement of British morale, and of the country's united resolve to stand up to the oppressor. The bombing took its toll, however. The RAF lost 415 of its 1,500 fighter pilots. There were 94 Canadians in the RAF during the Battle of Britain, of whom half were killed in action. Life expectancy for those brave men was 87 flying hours, or two weeks in time.

Britain's state of preparedness in 1939 and 1940 was deplorable, but the speed with which it improved was remarkable. The logistics of creating a defence mechanism were nothing short of miraculous. Picture a country of 50 million people and a capital city of eight million organized for its protection against a rain of bombs – the various agencies, the bureaux, gangs, teams, brigades, corps, schemes and systems, all needed at once, as well as their required equipment. In my short time in London I could see all of these organizations at work, and for the most part with success: the civil defence, made up of 400,000 volunteers, all contributing their time and effort as well as carrying on with their regular jobs. First aid, disposal of the dead, rescue, street repair, bomb disposal, decontamination; firefighters, blackout supervisors, ambulance drivers, air raid wardens, special police and members of the Observers Corps (who watched out for enemy aircraft). Talk about necessity being the mother of invention. It was of little consolation that Germany's civilian dead would amount to a million at war's end – the casualties in Hamburg alone matching the total sustained by Britain.

The first casualties of Britain's rush to prepare itself were the snakes in the London zoo. Imagine someone thinking that the snakes might escape if the zoo was bombed, and terrorize the population! They had to go. Imagine, too, the havoc caused on the streets when the lights went out. Many people were killed by cars whose drivers couldn't see pedestrians. In rural areas where open lights were hard to conceal, the cows that wandered on the roads were painted with broad white stripes so that they might be easily seen in the darkness.

Early in the Blitz, thousands of children were evacuated from London to billets in the country. Many went to Canada and the United States. Some of the evacuees returned to their homes in London before the war's end, especially when the Royal Family refused to leave after the palace was bombed.

Londoners took their plight seriously. The penalty for those who chose to loot in the chaos was death. For safekeeping, the treasures of the National Gallery were removed to a cave in Wales.

When the Germans changed their tactics and started to bomb other British cities, in 1940, they went first to Coventry (where Lady Godiva had ridden nude through the streets) and destroyed a third of the city, including the ancient cathedral. Five hundred and fifty-five lives were lost and 865 were wounded. Churchill had agonized over this controversial raid. He could have warned Coventry in advance, but if he had, the Germans would have known that the British had broken the Nazi code and thousands of lives would have been lost in other places. Churchill opted for silence "for the greater good." Coventry was added to the other demons that must have haunted his sleep.

The RAF retaliated for the Coventry assault by assigning the first of the thousand-bomber raids to the city of Cologne, a river port on the Rhine. Most of the central part of the city was destroyed, except for the 13th-century cathedral, which would survive the war.

CHAPTER 19

Getting Used to
Air Force Lingo

One wasn't in England long before he would encounter a language barrier. There were the dialects of Yorkshire and Lancashire, as well as the Cockney idiom (used by those living within the sound of the Bow Bells), all of which took a while to fathom. These simply had to be tolerated. Incidentally, Samuel Johnson in his celebrated *Dictionary* of 1755 defined the word Cockney as "any effeminate, ignorant, low, mean, despicable citizen of London." The word now identifies one of England's most fascinating dialects, one that has resisted the vagaries of time. The RAF lingo that embraced an airman just off the boat had to be studied and understood as well. Some time ago I asked Dr. A. C. Forrest, then editor of the United Church Observer and an RCAF veteran, if he would compile a glossary of RAF terms. He did that, and now I borrow greedily from what he gathered together.

I think the most durable word that comes from the RAF compendium is "copacetic," a word of unknown origin that dates back to 1919, and means "everything is just fine." Here is a listing of other wartime terms, some of which are now common in the English language (indeed I've used many of these terms freely throughout this narrative).

A/C Aircraft (not to be confused with Air Commodore).
ACEY DUCEY AC2, ground crew of the lowest rank.
AWOL Away without official leave.

BANG ON First rate.

BEAT UP THE TOWER Fly low over the tower without authorization.

BIND Dull, monotonous work.

BUCKSHEE Something unpaid for.

CANUCKS Canadians.

CHAUFFEUR or CABBIE The pilot.

CHUTE Parachute.

CIVVIES Street clothes.

CLEW Positive idea.

DECK The ground.

DIM VIEW Disapproving.

DITCH Make an emergency landing on water.

DROGUE Condom.

ERK Ground crew.

FLAK Exploding bomb pieces or oral abuse.

FLAP ON Worked-up situation.

PILOT OFFICER PRUNE A cartoon character created by Anthony Armstrong and used in the RAF training manual, "Tee Emm." P/O Prune was the embodiment of Murphy's Law, a blunderer, with a patched hat, and his top tunic button undone, and wearing a swashbuckler scarf.

GEN Information, of three categories: Duff (may be true), Cookhouse (never valid) and Pukka (bang on; reliable).

GPO General Post Office, which in England operated postal and telephone services.

GOLD BRICKING or SWINGING THE LEAD Goofing off.

GONE FOR BERTON, HAD IT, or BOUGHT IT Shot down.

GONG Medals.

GREENHOUSE Aircraft cockpit.

GROUPIE Group Captain.

HAD IT No chance of succeeding.

INHIBITED Shut down for inspection.

KITE An aircraft.

LAY ON Make arrangements for, as a party.

LMF Lacking Moral Fibre.

LORRY Truck to transport crews to their aircraft.

MEAT WAGON Ambulance.

OLD MAN The CO

ON THE BEAM Everything done correctly.

ON THE CARPET or ON THE PEG On charge for a misdemeanor.

OPS Operations. Aerial action against the enemy, 30 of which were required to complete a tour.

PACK IT UP Finish what you are doing.

PADRE or SKY PILOT Chaplain.

PIECE OF CAKE A breeze; easily done.

POOR TYPE A clot, stupid.

PRANG Smash up an aircraft or a good bombing raid

RUMBLE Fine paid for stupid act, such as landing downwind or pulling a parachute toggle by mistake.

SCRAMBLED EGGS The yellow braid on the hat of a senior officer (an officer more senior than Winco).

SCRUB Cancel an Op.

SECOND DICKIE A pilot's first operational flight, taken as the co-pilot for an experienced captain.

SHAKY DO A rough operation.

TAIL-END CHARLIE Rear gunner.

TIED ONE ON Had too many drinks.

TRIP, SORTIE, or OPERATION Bombing flight.

TYPES Aircrew, ground crew, RAF radio personnel.

The following is the RAF phonetic alphabet, used in radio-talk communication and to designate aircraft: A–*Able*, C–*Charlie*, F–*Freddie*, et cetera. Aircraft also had serial numbers which crews usually ignored in favour of the alphabetical designation. The serial number was the proper identification, however, as aircraft in all squadrons were labelled by phonetics. All aircraft in a squadron were of the same type – Halifax, Lancaster, Wellington, Canso. But sometimes the whole squadron would convert to another type of aircraft.

ABLE	NAN
BAKER	OBOE
CHAP or CHARLIE	PETER
DOG OR DARE	QUEENIE
EAGLE	ROGER
FREDDIE	SUGAR
GEORGE	TARE
HOW	UNCLE
INK	VICTOR
JAIL	WILCO or WILLIAM
KING	X-RAY
LOVE	YOLK
MIKE	ZEBRA

The radio-talk designation "repeat" was changed to "say again." With the former usage, ground artillery crews would fire again, hearing "repeat" on their radio frequency.

CHAPTER 20

More Training at
West Freugh, Scotland

Transportation routes in Britain ran north-south. Feeder lines operated across the island, but it was sometimes difficult to reach towns and villages off the beaten track. The London North East Railroad (LNER) took you from London to Edinburgh via Lincoln, Hull, Northallerton and Newcastle, while the London Midland and Scottish (LMS) rail line followed the central route to Glasgow. The Great Western Line served the area southwest of London. (After the war all of these railroads would amalgamate into British Rail.)

Since our ultimate posting was to West Freugh, a small flying field near the seaport town of Stranraer in southwest Scotland, we took the LMS, although we would not report to West Freugh until after our leave was up. West Freugh was a district in the burgh of Stranraer, in Wigtownshire. It carried on a regular mail service to Northern Ireland.

Although Coombs, Geddes, Hopper, Miller, Reid, Danburger and I all had first-class tickets, there weren't enough first-class seats to go around. When you boarded an English train you walked along a corridor the length of the car, entering the compartment allocated to you, and you stayed there until the train reached its destination. If a third-class passenger had your seat, however, you simply found a place somewhere else – and sometimes in the night it was out in the aisle, using your respirator as a pillow. This time the seven of us managed to commandeer an entire compartment. Of course, we knew that at Crewe we would all have to get out and board another train, and then the whole procedure would start again.

We could now determine when we might expect to join a squadron and get on operations. This was mid-February. We would be at West Freugh for four weeks. Then operational training would be another six weeks, followed by two weeks at an aircraft conversion unit, and then probably seven days leave. We would join a bomber squadron in mid-July. The scuttlebutt at the time was all about the impending invasion of the continent. Nobody had any real information, but we guessed it might take place about the time we got into operations. And that was good.

The rail trip to Scotland was uneventful, except for a memorable incident that occurred after we left Crewe and were settled into two compartments. Hopper and I shared space with several American soldiers and a dignified old gentleman with a crisp white mustache and a lean face. For a long while no one spoke, as the train clicked on. Finally, one of the soldiers who had been watching the landscape slip by started to talk about the bomb damage in London. He said he had relatives in Brighton whose house had been destroyed a year before. One of the victims was literally blown to bits and not even the pieces could be found. It was discovered later that a single hand had been blown into the exposed roof of the house across the street. It had mummified by the time it was found and was identified by a wedding ring. This set off a round of bizarre stories – the strange lore of war. Another Yank said he had heard about a marine fighting in the South Pacific who managed to jump into a foxhole just as a shell exploded. When the dust settled he noticed a metal fragment, which he examined when it cooled. There was a number engraved on it. The number matched his regimental number.

There was another long silence during which we opened our K-rations and ate some tasteless crackers and spam from a small tin. There would be nothing more until a cup of tea at the next train stop. I invited the old gent sitting next to me to join us, but he gently declined. Then just to break the silence someone remarked on the picturesque beauty of the British landscape, and this led into some surprisingly informed comments on how the English poets had captured this in verse. Someone mentioned the English poems of the sea, and, of course, John Masefield's name came up, as his sea poem "Cargoes" was printed in our English readers. We made stabs at quoting it –

> Dirty British coaster with a salt-caked smokestack,
> Butting through the Channel in the mad March days,
> With a cargo of Tyne coal,
> Road-rails, pig-lead,
> Firewood, ironware, and cheap tin trays.

Then someone (one of the Americans, I think, which surprised me) extended the Masefield connection and mentioned "Sea Fever." Another said it wasn't Masefield who wrote that but Joseph Conrad. This seemed probable, as Conrad was renowned for his stories about the sea. Another assured us that it *was* Masefield, and quoted a few lines of "Sea Fever:" "I must go down to the seas again, to the lonely sea and the sky, / And all I ask is a tall ship and a star to steer her by ... And all I ask is a merry tale ..."

"Yarn."

We looked at our mustachioed companion, who had just spoken for the first time.

"And all I ask is a merry *yarn*," he repeated, with emphasis on the word "yarn."

We gathered he was a literary scholar – perhaps a don from Oxford – in our midst, and no one wanted to press the issue before an expert. The conversation turned to other things. My thoughts remained with Masefield and the poetry he had written. The English poet laureate had been an apprentice on a windjammer in his youth, and in some respects his life did parallel that of Joseph Conrad. I remembered that Masefield's son, Lewis, had been killed in action in 1940.

When we stopped at Crewe to change trains we all spilled out onto the platform, along with our older companion, who dropped a fabric valise in the scramble. I picked it up and gave it to him, offering my hand as I did so. He accepted the gesture graciously and said, "My name is Masefield. John Masefield."

I was dumbfounded. I had shaken the hand of the Poet Laureate of England. And it has remained one of my favourite name drops.

The Knights of Columbus found lodging for us in Edinburgh, at 8 Royal Circus. The landlady couldn't understand our Canadian accents. I had my own agenda, so we went our separate ways. Reta had been born in Scotland, as I mentioned, at Dunfermline, just across the Firth of Forth in Fifeshire. At the first opportunity I took a bus and went across the great bridge. I had no contacts in Dunfermline, I just wanted to be there, to feel close to Reta. I walked past the school she had attended in Crossford and imagined her playing in the schoolyard as a child, dressed in a uniform: white blouse, blue pleated skirt and long black stockings. I browsed around the old city, where King Malcolm and Queen Margaret were married in the 11th century, though the Scots talked about it as though it were yesterday. (Queen Margaret is the only royal saint.) I visited the gardens of Pittencrieff Glen, a gift of the famous financier Andrew Carnegie, and I saw the house where he was born. As I walked alone along winding cobbled streets I felt the full age of the town, as though the past had challenged the future and won.

Back in Edinburgh, I walked the Royal Mile between the castle and the palace of Holyrood. St. Giles' Cathedral stands midway between them. I trod on Nova Scotian soil at the castle's esplanade. The Knight Baronets of Nova Scotia, formed in the 17th century, could only receive their title and grant by enduring the ocean voyage to accept the honour in Nova Scotia proper. To get around the hazardous voyage, they had transported a cargo of earth from my home province to Edinburgh, and scattered it around the esplanade of the castle, where the knights later knelt to be dubbed.

Scotland, the land of Robert Burns, Sir Walter Scott and Sir Harry Lauder, found its way into my imagination. I conjured up visions of Robert Louis Stevenson's Dr. Jekyll roaming the midnight streets of the Scottish capital, and of Burke and Hare skulking about in the graveyards looking for corpses. I bought an armload of books from a second-hand shop, not realizing that I would have to carry them with me wherever I went. I thought Scott's monument on Prince's Street impressive, but grotesque. I saw the Station Hotel, long spewed-upon by coal soot from the trains that ran right through the city centre. I discovered Tommy's Bar on High Street, across the glen, which I would visit on future occasions. Unlike Glasgow, which was, and is, industrially oriented, Edinburgh is a cultural centre. The Scots don't make automobiles, but they have historically supplied first-class engineers for the ships and shipyards of the world. And Scottish inventors, like John Loudon McAdam (macadamized roads) and James Watt (who invented the condenser that made a steam engine practical), have achieved world eminence. And Joseph Lister, of course. Lister, though he was born in England, made his important discoveries in antiseptic surgery while he was practising in Glasgow. All this inspired me so much that I wanted to know more about the history of Scotland. I met a chap in an Edinburgh pub, who was a fellow WAG from Canada. He informed me that the University of Edinburgh offered free courses to servicemen from the colonies. I went there and was accepted as a student of Scottish history. The deal was that when I was in Edinburgh on leave I would attend two classes a day, and I'd fill in at other times by correspondence. I would spend a year in this regimen. As a result, I would be able to say with pride that I had attended Edinburgh University.

M y small contingent of RCAF wireless-operators/air-gunners arrived at West Freugh and checked in at No. 4 Advanced Training Unit as WAG Entry 156. It was cold and forbidding at the training unit, and it was particularly discomforting for me because my metal suitcase and duffle bag had not arrived. There was not room in train compartments for large cases, so they were put into a boxcar, labelled with their owner's name and destination. While it was always a bind to be without a change of underwear, it was remarkable that more baggage wasn't sidetracked. Eventually, the luggage would show up – and if it didn't you lived with it because there was no one to sue.

We were billeted with a dozen or so others (some New Zealanders among them) in a typical "tomato tin" facility. We each had a good bed and a chest of drawers. There were two small coke-burning stoves, but there was no coke. We eventually organized foraging parties, which invaded the communal pile of coke, enclosed by a wire fence and a locked gate, to augment the daily ration. The ablution hut was just a few feet from the billet, and we could never understand why the excess heat in that rustic unit wasn't piped into the place where we slept instead of being vented out into the frigid February air. The billet was allotted two Women's Division girls as "batmen." Their duties were to make our beds and keep the place clean. Nothing more.

West Freugh had to be the least practical place for an airfield – and there were others in the area – as the weather, at least in February, was atrocious. We used Anson aircraft, which were called "Anson bombers," but to us they were still flying classrooms.

At once, I was appointed Class Senior. This was no longer flattering, but was just a joe job. But it was easier for the powers to communicate with the contingent through one person, so I didn't mind. I was, after all, the only Flying Officer in the group. We were all issued "battle dress," a comfortable alternative to No. 1 blues, which officers had to supply for themselves. (The battle dress was free.) We were also issued whistles, and I had one attached to my flying jacket from No. 5 (BR) Squadron. I never used it, but it could save lives if a crew had to ditch in the sea and searching aircraft or boats couldn't see through the fog.

It wasn't clear what we were supposed to learn at No. 4 ATU. Actually, it was a navigation school, but aircraft could not fly without a wireless operator aboard. Though I had gone through much of the training before, it would be good practice.

We were introduced to the RAF system of wasting time. The first parade was called for 0805 hours (why 05?) and at 0820 we were lined up and counted, and dismissed. Next we were herded to a classroom where we waited for someone to open the door. The classroom then had to be cleaned up and a fire lighted (shades of the old country schoolhouses back home).

An RAF Flying Officer Banks, with a Distinguished Flying Medal, introduced us to a New Zealand wireless operator (WOP), who had finished his operations and been seconded to No. 4 as an instructor. He spent the morning introducing us to Marconi wireless equipment, which we would be using throughout our operational experience. It was new to me, as Bendix had been used on Coastal Command. There were lots of coloured knobs, and the transmitter had about 19 valves (tubes) of which half could be bypassed in an emergency.

In the afternoon we were loaded into a bus, driven 45 miles to a Midland-London-Scotland (MLS) hotel, and given dinghy drill in the swimming pool. I had had this before as well, but an airman flying over water could not have too much drill.

As the days passed, we flew whenever weather would permit, mostly at night. Except for the absence of enemy fighters, the exercise was real. It was good training for a WAG. There were many wireless stations in the region, and as the broadcasting bands were close together it took some skill to distinguish one signal from another, in order to read a coded message in Morse. Direction-finding loops and radio/talk techniques were stressed. This was a good opportunity to practise procedure as well, to know what IMI, QDM, QDR, QEF and all the other coded signals meant, and what to do with them. A wireless operator who didn't know his job was a hazard in a crew. Although we were not on operations, we were flying in an operational environment and a training aircraft could easily be shot down by an enemy intruder.

Bad weather prevailed. Flights were scheduled and scrubbed. Classes were a farce. Instructors didn't show up.

We were assigned to parades and physical training classes, but nobody attended them. So we had a lot of time on our hands, which allowed us to cycle around the countryside. The lack of discipline was refreshing, but it was becoming apparent to us that we colonials – the Newsies, the Aussies and the Canucks – were not very popular with the RAF administrative officers. Some of them had been in the service for as long as we had been alive, and they had worked hard for their promotions. On the other hand, most of us had less than a year's service and were already sporting pilot officer's rings. The "Erks" (the ground crews) got along well with us, however. At any rate, the Canadian government was particularly concerned that Canadian airmen serving in the RAF would not be abused by politically incorrect treatment.

Two RAF WAGS, Bob Lacey and Reg Hughes, joined our class. We bonded with them, but after West Freugh we never heard of them again. They were both from Scotland, and I suppose I shouldn't have been surprised when I discovered their technique of filching from the GPO (General Post Office). Although postage stamps were only a penny, Bob and Reg would collect envelopes with the British stamps on them cancelled. They would select stamps that were only partially marked by the cancellation machine, that is, one might be marked on the top and the other on the bottom. The marks could be cut off with scissors. Then two partial stamps could be aligned, and pasted on a letter to be mailed.

We had a lot of days off, marking time as the navigators completed their ground work. Mail finally caught up with us, and I received about 20 letters all at once – mostly from Reta, who numbered her letters so I could read them in sequence. A letter came from my father telling me that my dog had died.

We also passed time with barrack discussions, huddled around the little stove. One of the subjects, I remember, was "Knowledge is responsible for the chaos in the world." I can only imagine what we said about it. Although I was anxious to go through the training program and get back on Ops, I chalked up what was happening to me as experience.

CHAPTER 21

Happy Days in
Shakespeare Country

It was March 28 when a few of the WAGs from Stean-
raer, including Leo Hopper – with whom I had developed
a friendship, although we did not have much in common –
arrived at Honeybourne in Worcestershire, central England, to
begin operational training. It was spring. Roses were bud-
ding, the grass was green and all seemed right with the world.
We had just checked in when we were told we would be on
leave for five days. That night we witnessed one of the mar-
vels of the 20th century. We stood looking upwards in awe as
wave after wave of aircraft – heavy bombers, medium bombers, fighters – passed overhead at low altitude, heading for
the continent. The sound of their de-synchronized engines
lasted for an hour. And I thought those men in those aircraft
up there were making history. We were convinced the invasion
had begun. In fact, even thousand-bomber raids were not then
uncommon. Still, I felt isolated from those hundreds of young
airmen who were dancing on the razor's edge, and I wondered
if I would ever get to join them.

I went off to Stratford-upon-Avon, which was not far away
by Canadian standards – a short bus ride. I would go often to
Stratford while I was in the area. I took pictures of the thes-
pian statues – Falstaff, Hamlet, King Richard – in front of the
Shakespeare Memorial Theatre, paddled a canoe on the idyl-
lic Avon River and had happy times in the town's most popular
pub. Its sign on one side read "The White Swan," and on the
other side, "The Dirty Duck." I was enjoying the experience of
war and all its opportunities, and in so doing felt a bit guilty.

The Gen Crew frolicking at the Shakespeare Memorial Theatre, Stratford-upon-Avon

Stratford was a small market town, as it had been in the bard's time. Now, of course, it was also tied to the fact of Shakespeare's birth there, in 1564. The brick and thatched houses were quaintly timbered in Elizabethan style, some dating back to the 1600s. The festival was on and I saw *The Merchant of Venice*, from the dress circle, for three shillings. I read

Roderick Eagle's settlement on the Shakespeare-Bacon issue, and concluded that William Shakespeare, the uneducated son of a tradesman, did perform a miracle in producing the literary works attributed to him, or he did not write them at all.

Leo Hopper and I went off to London for the balance of our leave. We checked in at the newly repaired No. 4 Officers Club and planned our program for the next two days. We took in all the popular amusements and managed to fit in a movie before the pubs opened. Leo, Jack Miller and I, along with an RAF aircrew engineer we'd met at Piccadilly, were walking through Green Park in the West End when the air-raid siren sounded. It wailed for a long time before anything happened, as though people in London were used to the bombing or didn't believe it was really a raid. Sometimes the sirens were turned on to make sure they were operating. When the earth shuddered from a bomb blast nearby we followed some people who were looking for a shelter. In addition to the eight deep shelters, there were, of course, small emergency shelters, and it was in one of them that I escaped the bombing. It was the first time I had ever been in a shelter. No one panicked. Another bomb exploded above us. Everyone was seated quietly and an air-raid warden came in to see if we were all right. Some were reading newspapers. There was little conversation. When the all-clear sounded everyone just got up and left, as though they had been waiting for a bus. It was dark outside and the fog was thickening. Eventually it was impossible to see anything, and we stumbled about in pitch dark. A taxicab appeared suddenly, with two tiny beams of light emitting from the holes in its otherwise blackened headlamps. The cab stopped and a man poked his head out of the window and said, "Want a lift?" We didn't know where we were or where we wanted to go, but we got in anyway. We sat on the little jumper seats facing the fare and engaged in generalities. In a short time the taxi stopped again, and our host got out and disappeared in the pea-souper. The driver leaned back and asked us if we knew who we were driving with. We said we didn't. "That's Jack Buchanan," he said. Jack Buchanan was a movie actor who was more known in Britain than to us, but I had heard of him. We were delighted when he returned to the car and asked if we wanted to go to a party. The question was rhetorical, I am sure, because airmen always wanted to go to a party. We got out and followed him, and the taxi drove away.

We followed Buchanan through a heavy door at the basement level (like the entrance to an old-fashioned New York speakeasy) and then into a brightly lit drawing-room where it seemed half of London was assembled for a grand celebration. The actor took us, seemingly with pride, and introduced us to some of the celebrants. Actually, he *showed* us to people, then got us each a drink and disappeared. We didn't see him again, but the drinks were on the house, and a number of people who had seen the "Canada" badges on our shoulders came to speak to us. They were all theatrical and radio people, most of whose names were not familiar to us, though they may well have been famous figures in London's theatrical coterie. Sarah Churchill was there, and I remember Vic Oliver, a popular radio and stage personality, who at the time was married to Sarah, much to the displeasure of her father. I was pleased to meet the man who played Squadron Leader Murdoch in the hilarious radio show called "Much Binding in the Marsh," which was popular with the air force.

The stage and film world was proud of its participation in the war effort, particularly in view of the criticism sometimes levelled at actors for hiding behind microphones and cameras. Donald Crisp served in the Boer War; J. Arthur Rank, a big man in films in Britain, was in the ambulance corps in World War I, and the silent screen idol Ivor Novello was in the Royal Flying Corps in the same war. Many stage and screen actors were currently doing the servicemen's-camp circuit. American headliners like Henry Fonda, Jimmy Stewart, Clark Gable, Dana Andrews and Jack Lemmon were in uniform, and there were many nondescript servicemen who would later become famous entertainers. In fact, Bing Crosby was in London at the time, and I (along with hundreds of others) met him during his brief appearance at the Whitehall.

I don't remember how we got back to No. 4 that night, but we were up early and bushy-tailed next morning, prepared to make the rounds of the pubs again. It was a favourite pastime of servicemen on leave in London (and anywhere else in England for that matter). Usually we didn't get to more than three or four, as we were continually running into chaps we had known at training schools and who were now on air squadrons in Britain. It didn't matter where you were stationed; London was the mecca, and drinking was the objective. The pubs were colourful and interesting. We didn't have pubs of any kind at home, and most of us had never tasted liquor before we enlisted. But we quickly adapted to the routine in Britain. Drinking places were open during the day from 11:00 AM until 3:00 PM, ostensibly to prevent over-indulgence, but practically to allow time to clean up. They opened again at 5:30 PM and closed for the night at 11:00 o'clock, when the familiar "Time, Gentlemen, please!" echoed through watering places all over Britain.

Pub life was fascinating. The pubs' names were quaint and used without licence. London had pubs for every interest – music, literature, theatre, sports. There were also pubs with thematic decor: dockside, architectural, et cetera. People frequented a certain pub because others with similar interests did, and Canadian airmen would go anywhere they could get a brew to their taste in an interesting environment, with congenial people, civilian and military alike. Beer was the main beverage served, as hard liquor was rationed. However, when it was available, Nelson's Blood (rum) and Bloody Marys (vodka and tomato juice) were welcome. The Shandy (sometimes called Chandy) was a pleasantly fizzy drink of bitter ale mixed with a mineral water, and it was popular with the ladies.

Light, bitter, stout and lager were the common varieties of brewed drink. They were served in bottles or on tap, the latter being most popular and selling for less than a shilling a pint, which remained the price throughout the war. Brewers' names became familiar – Bass, Worthingtons, Charrington, Courage, Witney, Whitbread, Guinness, Young and Younger. Most of the public houses belonged to the brewers, who pushed their own brands, but also served other kinds. In London, pub names like Gilbert and Sullivan, Sherlock Holmes, Red Fox, Fox and Hounds, John Bull, King's Arms, Cutty Sark, Crown and Anchor, and Washington, were common. Some pubs, like Old Bailey, Jack the Ripper and Crippen, had decorative motifs pertinent to their names. Some of the London pubs were ancient, like Ye Olde Castle on Battersea High Street, built in 1600. (One day I would make a special trip to Nottingham just to see the oldest public house in Britain, Ye Olde Jerusalem Inn, dating back to 1189.)

Service personnel on leave in London usually ate at the pubs, which did a lively business at noon time in ploughman's lunches (with ersatz sausage), soup, shepherd's pie and sometimes dishes made with powdered eggs – the beginning of fast food.

CHAPTER 22

The Gen Crew is Formed

Bomber crews were formed at Honeybourne. All of the assorted air tradesmen had flown with a variety of temporary crews, but this was the inherently definitive – the most important of all our training – selection of crews. The objective was to bring together an energized, spirited, hard-hitting unit of fighting men who could work compatibly in the cramped space of an air bomber. We were looking for two gunners, a navigator, a bomb-aimer, an engineer, a WAG and a pilot: seven trained and willing warriors. We were given complete freedom in this exercise. No unwelcome bodies were forced upon us. We considered personality, age, attitude and even marital status. Some airmen had a thing about a married man being a better crew member because he would want to return to his family and wouldn't do anything foolish that would jeopardize the safety of the crew. This was nonsense. We were assembled in a compound, like a herd of cattle being selected for their breeding qualities. We knew absolutely nothing about the other airmen milling about, and crew members were selected for the least pertinent reasons. A navigator in the group had selected an air gunner because they had known each other back in their hometown of Peterborough, Ontario. Another air gunner teamed up with the Peterborough chap because they had trained together. The air gunners and the navigator approached me as they heard I had done a tour on Coastal Command and thought my experience would be an asset to the crew. Reta was now living with her sister in Peterborough, so I agreed to crew with them. So we were four. Someone had been talking with a pilot who had teamed up with a bomb-aimer from Calgary. We had a consultation and decided to ask him to be our pilot, to which he agreed. It seemed like a compatible group, but actually the chances were that another combination would be just as good. We needed an engineer. All the engineers were RAF at this point. (Later in the war, when the Commonwealth Air Training Plan was turning out more pilots than were needed, new pilots from Canada were assigned to aircraft engineering positions on Canadian squadrons.)

Bruce Wallace of Toronto was the designated pilot. Howie Reid of Peterborough was named rear-gunner. Al Rothwell of Dauphin, Manitoba, was the mid-upper gunner. Jim (Hamish) Murdoch of Calgary was the bomb-aimer. Vaughan Glover, a grocer from Peterborough, was the navigator. I was the WAG, and an engineer was assigned to us – George Read of London, England. We all wanted to get home again. Four of us were married. Apart from George, who was over 30 (he had been a furniture dealer), we were all under 25. The gunners were only 18.

This was the "Gen Crew," by our own estimation the most competent crew in Bomber Command. Fate had thrown us together, to "slip the surly bonds of earth," and top "the windswept heights with easy grace / where never lark, or even eagle flew...." We would do the rest of the war together, with our lives, our very souls bonded together.

We were two weeks at Honeybourne, each crewman taking separate courses in his specialty. The pilot would learn how to feather and un-feather the aircraft's engines, how to put out a fire, how to deal with an engine-failure in flight, how to deal with an under-carriage emergency, and how to evade enemy fighters and the blue beams of searchlights. The bomb-aimer would practise using a new bombsight; the gunners would assemble and disassemble their guns and sharpen their aircraft recognition. The navigator would study his sky charts and manipulate his radar aids. The engineer would improve his knowledge of aero-engines. I would practise how to deal with radio equipment in emergencies. Our lives depended on each other.

The WAGS were assembled in a classroom, and an RAF bloke strode in with an armful of books and started asking us questions about what I took to be meteorology. He said there would be a test, but no one knew what he was talking about. Finally he acknowledged he was in the wrong classroom. Shades of West Freugh! Actually, we didn't seem to be getting any new instruction, just polishing up on what we had already learned. We did, however, receive new information about bailing out of an aircraft, and about security and intelligence.

Honeybourne was still run by the RAF, although it was quickly being converted to an RCAF station in an RCAF group with Canadian crews. Some of the Canadian crews still had a mixture of Commonwealth fliers, most of them Aussies and Newsies. The station was still lax and sloppy from the earlier regime, but there was a new CO, 28-year-old G/C Lane, DSO, DFC and bar, who had excelled in the No. 617 Dambuster Squadron. Now grounded, he had no intention of wasting his time.

Saluting became imperative. The barriers went up between ranks and a new pecking order was introduced. He had flight sergeants digging in the spring gardens, and one reluctant sergeant was assigned latrine duty. Others were painting the buildings. The officers were put on charge for rolling dice in a classroom. Dinner was changed from 7:00 PM to 6:00 PM, to conform, it would seem, with the traditional Canadian custom. High teas were served in the mess at 4:00 PM. Of course, you could almost always get a hot cup of tea from the NAAFI (the Navy, Army, Air Force Institute), if you had a cup. Lane thought tea was a waste of time.

I acquired a bicycle for five pounds. This was the only means of transportation from billets to flights, where squadron offices were located. Sometimes (outside a pub before closing) there would be so many bicycles you couldn't find your own. It didn't matter. Usually you just commandeered the bicycle closest to you and rode it away. The last man out of the pub rarely got his own bike. Unfortunately, there was a thriving traffic in missing bicycles.

On 18 April 1944, the British government put a ban on sending coded and uncensored messages and documents to embassies and representatives of foreign governments other than the US and Russia. We learned from the wireless that the Russians were making rapid moves through German positions on the Eastern Front and that Allied forces had taken Nuremberg and Stuttgart. The campaign in the Admiralty Islands in the Pacific had ended with the loss of 3,280 Japanese and 326 Americans. The British 8th Army had failed to breach the Hitler line in Aquino. It was publicly revealed that 47 of the Allied officers who were captured after they had escaped from Stalag-Luft III POW camp were summarily executed.

On April 20, the new Honeybourne crews were transferred to Long Marston, a satellite station of No. 24 OTU, where each crew would concentrate on working as a single unit.

The practice at training stations was to employ second-line used- and abused-aircraft, like the Hampden and Whitley medium bombers. These were too useful to abandon entirely, and could be put into operations if necessary. An Armstrong Whitley was allocated to the Gen Crew. It had a strange configuration and looked as though it was diving when it was actually climbing, which it didn't do very well. It took almost to target time before it could attain operational height. The Whitley, which had been around since 1939, was already phased out when we arrived at Long Marston. It had been the first British bomber to fly over Berlin, so it had accumulated its share of glory.

The Whitley was powered by excellent Rolls-Royce Merlin engines. The latest model (Mark V), which was the one we used, could cruise to Germany at 165 mph. It reached its maximum speed of about 228 mph at 17,000 feet, about as high as it could go. When it was first introduced, it served as a night bomber and did coastal reconnaissance and anti-sub work. Its wingspan was 84 feet. It could carry a bombload of 8,000 lbs. with fuel for 650 miles, and 3,500 lbs. with fuel for 1,930 miles. There were no crew comforts, and it was cold. The sandwiches and chocolate bars we took along with us froze before we could eat them. The Whitley had one .303 Browning gun in the nose and four .303 guns in the rear turret.

The ominous thing about the Whitley was that it sometimes blew up because of a short-circuit in a generator that ignited petrol in the wing. On one occasion the rear turret of a Whitley fell off into a street in the village of Broadway, near Honeybourne.

The Hampden, another ancient aircraft on the station, was originally received by the RAF at the end of 1936. The models were designated No. 49, No. 83 and No. 50. The forward guns were fixed and in the beginning they were Vickers gas operated. There were single guns in the mid-upper and tail-gun positions, which were later replaced by twin guns. The Hampden was first used in daylight raids on the German mainland as early as 1940, with disastrous results for the RAF.

There was more talk about the invasion, and from the air we saw gliders lined up in the fields. Overhead there was an increased number of aircraft – American Lightnings, Mauraders and Bostons, and British Beaufighters, Whitleys and Ansons. Every aircraft available, regardless of vintage, was being dusted off for the long-awaited invasion. Lord Haw Haw and the American traitor Robert Best were ignoring these activities in their daily broadcasts from the continent – and we were ignoring their broadcasts in Britain.

I met a few old faces at Long Marston, including Bob Myers, who was on my lending list at Guelph. He was now a flight sergeant, still sloppy and unkempt (and probably still broke), and was waiting for a transfer to the US Air Force, where the pay was better. I met a man whom I remembered from Acadia University. He asked me if I knew Glen Hancock. For the past few years, no one had called me anything but "Hank."

CHAPTER 23

Learning to Fly
Lancasters & Halifaxes

Bruce Wallace's Gen Crew spent two months at Long Marston, honing our composite skills and bonding as friends. The flying was done mostly at night, circuits and bumps around the field for Wally, and cross-country exercises (lasting five and six hours) for Vaughan, the navigator, and for me, the WAG. The Whitley had a crew of five; the engineer and one of the gunners always had the night off. The weather was perfect, and since we often had the day off – sometimes even a 48-hour pass – we cycled often into Stratford. Pete Heron of Kamloops, one of the pilots, and I went off to the castle town of Ludlow in Shropshire to see a cousin of mine in the United States Army stationed there. I never actually got to see Jimmy – there were 17,000 soldiers in the camp – but we stayed at the Compass Inn, dined in one of the best of the English pubs, the Feathers, and talked with several old men, who were swigging from pints, and, apparently, pleased to see someone who didn't have an American drawl.

On June 5 we were selected to go on a nickel raid to France, carrying a load of propaganda leaflets that offered information to the French and advice to the Germans. The adrenalin rushed in our veins as we anticipated our first venture into enemy territory. At the last minute the operation was scrubbed without explanation, but we knew why. Next morning an announcement was made over the wireless: "Under General D. Eisenhower, supreme commander of the Allied Expeditionary Forces, Allied naval detachments, supported by air forces, landed this morning in Northern France." It sounded like a public relations release, but the invasion at Normandy had begun. Paratroops had landed, and that night the sound of many aircraft going east could be heard. Although we were a bit unhappy that we were not in on that big push, the invasion was welcome.

Our Gen Crew, under Wallace, along with another crew under a pilot named Pete Heron, embarked on the last stage of operational training at an RAF conversion unit, at Wombelton (in the mud), where we would move from twin engine aircraft to four-engine machines. This was a greater conversion for Wally than for the rest of us. We were taking on Halifaxes Mark II.

The Halifax bomber (or Hally) suffered through most of its lifetime in the shadow of the Lancaster, the best operational aircraft of the war. But it performed well and we liked it. It dated back to 1935, when Bomber Command had drawn up specifications for a twin-engine aircraft to replace the Hampdens and Wellingtons, which had been around for quite some time. The specifications called for a medium bomber that would carry a bomb-load of 8,000 pounds. (The Hampden could carry only half that much.) It would have power-operated nose and tail-gun turrets, and would be powered by two Rolls-Royce engines. The prototypes presented by the Handley-Page manufacturers were so wrought with problems that the project was shelved.

This was an important time for the war-aircraft industry in Britain. Germany had led in aircraft production up to that point, but by 1941 and 1942 the RAF would command a force of medium and heavy bombers that the Nazis never did match. The Stirling, the Halifax and the Lancaster were in the forefront of this development. The four-engine Lancaster developed from the twin-engine prototype of the Manchester. Meanwhile, Handley-Page went back to their old prototype, installing Rolls-Royce Merlin engines, and Boulton-Paul gun turrets in the mid-upper and tail positions. The first of these new Halifaxes was delivered to No.35 Squadron at Linton-on-Ouse in December 1940.

The Halifax never stopped going through modifications – a change in the twin tail assembly, alterations to the electronics, changes to the landing gear and the wing tanks – but this aircraft, with its 99-foot wingspan, a 13,000-pound bomb-load capability and a range of more than a thousand miles, went on the first daylight raids against Kiel on 30 June 1941.

It was discovered after the initial operation of the Halifax that the two Browning guns in the nose turret and the four in the tail caused drag. The nose turret was then fitted with a hand-operated Vickers gun. Mark II, our Wombleton aircraft, had inline engines. (Mark III had been delivered to No. 433 Canadian Squadron in November 1943. Marks VI and VII would be the final versions of the Halifax.)

The Avro Lancaster, the flagship of the RAF's air fleet, dropped its first bombs in March 1942, and it was involved in the dam raids of 1943 and in the sinking of the Tirpitz in November 1944, using a bombing technique which, alas, had come too late in the war to achieve its full worth. It was a supreme aircraft for a crew to man. Equipped with Rolls-Royce engines (1,130 hp.), it had a maximum speed of 287 miles per hour, a ceiling of 24,500 feet, a range of 1,660 miles and a bomb-load of up to 14,000 pounds. More than 7,000 of these aircraft were built, some of them (Mark X) in Canada. The Lancaster was one of the few wartime aircraft that survived the war. Mark IV and V eventually became the Lincoln, which was assigned to the Second Phase in the Pacific.

Although the great US bomber, the B-29 Super Fortress, was employed in the Japanese war, there were lots of Boeing Fortresses of other marks included in the bombing raids against the Germans. The B-17 was a bit faster than the Lanc and could fly easily at 30,000 feet. Its range depended on the bomb-load. We claimed the Lanc could take a heavier bomb-load to Berlin, but the Fortress could carry more than we could in a short run. The USAAF was committed to daylight bombing, and while we bombed around the clock we had a strong sympathy for Fortress crews. There were 10 in a crew, mostly gunners, and their mortality rate was colossal, in spite of the firing power they commanded.

RCAF crews achieved a good knowledge of German aircraft, but we were most interested in the ones that could shoot us down. We could recognize the Dornier 17, which we called the "flying pencil." It was a medium bomber with two engines. The Blohm & Voss reconnaissance aircraft looked like a "flying horseshoe" and it had three engines, with a crew of five, and was armed with two cannon. We had a special respect for the Heinkel III medium bomber, the Junkers 88, a bomber-fighter, and particularly for the ME-109, the Germans' proud fighter that could outrace both the Spitfire and the Mosquito at a speed of 428 mph.

At Wombleton, the morale was not very high. In fact, the ground-crew personnel had balked and were in a strike position when we arrived. They objected to the petty discipline. They stopped work and went to church en masse, assuming the commanding officer would not interfere with their religion. Only 50 of a total complement of 700 men and women would eat in the mess hall. A squadron leader Admin. Officer gave us shovels and ordered us to repair the runway, which had been bombed. We balked, too. Pete Heron gave a splendid speech outlining the reasons why we should not be asked to do manual labour, and there was a stalemate until another squadron leader with a better perspective suggested that we do the digging first and complain about it afterwards. We did the digging, but we didn't bother to follow through with our complaint. We had only one other grievance – that one of the ground officers, all of whom seemed to outrank us, had a habit of warming his ample backside against the less ample fireplace in the mess, and of arbitrarily switching the radio dial from the Forces Radio to the BBC News.

Like the Whitley, the Mark II Halifax had an unfortunate habit of blowing up spontaneously. One of them blew up after returning from a cross-country exercise. It was U-Uncle, which the Gen Crew had refused to fly a few days before because of engine problems. The pilot was one of our friends, Doug Moffat, who had just received his commission. Frankie Green, the WAG, had been married only a week before to a beautiful WREN, and George Luftwaite, the navigator, had married on his embarkation leave in Canada. The crew could only be recognized by their positions in the burned aircraft.

This didn't do much to raise morale.

Our batwoman, however, had just become engaged, and she was bubbling over with happiness that spread throughout the barracks. She had placed a bouquet of lilacs on the table. Also, mail caught up with us again. Nothing could boost morale better than mail from home. I devoured a clutch of letters from Reta. She had sent a parcel containing a bottle of sodium perborate (for dental use), a package of gum, a tin of sardines, cheese, a cake (which had hardened) and a billfold. One of the other chaps got a turnip. Sometimes the parcels contained cigarettes, although the Red Cross kept Canadians well supplied. Woodbine was a British brand that smokers only smoked when they couldn't get anything else.

A boy from my hometown, Warrant Officer Ron Smith, showed up at Wombleton with a crew. I was surprised to see that he was in the air force, and as a pilot, since he had always had trouble with his vision. He wore those "bottle" type glasses that prevented you from seeing his eyes. In civilian life Ron was a well-known ornithologist who had once been research director aboard George Vanderbilt's yacht in the Caribbean.

Before leaving Wombleton for posting to an operational squadron – No. 408 Goose Squadron at Linton-on-Ouse, Yorkshire – we were sent on leave again. The frequent leave-taking had delayed our finishing the training program, but it gave us leisure to explore the English countryside. I was able to keep my commitment to the University of Edinburgh, and was actually putting more into the program than was necessary; I was also learning a lot about British history. As often as I could, I visited castles, and battlefields like Culloden in Inverness, where Cumberland thrashed the Scots in 1746; and Runnymede in Surrey, near London, where King John was forced to sign the Magna Carta in 1215, that most famous document in the story of British freedom; and Hastings, where William the Conqueror defeated the Saxons in 1066.

Usually Pete Heron and his crew teamed up with us on leaves, and on this occasion we went to London together. George Read invited us to go to his home in Richmond, a comfortable train ride on the Metropolitan system. It was interesting to see George and his wife putting their five-year-old daughter, Ann, to bed in a Morrison shelter in the dining room. They did it as methodically as if they had learned the procedure from their own parents.

One of the saddest attributes of the war was the disfigurement of airmen who were caught in burning aircraft. At the George and Dragon, just off Piccadilly, we met a young RAF gunner who could not get out of his rear turret in time to avoid serious burns to his face and hands. I started a conversation with him and happily he was not reluctant to talk about it. His face was grotesquely damaged, and at first I found it difficult to look him in the eyes, from which the lids had been burned off. He had undergone numerous operations at the Queen Victoria Hospital at East Grinstead, in South London, where a plastic-surgery clinic had been performing miracles in putting airmen back together again. Considerable restoration had been made of his lips, ears and nose, as well as to his hands, although his thumbs no longer had the opposable ability. He was a grisly sight, but he seemed glad to be alive. He told me the most difficult situations he had to deal with were times when children pointed to him on the Underground. I forget the man's name, but I know that victims like him eventually formed an organization called the Guinea Pig Club, with almost 700 members. It was of no comfort to our gunners that most of these unfortunate casualties had occupied gun turrets in burning aircraft.

CHAPTER 24

Life on a Bomber Squadron

The Gen Crew arrived at Linton-on-Ouse on 26 July 1944. It was the end of a long trail for me. At last I was where I wanted to be – and there was nowhere else to go. We discovered that they were really not ready for us when we got to Linton. On the first night I slept in a bed used the night before by a member of the Jones crew, which had not returned from operations. It felt a bit creepy, but it would happen again and one had to get used to it. Linton was a peacetime RAF station, with multi-storey buildings, and was well winterized. Our crew slept wherever there was room for a few nights, until two crews were screened (finished their tours) and space loosened up. The four officers in my crew were billeted at the former Women's Auxiliary Air Force (WAAF) site on the perimeter of the airfield, recently vacated by a crew that went for Burton. It was excellent (although not fancy) accommodation – four beds in a large room, and a larder, where we could cook eggs if the NCOs could scrounge them. The larder was used as a utility room by our batman, a shady looking character. The first thing we did was buy a record turntable and two 78-rpm records. One of them had "Canadian Capers" on one side and "American Patrol" on the other. Both sides of the second record were devoted to Richard Addinsell's "Warsaw Concerto," which he had written for the 1941 film *Dangerous Moonlight*.

The NCOs in the crew – Al, Howie and George – had quite different accommodations. They shared a large oak-panelled room on the second floor of a country mansion called Beninbrough Hall, the summer home of Lady Chesterfield. (Many of the aristocratic element in Britain did this as their contribution to the war effort.) The room had a massive fireplace in which

Junior officers' quarters at Linton-on-Ouse

they cooked Spam, and eggs they foraged from the countryside, for soirees to which we were invited. Lady Chesterfield at
times occupied the gardener's cottage, in which she had gathered many of her books. Beningbrough was some distance
from the dining hall and flights, so shuttles transported the
NCOs several times a day, when they didn't ride their bicycles.

It was apparent that discipline on the station was lax, rela-
tive to training units we had lived at. We were even allowed to
wear battle dress when we went to York, the nearest big city.
Now that we were "operational" we had a lot of new privileges.
There were no parades, for instance – except burial parades.
Airmen lived well at Linton, though briefly. Many familiar
faces were showing up, people from home and former classmates from training stations. The war had homogenized the
Canadian population like nothing else could have done. Wing
Commander Gerry Edwards appeared in the mess one day
with a string of gongs and three rings on his arm. From copy
boy to commander of the Snowy Owl Squadron, and later to

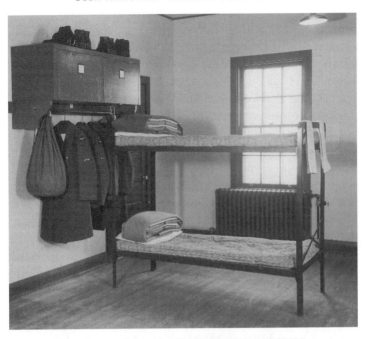

(Top) Typical airmen's living quarters. (Bottom) NCOs hamming it up at Beningbrough Hall, April 1944. Joe Milligan, Andrew Blais and Jack Moore

general, wasn't a small achievement. P/O Everett Cameron, another Acadia University man, showed up as well. He was a bomb-aimer who went missing a few days later. You just didn't know. Two boys I'd known in wireless school in Guelph were there, Clyde Sherwood and Ross Hodgeson, and I recognized the squadron adjutant who had been in Brandon with me. Ron Smith, the ornithologist, came from Wombleton to join the squadron with his crew around this time. Jack McCulloch, from Portage la Prairie, of the 47th Entry at Guelph, was a senior NCO on 426, and Greg Titus of Yarmouth, Nova Scotia, was a pilot with the Thunderbirds. The commanding officer of Linton station (which linked the two squadrons, 408 Goose and 426 Thunderbird) was Clare Annis, who had commanded Gander when I was in Newfoundland. Annis was probably the most popular CO in the RCAF. A tall, good looking man, he understood morale and good communications. Every noon-time you could hear him on the tannoy, bringing the whole station up to date on what was going on in the war. In particular, he would let us know what had been heard from the Red Cross concerning airmen who had been shot down. When Annis made his rounds of the ground crew flights at night he would call the erks by their names.

The daily routine was for the WAGs to make radio inspections of operational aircraft, and then hang around the flights, playing cards or darts, yacking and waiting for aircraft to come back. Aircraft were identified as "S-Sugar," "V-Victor," or by the captain's name. In the Ops room we would watch with solemn concern as each crew was chalked off the board when it returned. We always hoped that those that didn't return had been diverted to another landing field, or, at worst, captured by the Germans.

Linton was in the process of converting from Lancasters to Hally IIIs. It was the practice for new pilots to do their first operational sortie as a co-pilot, called "Second Dickie," with an experienced crew in order to gain some idea of what to expect. Pete Heron had arrived the day before we did, to join 426, and he was sent out at once on his Second Dickie with

F/L Thompson in a Lancaster. Six aircraft from the station were lost on that operation, and 6 Group, the bomber group to which we belonged, lost a total of 24 aircraft and 168 men from enemy action. Pete's aircraft was one of the missing. It was a distressing happening, but we would get used to this sort of thing. Pete's crew, incidentally, received a new pilot (they had to go back and train together) and early in their tour they, too, were shot down.

Around this time we learned that in the French village of Oradour-sur-Glane, the German S.S. had shot all the men, and locked the women in a church and burned it down, as reprisal for sabotage. It was this kind of ruthlessness that gave credence to some of the atrocities we had been hearing about, but had found hard to believe.

Aircrews at Linton were busy, but our baptism of fire was being delayed because there were not enough aircraft. In the first week of August they did two daylight raids every 24 hours. My skipper, Bruce Wallace, did his Second Dickie in a Lancaster on August 7. It came off well, and he was delighted to have flown in a Lanc. We were all keyed up to start on our own tour. On August 13, our squadron aircraft bombed Calais and Kiel. Now that the Allies had fought a brutal battle on the beaches of Normandy, Bomber Command had stepped up its aerial onslaught against targets in France and Germany, the objective being to damage industries and morale, all at a cost.

Meanwhile, Linton was visited by King George and Queen Elizabeth, accompanied by the young Princess Elizabeth. They had come to present medals to members of the squadron. We were delighted when they made a "walk-around" among station personnel, and many of us were able to meet them. Also in the group were the Lord Mayor of York, Canada's High Commissioner Vincent Massey and Air Marshal Breadner of the RCAF.

Elizabeth, the Queen Mother, inspects the Canadian Women's Division at Linton in 1944

CHAPTER 25

The Anatomy of the
Goose Squadron

My crew had its baptism of fire on 22 August 1944, when we were sent to bomb a VI rocket site at L'Hey, France. The first of Hitler's secret weapons – the "Doodle Bug" or "Buzz Bomb" – had been launched six days after D-Day. Fifty launching rails had been set up at locations on the continent, and L'Hey was one of them. Ten missiles were fired on the morning of June 13. The first of these crossed the English coast and exploded in the village of Swanacombe, 20 miles east of Tower Bridge. A second fell at Cuckfield. Only four of the 10 reached London, but six people were killed. This new Nazi menace was really a continuation (a last assault) of the Blitz, and Londoners took it seriously. Thirty-two thousand VIs would be built by Volkswagen before the war's end, but only 8,000 of them would be activated. Unfortunately for the Germans, the VI was too late – like many of Hitler's innovations. It is said that, had the Doodle Bug been introduced earlier, the invasion would have been delayed. The VI required 130 gallons of low-grade fuel and had a range of 150 miles, flying at an altitude of between two and three thousand feet. Launching ramps on the Channel coast of France, for rockets aimed at London, had been observed as early as 1943, and guns to shoot them down were set up on the south coast of England.

By the end of the war, the VI rockets that reached London would have killed nearly 6,000 people, injuring 40,000 more and destroying 75,000 homes. The rockets were vulnerable, fortunately, to anti-aircraft guns and to fighters. More than 630 were shot down by Tempest aircraft alone.

The V11 would come along in September 1944 and cause even greater havoc, part of Germany's ferocious resistance in the face of certain defeat. This second rocket was more sophisticated than its predecessor, and much more lethal. It had taken the Germans more than 12 years to develop. The rocket was 46-feet long and had a range of 250 miles. It carried eight tons of fuel, primarily alcohol and liquid oxygen, and a 2,000-lb. warhead. The V11 was more deadly. Actually, it opened the space age. It had greater range, was too fast to be shot down and when it reached its target, the warhead rushed to the earth at four times the speed of sound, causing great damage – five hundred of them caused nearly 10,000 casualties. The last of Hitler's secret weapons could only be stopped by destroying its launching pads.

The first V11 was fired at Paris, a kind of dummy run, and the next two were pointed in the direction of London, the first of a total of 1,145 that would be fired on the city.

Our task on August 22 was to destroy one of the V1 launching pads. It seemed a minuscule contribution, given all the other things that were happening on the front. Senior Allied personnel were meeting to discuss post-war security and to establish an international court of justice. In the Arctic three naval carriers were engaging the German battleship Tirpitz in a Norwegian fjord. The Allied vessels suffered damage from ack-ack barrages and fighters. Germany's army had lost its ability to fight. Rumania's King Michael had accepted the Soviet surrender terms. (Rumania had joined the Axis in 1941.) The situation seemed to suggest that the war was winding down, and although this was enough to make us confident of the ultimate outcome, it would take almost another year before the end would be a reality.

The V1 operation on L'Hey took us three hours and 35 minutes. Only a few aircraft were involved. We bombed the target at a low altitude and encountered only slight flak. Wally kept the Hally flying straight and level until the camera caught the bombs landing on target. We were all a bit nervous, this being our first Op, and we were surprised that there was so little resistance from the Germans. Is this what Ops is like, we

Hank meets his brother Ron at Linton. Ron was a 6 Group aero-engine mechanic.

thought? (We would learn that it wasn't.) This maiden sortie of ours tested the way we could work together under fire. Navigation was perfect. The bomb-aimer was satisfied that he had hit the target. I had maintained contact with Group Operations without any hitches, and our intercom discipline, which we had honed to perfection in training, was excellent. We were on R/T and W/T silence, and the intercom was silent, except for necessary communications between members of the crew. All of our aircraft returned safely to Linton. This discipline would serve the Gen Crew well during its tour of duty.

We were not unaware that we had joined one of the most successful and acclaimed squadrons in 6 Group, which had been formed expressly to mother Canadian airmen in squadrons of their own. Prime Minister Mackenzie King had long hankered for this to happen, and "Bomber" Harris, commander-in-chief of Bomber Command, had been just as much

Z for Zombie, showing maple leaf sortie

against it. Harris wanted the Canadians to "augment" existing
units of the RAF Bomber Command, but to King this would
put Canada in a position of subordination. So 6 Group was
formed on 1 January 1943, and located in Yorkshire. Under the
command of RCAF Air Vice-Marshal G. E. Brookes, it started
out with eight squadrons that had previously been attached to
RAF No. 4 Group.

In the beginning the group had many Commonwealth
airmen in its squadrons – former crews of No. 4 – and while
the clutch of squadrons, 14 of them eventually, was adjusting
to its new command it suffered a large number of casualties.
In the first six months of 6 Group's existence, up to about the
time we joined 408 Squadron, 43 aircraft and crews were lost –
313 aircrew in 364 sorties. Many of the casualties were due to
factors other than enemy action – weather, icing, aerodrome
prangs and bombs falling from aircraft flying above. Also, 6
Group suffered from development syndrome: the dangers of
inexperience, when airmen thought they knew all there was to
know, and the dangers of overconfidence, when they became
lazy and indifferent to things that could go wrong.

Wing Commander Nelles Timmerman, DSO, DFC (second from right, back row), who was the first officer commanding the Goose Squadron when it became part of the Canadian 6 Group in Yorkshire. Other early members of the squadron include: (Back Row, L to R) P/O Tom Dench, P/O Roy Campbell, S/L Pitt Clayton (DFC), Timmerman, S/L Wilf Burnett (DFC); (Front Row, L to R) Sgts. Alex McMillan, John Ross, Eric Marshall, Ken McGrail and Bill Reinhart. This photo was taken when the squadron was stationed at Syerston in 1941

No one asked at the time, but the cost of running the wholly Canadian 6 Group was borne by Canada, and the cost of the full upkeep of the operational squadrons, including the cost of fuel and ammunition, was defrayed by Canadian taxes and loans. Canada would consider the investment to be a good one.

No. 408 Squadron – adopted by the Ontario town of Kingsville and designated "Goose Squadron" after Jack Miner's goose sanctuary located there – came into being on 24 June 1941, and set up in Lindholm, Yorkshire. It was the second RCAF squadron to be formed, No. 427 having been the first. The first commanding officer of 408 was W/C Nelles Timmerman, one of 400 Canadians who had become pilots in the RAF before the war. Shortly after this, No. 408 moved to Syerston,

Nottinghamshire, and on the night of 11 August 1941, it carried out its first mission, on the docks of Rotterdam, flying Hampden medium-bombers. For a time the squadron flew daylight raids, escorted by fighters. The first airmen to die were Sgt. A. T. McMillan of Windsor, Ontario, and Sgt. R. M. Gifford of Sherbrooke, Quebec.

In December 1941 the squadron moved again, to Balderdon, Nottinghamshire, and remained there until September 1942. In May 1942, the Goosers had taken part in the first of the thousand-bomber raids, on Cologne. W/C J. D. Twigg succeeded Timmerman in May, and was the first RCAF officer to command the squadron. He was the first of three commanding officers of the squadron to be killed in action, over Saarbrucken on August 28. The squadron did 1,271 sorties in Hampdens, and then converted to Lancasters (Mark II) and moved to Linton-on-Ouse, where it again changed aircraft, to Halifaxes (Mark III).

From 1943 to January 1944, the squadron directed most of its efforts against Berlin, and lost 20 crews in so doing. When we arrived, 408 was involved in both day and night raids. Three aircraft were lost over Hamburg around the time of our arrival.

CHAPTER 26

Air Force Heroes Identified

When my crew arrived at No. 408 Squadron at Linton-on-Ouse in mid-August 1944, the signs of victory over the Germans were appearing all over Europe. The Polish underground army in Warsaw began a full scale offensive against the Germans, abetted by an airlift of weapons from the Allies. The Germans had destroyed the bridges in Florence, and Allied losses in Burma were heavy. The Russian army offensive had stalled because they had run out of fuel. Eight German officers were hanged for their part in the assassination attempt on Hitler's life. Eisenhower had moved his headquarters from England to France. Japanese resistance had ended in Guam. Canadian forces had completed the encirclement of Falaise after the RAF dropped 3,723 tons of bombs on German positions in the Caen area.

Even though the Germans were on the run in some areas in France and Germany, it was clear that the war was far from over.

Most of the Commonwealth heroes of World War II had already trod the paths of glory and were either consigned to desks or were resting in that corner of human destiny that is forever green.

Knowing that there was still fighting to do, it must have been frustrating for the likes of Basil Embry, Arthur Donaldson, "Buck" McNair, Johnnie Fauquier, Ginger Lacy, Johnny Johnson, Roy Gordie McGregor, Reg Lane, Leonard Cheshire, Len Birchill, Hank Burden and Kane, the Australian, to be grounded behind desks.

Perhaps the opportunity didn't arise for pilots and other airmen who followed them to score so many hits and win so many medals. The fighter pilots, of course, were the media heroes of the war. Standing high among them in the RCAF was George "Buzz" Beurling of Verdun, Quebec. When he was a sergeant, serving in Malta in 1942, he shot down 28 planes. Later in his career he added three more. Beurling was Canada's greatest fighter pilot, but was also a screwball. He was originally turned down by the RCAF in 1939, although he could already fly. He lacked the required formal education, so instead worked his way to Britain on a ship, and was finally accepted by the RAF. On squadron he was a loner, and conceited. He bragged about being the best (and he was). His complicated personality did not make him popular with senior officers. He turned down a commission because he didn't want the responsibility. Eventually, however, he became a flight lieutenant and was awarded the Distinguished Flying Medal and bar, as well as the DFC and bar.

Among the RAF fighters in the Battle of Britain, James "Ginger" Lacey shot down more German planes than any other pilot. He destroyed 18 in 1940, and would claim nine more before the war's end. He himself was shot down nine times. Roy Gordie McGregor was also a Battle of Britain pilot. He shot down four enemy aircraft, but to be considered an ace he would have had to shoot down five. (He had claimed a fifth, but it was not confirmed until the wreckage of a German aircraft was discovered 37 years later.) At 39, he was the oldest RAF fighter to see action.

Douglas Bader was also older than most pilots. He was born in 1910 and had lost both legs in a crash before the war; however, he commanded No. 242 fighter squadron and was able to shoot down 22.5 German aircraft before he was taken prisoner in August 1941. He was awarded the DSO and bar and the DFC and bar.

Memorable among Commonwealth pilots were the sons of the Donaldson family of England. Three Donaldson brothers served in the RAF and each of them won the DFC, among other awards, including the Air Force Cross. Group Captain Arthur Donaldson joined the air force in 1934. In February

1941, he led a low-level attack on Morlaix, on the French coast. He was hit in the head by a piece of cannon shell and knocked unconscious. When he came to, his aircraft was heading back across the Channel. The oldest Donaldson was a squadron leader who was lost when the carrier on which his squadron had landed was sunk off Norway. The second son, eventually an Air Commodore, was E. M. Donaldson, a fighter pilot. Their mother went to Buckingham Palace 13 times to see King George present medals to her sons.

Canadian bomber pilots were no slouches, either. Standing high among all World War II pilots was Johnny Fauquier. Born in Ottawa in 1909, with a "silver spoon in his mouth," he was the only Canadian airman (and perhaps the only Commonwealth pilot) to win three Distinguished Service Orders, as well as a couple of DFCs. He had learned to fly before the war and enlisted in the RCAF as a Flight Lieutenant instructor. In September 1941 he was posted to the famous 405 Pathfinder Squadron, flying Halifaxes. (The Pathfinders were the elite of Bomber Command. Most of them were in their third tour. Their job was to mark the target with coloured flares, so bomb-aimers would know where to place their bombs.) By June 1944, Fauquier had completed two tours of operations. He handed 405 over to Wing Commander Reg Lane, DSO, DFC, and retired as the undisputed "King of the Pathfinders."

Courage was in no short supply during the war. Two notable examples of this occurred just weeks before I arrived at Linton. One was the heroic action on the part of a mid-upper gunner whose aircraft was shot up over Cambrai in France. Pilot Officer Andy Mynarski, of Winnipeg, had attempted to extricate the rear-gunner from a jammed turret after the aircraft burst into flame. His own parachute caught fire and he was killed, however, the rear-gunner was saved. Mynarski was awarded the Victoria Cross, posthumously.

The second example involved 34-year-old David Hornell from Mimico, Ontario. He had left his base in Northern Scotland on his 60th trip. Flying an amphibious Canso, he spotted a surfaced U-boat (later identified as U-1225) and dived to attack, but the sub opened fire from its deck guns and the Canso was hit. A fire broke out in one of its two engines but Hornell pursued the attack and dropped the depth charges attached under each wing. One of the wings of the Canso fell away completely and the plane tumbled into the sea. Only one of the two dinghies inflated and while six of the crew occupied it, the other two stayed in the water. After 21 hours a rescue boat picked them up, but Hornell died from exposure and injuries. He won the Victoria Cross. The co-pilot, Canadian Bernard Denomy, won the DSO, and other crew members were decorated as well.

CHAPTER 27

Operational Procedures

Preparations for an operation (also called a trip, a sortie, a raid and a number of other euphemisms) were consistent. The captain looked at the Battle Order and would alert the crew if his name was on it. Operational bods were shamelessly pampered. We would go to the dining room for whatever meal was appropriate. It was good fare, for a country bogged down with rationing, and certainly better than the army was getting in the flooded lands of Holland. But the bacon-and-eggs bills of fare would be withheld until we got back. We complained that since we might not get back, it would be more appropriate for them to give us dinner *before* we left.

Each of us had a locker at the flights in which we kept our flying gear: jackets and wool-lined boots, maps, charts, a helmet, with earphones and goggles, and a standard-issue service revolver, which we had fired on the range. (I took mine with me on Ops, but some crewmen didn't bother.) We kept our parachutes in the lockers as well, packed so that they could be hooked to clamps on the chute's harness that we wore all the time. We kept our packs near our working position on the aircraft, in case we needed to get to our gear. There was, of course, no heat in the aircraft so we usually wore the warm gear throughout.

All the crews involved in the Op then gathered at the briefing room. We entered from the end, where we could not see the map on the wall, the target and flight plan indicated on it with bits of coloured string held in place by pegs. We craned our necks going in to see the target, as we knew the easy ones and those where we usually encountered heavy flak. When all the crews were seated – as many as 140 bodies, if all our aircraft were on the roster – the wing commander entered and we would rise to our feet. We stood at attention and he would address us from the platform about the particulars of the sortie. Then the met-man would have his say about the weather to expect over the target. This was important to all of us – the bomb-aimer wanted to know if he would see the target or have to depend on radar, and the navigator wanted to know what kind of winds to expect along the route. The pilot was concerned about ice forming on the wings. Weather was difficult to predict, and the meteorologist was wrong as often as he was right. Sometimes the intelligence officer would tell us to expect anything from light to medium flak, depending on information received from the spy network. We learned not to count too much on the information because we would often run into heavy flak where we had expected none. The briefings were informal, and a lot of questions were asked. Good spirits prevailed, and a sense of humour was an asset. There was always a certain tenseness among the assembled crews, but if there was outright fear it wasn't expressed. In fact, there was a kind of morbid thrill in knowing that you might not come home again.

Crews climbed into a stake truck, called a lorry, and were taken to the site where their aircraft were dispersed. Almost everyone smoked.

On one occasion a gunner grabbed for his parachute pack in the dark and pulled the release toggle instead of the handle of the pack. Instead of a silk parachute, a blanket fell out. Someone had stolen the silk and put a blanket in its place.

Crew members would loll around the aircraft, waiting for takeoff. We would all have done inspections on our equipment (which would have been done by the ground crews as well) and it was reassuring to know that the guns were assembled properly, that the radar (radio detection and ranging), like Gee, H2S, Fish Pond and IFF, was properly inspected, and that the instruments in the pilot's cabin were in working order. Not

Members of the Gen Crew waiting for takeoff instructions (L to R): Al Roth-well (mid-upper gunner), Hank Hancock (WAG), Wally Wallace (pilot), Howie Reid (rear-gunner)

until we were airborne would we know whether the undercarriage and bomb doors were working properly.

Sometimes, while we were waiting for takeoff, someone would come out in a Jeep to say the trip had been scrubbed. This could be for any number of reasons, from deteriorating weather to breach of security.

The padre would cycle around the dispersal sites and offer a short prayer. We would say our own prayers as well, but they were never ostentatious. Many airmen carried talismans of one sort or another, for good luck – crosses, pictures of girl-friends, icons, teddy bears. There were various superstitions that harassed fliers. For instance, the anxiety-level rose on a crew's first trip, on the 13th trip and on the last trip before screening. It seemed that too many aircraft were lost on those sorties.

It was difficult to identify fear and what effect it had on a crew member's ability to do his job. Rear-gunner Howie Reid of the Gen Crew was always frightened, but his greatest concern was that his fear would impair his ability as an air gunner. He suffered phobia gallantly. Vaughan Glover, the navigator, never looked out at the sky from behind his screening to see the hordes of aircraft creeping over the carpet of bursting shells.

I have always looked upon fear as a motivator. We do things in our lives, or we fail to do them, because we are frightened of the consequences. Symptoms of fear are sweating, coldness, trembling and difficulty in speaking. We could sometimes recognize these symptoms in ourselves, but we never knew whether we were more frightened of being hurt or of being seen as a coward. Are some people braver than others? Well, yes; some people handle their apprehensions better than others. Anyone who flew in a bomber aircraft expected all the hazards of warfare. Doug Harvey, a 408 pilot, once had a WAG who was so frightened of dying that he bailed out of the aircraft in panic. I knew that would never happen to me since I was more frightened of bailing out than I was of crash-landing.

It was not until I joined an operational bomber squadron that I fully realized the role of the wireless operator, and my appreciation of the importance of the things the WAG did destroyed forever my feeling of inferiority in the crew. The first thing the WAG did after takeoff was to let out the trailing aerial so signals could be received from distant transmitters. Then the process of listening began. This was crucial. Missing a coded signal could put everybody in jeopardy. It was not unusual for a whole bombing operation to be scrubbed – even after the wave had reached the North Sea. This could be because the enemy knew we were on the way, and Bomber Command would rather retreat than run into disaster. If a message was sent from Bomber Command to this effect, and the wireless operator failed to receive it, the aircraft would continue on alone. All the other aircraft, having received the message, would be on their way home.

Unlike the Americans, who had a master-navigator in the aircraft leading the formation, we had a navigator in each aircraft, who charted the course as though his was the only aircraft in the sky. Part of the strategy of surprise was to employ diversional tactics. Often, part of the advancing wave would break off from the main stream and take a course to a minor target, while the main force would continue on to the main target, be it a marshalling yard, oil refinery or munitions factory. It was hoped that the diversional segment would lead enemy fighters away from the main target so that the prime force could drop its bombs with less resistance. This meant, of course, that the diversional group would bear the brunt of enemy defences, unless the fighters caught on to the ruse and concentrated on the main force.

After the various squadrons had rendezvoused over England, they would set off in waves in the direction of the continent. When we were over the North Sea, at operational altitudes of about 20,000 feet, we could look out through the Perspex and marvel at the spectacle of hundreds of aircraft from various groups and squadrons in Bomber Command, stretching away as far as the eye could see.

We would look up to check that our fighter squadrons were in evidence, and we would see them high above us, patrolling in groups, waiting for enemy fighters to show. It was always reassuring to see them, as they would distract the fighters from us.

As we neared the target (some strategic objective like Kiel or Hamburg or Berlin), we expected ground defences to open fire with predicted flak, shells that were calibrated to burst at a certain level. Black puffs of cordite smoke filling our nostrils with acrid fumes. We were consoled by the adage that what you could see wouldn't hurt you. Looking out, we'd often see our own aircraft – Y-Yolk, A-Able, R-Roger – veering away from the stream with smoke and fire belching from an engine, or plummeting toward the earth in a holocaust of burning fuel, no parachute appearing, and finally discern a fire on the ground that had not been made by a bomb. This item would be communicated to the intelligence officer during debriefing.

As the target neared, and the flares from the Pathfinder's aircraft appeared brilliant upon the ground, and the bomb doors opened, it was then that the pilot exercised his skill in keeping the aircraft on a steady course. There was nothing we could do to avoid being hit by bombs falling from our own aircraft above us. And sometimes they came close.

When the bomber-aimer announced over the intercom that the bombs were away, then, and only then, would the pilot ask the navigator for a course to steer for home and clear the target area. We knew that the flight home was always fraught with hazards. One of the things that all members of the crew sweated over was a rerun. Something had happened to the bomb doors and they wouldn't open. The target was obscured by cloud or smoke. Sometimes the pilot would orbit the target two or three times to achieve his purpose. Sometimes the bomb-load had to be contained, and, if possible, jettisoned over the North Sea.

The WAG had a role to play in the return procedure as well, as during the six to eight hours we had been airborne the weather back in England might have changed. Perhaps our base was fogged in. Command would designate another aerodrome in Britain which was clear to land. If the WAG missed the message, anything could happen. The aircraft might be low on fuel.

On the homeward flight, the triumph of having made a successful prang was mixed with the knowledge that danger still lurked in the skies. Over the North Sea we would watch for two-engine aircraft. All the aircraft on the raid would be four-engine, and at night a two-engine aircraft would probably be an intruder, an enemy fighter or medium-bomber flying in our formation, undetected by radar, waiting for an opportunity to shoot one of us down and then hit for home.

One time after a sortie on a moonlit night, we watched a bomber below us silhouetted against the clouds, and though it was out of place we were reluctant to take any action. To our chagrin, we eventually realized that the aircraft below us was our own shadow cast by the moon.

Now it was time for our sandwiches and bars of Rowntree's

Some of my squadron buddies relaxing in front of their quarters following a night operation

chocolate, but they would be frozen. We ate them anyway, or took them home with us.

After landing and being interrogated, we would go to the dining hall for those eggs and bacon, and then collapse in our beds while the Warsaw Concerto played itself out on the record player. Sometimes we would be alerted before the light went out that we would be on the Battle Order again in the morning.

CHAPTER 28

A Rough Trip Over
Castrop-Rauxel

Having successfully bombed a Buzz Bomb site in France on our first operation, we were gung-ho for our second. The red pin on the wall map was stuck in a place called Castrop-Rauxel, a fairly small city in West Germany, 32 miles from Munster. None of us had ever heard of Castrop-Rauxel before, but it had war factories and, particularly, synthetic oil refineries. When the Germans were having trouble getting equipment to where it was needed we bombed their rail yards and made it even more difficult. When the Luftwaffe and the German tank corps were running low on fuel, we bombed their oil refineries – and this is what 408 Squadron (with a host of other squadrons) was doing on Monday, 11 September 1944. A daylight raid.

We taxied away from the dispersal area as usual, and when the Aldis lamp signalled us from the control tower, Wally took off. The gravity force displaced our innards for a few minutes as the aircraft climbed over the aerodrome. Then Wally set course to join the stream on its way to Germany. There were perhaps 500 bombers on this mission. The weather was good and visibility was unlimited. We looked out at the Hallies and the Lancs, and wondered how many of their crews would complete their tours and go home again. As we crossed the English coast-out, I let the trailing aerial out and it bent in the slipstream. The gunners asked the captain for permission to test their Brownings, and fired a few rounds into the air. When we reached 10,000 feet we hooked up our oxygen masks, in which were embedded the intercom mikes. After all the checks were made, there was silence. As we crossed the enemy coast-in, our senses sharpened. German fighters liked to lurk along the coast, and they'd try to get some shots in with their ack-ack guns as we were climbing to cruising height.

This being a daylight operation, we were particularly concerned about fighters, and there was reason to be. One of the gunners broke the silence to say, in a voice that only partially concealed his tension, "Enemy fighters, starboard beam high!" Vaughan pored over his charts in his canvas enclosure (to keep the light from the radar panels) and I concentrated on radio signals from Bomber Command. The eyes of everyone else followed the gunner's directions and wondered where our own fighters were. There is little that can be done when fighters attack, except to stay on course, straight and level, and hope that the gunners, or those flying in aircraft alongside us, would take care of them. In this case, the ME-109s disappeared, perhaps to look for a more vulnerable part of the stream, as a predator seeks out the weakest of the herd before attacking.

From the enemy coast-in, almost to the target, there was no action, and the intercom was silent. Then suddenly, the air was filled with bursting shells and the stench of cordite. Now and then a shell, accurately predicted by the ground defences, would explode directly under us and we would hear the flak particles as they abraded the fuselage – too spent to do any real damage, but making us wonder if the next barrage would be more accurate. No evasive action could be taken as we went into the bombing run. We had nothing going for us except luck. And this time it ran out before we could drop our bombs.

The right starboard engine was hit and caught fire. Fire was the most frightening thing about getting hit, and for a moment I thought of London and my pub friend with the burned face. This was the time when pilots become heroes, and ours, a veteran of three flights into enemy territory, was up to the task. He feathered the engine and, with the help of the engineer, extinguished the fire. Wally held the aircraft steady until the bombs were released – 16 two-hundred pounders and one 2,000-pound cookie. The Halifax heaved upwards violently as the bombs left the bomb bay, lightening the aircraft. But Wally held us on an even course until the camera had recorded the effect of the bombs.

Then Wally asked the navigator for a course to steer us home.

The fires from our bombs striking the oil installations faded away behind us, and we began to breathe evenly again. As we left Castrop-Rauxel and started to think of the bacon and eggs waiting for us in the mess hall, I thought about how well our crew worked together under duress. Yet, as individuals, we really didn't have that much in common. Wally made furniture as a hobby. I couldn't drive a nail straight. Howie worked for his father's transport business. I couldn't even drive a car. Vaughan, the clergyman's son, ran a grocery store. I had once worked in one. George was a furniture salesman, and Al and Hamish had not yet begun working careers. I was a student and an embryo writer.

This reverie crashed as our aircraft – Z-Zebra – suddenly leapt upward, reacting to the explosions of 88-mm shells directly below us. The Hally shuddered and we heard pieces of flak striking its belly. Cordite came right into our oxygen masks. There was another bump, and I realized that I had been hit. It was so sudden and unnerving that I wasn't sure how much damage had been done, but when I saw blood streaming from a wound in my leg I began to think that war was hell after all. A piece of shrapnel had entered my left leg above the knee and had plowed its way up to my groin. Another piece of flak had become embedded in my shoulder. I recall that my chief concern at that moment was that the hot metal had destroyed the new pair of No.1 blue trousers that I was wearing. And I condemned the Germans for that.

In a few moments all was calm again. The Jerries down below had given up easily.

The captain checked all crew positions and discovered that the engineer had also been wounded, in the hand, but that the other crew members were unhurt, although shaken. A piece of shrapnel had torn a big hole in the pilot's metal seat and had rebounded to some other place in the aircraft. The calm in the aircraft was amazing. We had just experienced a traumatic operational happening, yet no one panicked. No one had raised his voice or made irrelevant comments in the intercom. We had beaten the Hun on our first encounter. Wally's concern now was to get his wounded crew members to the nearest medical aid station, and hope that nothing serious had happened to the Hally.

We were two-and-a-half hours from home base, so Wally looked in his bag of instructions and discovered two emergency air strips, closer than Linton, that could provide the kind of service we needed – landing facilities and medical help. We landed at Carnaby, on the English coast. The emergency services had been alerted, and we were amused at the melodramatic attention being given us. As we landed we could see an ambulance, a fire engine, and people racing on bicycles and Jeeps alongside of us. Perhaps they didn't have this kind of excitement very often and wanted to demonstrate how well they could handle it. And they handled it well. They took me from the aircraft on a stretcher. I think I could have managed without it, but I enjoyed the attention and didn't want to rain on their parade.

Part of the emergency ritual was the serving of a rum toddy, drained from a properly wickered jug by the medical officer in charge. I thought I caught a look of distress on his face when it appeared that the jug of Nelson's Blood was about empty after I had taken a good swig.

CHAPTER 29

Bedridden at No. 19
Canadian Field Hospital

At this point I was separated from my crew, and the others, including George, whose wound was only superficial, returned without me to Linton the next day.

At Carnaby the medical officer did all that he could do and put me in an ambulance for a hospital in Driffield, where I was wheeled to a ward. There I waited – my wounds were now beginning to hurt – until a gaggle of nurses, doctors and orderlies came to look me over. I thought it curious that no one spoke to me directly, only *about* me to each other. Eventually I made a comment and a nurse exclaimed, "O, you can speak English!" I assured her that I could, and I gave my name, rank and regimental number. With considerable fluster my bed was quickly surrounded by a screen to isolate me from the other patients in the ward, whom it turned out were Italian and German prisoners. The next day I was operated on and placed in a ward for Canadians. I think I was only at Driffield for two days, and then put into an ambulance and driven off by a good-looking ATS driver, whose husband, an RAF wing commander, was missing in action. Our destination was No. 19 Canadian Field Hospital at Marston Green, near Birmingham. On arrival I was wheeled into the hospital's busy reception room and left there, the good-looking driver departing for her return to Driffield. People dashed about carrying sheaves of paper, bedpans and surgical equipment. I am a patient person by nature, but after a long while I began to feel like a slab of beef on a table. I knew other people needed attention more than I did, but I was becoming uncomfortable. I hailed a sergeant major, who seemed to be in charge, and asked him if I could get into a proper bed. He didn't know anything about me. My file was missing. But he was sympathetic, and I was soon ensconced in a large ward with other Canadian officers, mostly army men who had come up from Italy. The bed on one side of me was occupied by a Capt. Normandeau from Quebec. On my other side was Capt. Greg Cann, of Yarmouth, Nova Scotia, whom I knew. They had both been injured in accidents involving Jeeps, one of the most dangerous "friendly" weapons of the war. The matron was from Port Williams, three miles from my hometown.

I received a telegram from my sister-in-law, Cathy Nash, informing me that Reta had given birth to a baby daughter on September 15, and I was elated. She had received an official notice the day before informing her that her husband had been wounded in action. It was an unfortunate coincidence.

I was at No. 19 for about three weeks. Letters from Wally informed me that they had picked up a spare WAG and had had a couple of shaky-dos, at Osnabruck and Kiel – both daylight raids, and both targets well defended. They had also gone to Boulogne to drop bombs on enemy troops, and then made another daylight raid on Calais, where the Germans were putting up stiff resistance. I felt badly about all this – that I was missing Ops, and particularly that another WAG was occupying my place on the Gen Crew. Wally told me that my friend Ron Smith, the one with the thick glasses, had been killed on the Castrop-Rauxel raid. He had returned to Linton with an engine gone and had asked for emergency landing instructions. The control tower heard nothing more until Smith's Hally crashed into the Motor Transport Section, killing a dozen people there, and all seven members of the crew.

One day at Marston Green I saw an orderly passing my bed, and I could not believe my eyes. It was my brother Doug. Our father had "gotten him off the boat" some time before, when he had lied about his age and joined the army. But he finally made it. We had a great reunion, and when I was able we would go out to a local pub and talk about home.

I had run out of money. We never took much with us when we went on Ops, although Ron Smith used to carry a wad of notes on his person wherever he went, even on operations. (I had borrowed five pounds from him before the fatal trip, and I did the right thing and gave the money to the Salvation Army.) One day I hobbled into Birmingham to get some beer money. I had an account at the Royal Bank of Canada branch on Cockspur Street in London, but there was no branch in Birmingham, so I went to the famous Lloyd's of London counting house. I looked bedraggled. A nurse at Driffield had patched my shirt, but my trousers were still ripped. I had no identification, it being taboo to carry any on Ops.

I entered the cavernous lobby of Lloyd's, which insured ships and the legs of film stars, and told them my problem. A uniformed person was summoned to my side and I described my predicament again, whereupon he took me to a wicket, behind which a nattily-attired clerk listened to my tale and then called another liveried person, who escorted me to the outer office of someone of importance. Eventually I found myself in the office of the manager. He courteously – I might even say *enthusiastically* – received me and invited me to sit. I had never been in the office of a bank manager before. The manager had a nephew in the air force, and he was anxious to learn what it was like. The telephone rang now and then, and he impatiently conducted bank business, quoting figures like 10,000 pounds. I was impressed. But my friend the manager really wasn't interested in business at the moment. He was interested in me. Eventually, he asked me what he could do for me, and I said I didn't have any identification but I needed some money.

"Of course," he said, "how much do you need?" I kept thinking of those large amounts he had mentioned on the phone, and I squirmed as I said, "Could I please have five pounds?" And he said, "Certainly," without batting an eye (the mark of a professional). He told me he would have to send a telegram to Cockspur Street to verify my balance, so he wrote something on a piece of paper and rang a bell. Almost instantly a liveried person appeared and left with the paper, presumably the telegram. Following more pleasant conversation, the courier reappeared with another piece of paper, presumably a reply. The manager then wrote out a withdrawal slip and rang the bell again. Another person in uniform appeared, and left with the slip. He quickly returned, bearing a tray on which were four one-pound notes and some change. "You realize, of course," said the manager, "I'll have to charge you for the telegram to the Royal." I nodded, and he took the price of the telegram from the change on the tray and gave me the rest. "If you need any more, just come right in to see me."

I will never forget my business transaction with Lloyd's of London.

I boarded a train in Birmingham, carrying a cane, which I really didn't need, and looking for all the world like the stereotypical hero: ragged pants stained with dried blood, no hat, and a gas mask issued to me in the hospital. I was going back to duty and I was excited about it. I found a compartment, empty except for an elderly gentleman sitting alone behind a newspaper. I took a seat next to the window and waited for the compartment to fill. I was surprised when the train started to move and we were the only passengers, the old gentleman and I.

From time to time I would look over at my companion and exercise my newspaperman's instinct for observing details. On the luggage rack above him were three items – a bowler hat, a lunch box and a briefcase. The man was heavy-set and fleshy, but not stout. He was dressed like a member of parliament, or a minister of the church, but for all I knew he was just somebody's grandfather on his way to a family reunion. I noted a gold chain on his vest, leading, I assumed, to a gold watch in his pocket. I decided he was a man of the cloth.

After a while my fellow traveller folded the newspaper and put it in the briefcase. I thought he could have offered it to me. I was beginning to create a personality for him – a stuffy Englishman, who just barely tolerated travelling with a dishevelled young man from the colonies. But he couldn't have known that, for we hadn't spoken. I watched the landscape pass for a while, and then he spoke. While I'd been looking out the window, he had reached up for the lunch box and had opened it, revealing two or three large sandwiches and an apple. He unfolded a linen napkin on his lap. My first thought had been that he might have offered me one of the sandwiches. And now he did. I was so embarrassed for the thoughts that I'd had of him that I declined his courtesy. However, the ice was broken and we had an absorbing conversation – about the war and life in general – for the remainder of the journey.

When we arrived at York, we scrambled out onto the platform with our luggage. My friend had dropped his briefcase and I stooped to pick it up for him. Then he said a strange thing. "Do you mind if I pray for you?" I was startled, as no one had ever asked me that before. I assented humbly. He gave me his card, and we parted. I noted the name on the card: "H. E. Helliman, Harrogate." I would later have reason not to forget it.

CHAPTER 30

Making the Best
of Furloughs

When I reached Linton my crew was just going on leave. We spent an evening at the Blacksmith's Arms recounting all that had happened since that day over Castrop-Rauxel, and it gave us all a chance to think about what life was like on a bomber squadron.

Things happened quickly on a squadron. G/C Annis announced in his noonday tannoy report that Pete Heron, who had gone missing on his Second Dickie, was a prisoner of war. Pete told me later that he had jumped from the burning Lancaster and landed in a freshly harvested wheat field. He had lost his boots and socks in the descent and found it painful to walk on the stubble. For six days he travelled by night and slept during the day, making for the port of Lubeck where he planned to stow away on a ship. Suffering from hunger and frustration, he surrendered one morning to a farmer with a pitchfork. He was taken to a farm where a kind woman fed him, and he was eventually turned over to a village policeman on a bicycle. Other members of his crew did not fare so well.

The Linton mess seemed to be a crossroads. If you stayed in one spot long enough all of your old buddies from home would pass by, squadron leaders and wing commanders, sporting gongs and suffering from the operational twitch. G/C Annis was replaced by G/C Pleasance as station commander, and Squadron Leader Jake Eastman succeeded W/C McLernon as 408 Squadron commander. McLernon was a big man who had sufficiently irritated the Germans during an escape from a crash as to have had a price put on his head. I had just been

[237]

promoted to flight lieutenant, but I felt out of place among the big shots, except when my friend W/C Gerry Edwards visited. P/O Jones, who had lived in one of the Nissen huts we passed every day en route to our tomato-can quarters, had committed suicide. There was quite a bit of that going around, much of it, I think, as a result of "Dear John" letters. Russ Hubley, an air-gunner from Halifax, Nova Scotia, had won the DFC with the Pathfinders and was on his way to completing 71 missions, which was about as close to getting the chop as you could get. Jim Lovelace, another Nova Scotian from Cape Breton, had won the DFC as a WAG. When he first applied to the RCAF in 1940 he was rejected because he couldn't hold the standard column of mercury up by lung power. He tried again after two months and was again refused. Finally, on the third try, which coincided with the fall of France, the medical officer said, "Oh, what the hell," and passed him. He would go on to complete 68 trips.

The Gen Crew had discovered Scarborough, a resort on the North Sea and the site of a Bronze-Age village. It was not far from York, and we went there often on leave. Hamish bought an old car, for which he finagled 100-octane petrol from the ground crew, and we used that when it wasn't broken down. We were regular guests at "Doris's," a private home which offered adequate lodging for a good price. Dorothy was our hostess. In the evenings we haunted the Royal Hotel, which had seen better days (as well as better clientele), but it satisfied our needs. A good band, and bar facilities. There was no bar as such, only a small table behind which a little old lady dispensed drinks judiciously, and firmly refused to serve Howie Reid after the second Laughton's Nut-brown Ale. The hotel was run by the Laughton family, who made the beer. Charles had gone into the theatre, like Raymond Massey (of the Massey-Harris family in Canada), but Frank Laughton had been left to run the hotel. He took a special interest in the Gen Crew. On the second floor of the hotel there was a room with the name "Earl Haig" on the door. It was apparently a special sanctuary for the famous World-War-I hero. There was also a grand piano, and a girl would play it brilliantly for anyone who would listen. I was very fond of that girl, in a platonic way, and we went together to music recitals, and hiked to historic sites in the area, to the castle ruins and to the museum.

I didn't mention that I was married, and she didn't ask me. I think had I told her she would have dropped me like a hot potato. As time went on it was difficult for me to be honest with her. I enjoyed her company and rationalized that everything would work out well in the end. She had a boyfriend in the army. Later I would complete my tour, and the problem would be resolved.

On occasion, our crew would go swimming in the public pool on the sea front. It had received a direct hit from a bomb, but it was still in operation, although when we were there no one else was around. We rented bathing suits, the Gay-Nineties style, for three pence. The coastline behind the swimming pool was barricaded with huge rocks, steel rods and barbed wire.

There was a rustic theatre on the perimeter of the station, which accommodated films and ENSA shows, the latter performed by volunteers, who gave their talents freely because they couldn't sell them. Italian prisoners, who were employed to harvest sugar beets in the fields surrounding the aerodrome, were allowed to use the cinema, and they sat on the benches with us, with large red patches sewed to their shirt-backs. The cinema was a major source of entertainment for the troops, and there were 4,000 film-houses in Britain, 160 of which were destroyed by German bombs.

York City was another attraction. We explored the famous York Minster, established in 627. But Betty's Bar was more popular than the minster. It was amazing how the entire 6 Group could crowd into such a small space. There was a wall-size mirror there, and airmen scratched their names into it for posterity.

The Punch Bowl also drew an enthusiastic crowd, as did Alice Hawthorn's Inn, which we could reach from Linton by hiring a boat to cross the river. The boatman could have improved his income by doubling the fare on the return journey, but he did not; the boat-ride cost a penny either way.

We cycled to small communities near the station, and sampled their pubs, too. The Yorkshire moors and the peat bogs were eerie in the mist, suggestive of *Wuthering Heights* and *Rebecca*.

Shooting dice was still a favourite pastime. I don't remember anyone in our crowd playing poker. Not all the entertainment was frivolous, however, and we often had serious discussions about things like "double-standard" relationships, the merits of war, the ethics of shooting enemy fliers who were parachuting to the ground, of anti-personnel bombs and of the zombie situation in Quebec. The Prime Minister was extremely sensitive towards the general reluctance of men in Quebec to volunteer for service. I don't think young Quebecers were any less courageous than men in other parts of Canada. It was just that, to them, the Plains of Abraham had not resolved the question of sovereignty in Canada.

The government had conscription for home defence, but it never quite got around to declaring conscription for service at the front lines. Many French Canadians served bravely in the RCAF, however, and there was never any prejudice shown against them in operations.

One time our discussion pursued the subject of volunteering, and it was felt that some people at home, some of the VIPs and those who were well connected, managed to stay out of uniforms because of who they were. Many prominent entertainers managed to skip the draft, and many film celebrities didn't serve because they were rejected: Marlon Brando, Gary Cooper, Errol Flynn, Richard Widmark, Dean Martin and John Wayne, all of whom played swashbuckling roles in films of action, tried and failed to pass the test for military service.

I had a yen to visit Stoke Poges, a small parish in the Eton rural district in Buckinghamshire, to explore the graveyard where Thomas Gray wrote his immortal poem "Elegy Written in a Country Church-Yard." I inveigled Leo Hopper to go with me. Leo wasn't much of a scholar, and though he'd probably learned what he was taught in school, it hadn't inspired him to know more. He was unpretentious and unambitious, and summed up his occupational background by stating unceremoniously, "The only job I ever had was shovelling shit in the Calgary stockyards." He wasn't boasting or apologizing. He had married just before coming Overseas, and I had a feeling the marriage wasn't going well. Leo was a good WAG, but I didn't think it was taking him anywhere. He had a commission but he wore it carelessly. I pegged Leo as someone who had a death wish. He refused to wear his parachute harness when he was flying.

Anyway, we both went to Stoke Poges and walked quietly in the graveyard there. For me it was thrilling to tread among those hoary stones, where Thomas Gray had walked, to sit on the stone steps where, perhaps, Gray had sat composing those immortal words on human mortality: "The paths of glory lead but to the grave." "Full many a flow'r is born to blush unseen, / And waste its sweetness on the desert air." "Far from the madding crowd's ignoble strife...." Actually, Gray wrote most of the elegy at his mother's home – she was a milliner – and finished it on 12 June 1750. He was the only one of his 12 siblings to survive. It is hardly believable that the same man who wrote the Elegy also wrote "Ode on the Death of a Favourite Cat Drowned in a Tub of Goldfishes."

Leo and I went down to London after that and returned to the pub where I had met the man with the burned face. He was there again, and he told me that he had gone back to East Grinstead, where they had given him some psychological coaching. "Did it help you?" I asked. "Yes, it did," he said. "The kids still point their fingers at me – but it doesn't bother me anymore."

I saw my first buzz bomb on this leave. It was now October 1944. Although the Allied armies were now disarming their launching pads, the German's Doodle Bugs continued to harass the Brits. Some, in fact, were launched from special racks attached to Heinkel III bombers that sneaked across the Channel at night, usually in bad weather, and released the

V1s about a hundred miles from London. These were not precision weapons, but it was not difficult to set a timing mechanism on the rocket before launching (using calculations that any navigator could do, given weather, pressure, wind, speed and distance), and expect the bomb to cut off somewhere over London.

Leo and I were watching the pigeons around Nelson's monument at Trafalgar Square when we heard a sputtering sound above us. We looked up to see a Doodle Bug jetting over at about a thousand feet. Actually, we had hoped to see one of these fascinating instruments, and the performance delighted us. We had long since ceased carrying our steel helmets, unlike most Londoners, who would continue to take what precautions they could as long as they were threatened. The V1 cruised for about a half a mile from where we stood. Then the motor stopped, and the Vergeltungswaffe, as the Germans called it, simply fell to the ground, exploding among some buildings in the West End. We saw another one before we returned to Linton. This time, a fighter aircraft was in pursuit. Unfortunately, the fighter was too late to be effective. The Buzz Bomb had to be shot down over the Channel or in open space, for it would explode on impact.

CHAPTER 31

Strange Quiet Over Duisburg

It felt good to get back with my crew again. We were on the battle order for 0700 hours on October 14. I was filled with anxiety as we filed into the Ops room and stretched our necks to see where the red peg was on the map. I was frightened it would be Castrop-Rauxel again. But we all smiled when we saw Duisburg was the target. Not that Duisburg was a piece of cake. It was up there with Essen, Düsseldorf and Dortmund as one of the rougher targets in the industrial Ruhr valley.

As early as 1942 the Air Ministry had named Duisburg as one of its prime targets and had launched attack after attack on the chemical, steel and shipbuilding factories there. Production would be cut in half by a single raid, but the city would have tied its broken parts together and would be back at almost full strength before the next onslaught. The Germans were remarkable for their ability to recover. As attacks continued, Hitler had strengthened the city's defences, and crew from the British Air Command now had a healthy respect for the ground defences there.

We were to hit Duisburg with all the strength of 1,000 heavy-bombers, gathered from operational stations all over the British Isles. It was thrilling to be part of such a mighty air armada. In these last three months of 1944, there would be 14,254 sorties based out of Britain, dropping 60,830 tons of bombs. Bomber Harris would be so pleased with the results that the Command would unfeelingly boast that "only" 136 Allied aircraft had been lost in the campaign.

Again, we were told to expect light to moderate flak.

As we approached the enemy coast-in, the gunners could see German fighters high above us, and we wondered what their pilots were thinking as they encountered a stream of air-craft that covered 50 miles of sky. Our gunners were at a dis-advantage, as they could not effectively fire their guns until the enemy aircraft filled the ring-sight. The JUS and MES were equipped with 7.9-mm guns – and some carried 20-mm canons – which allowed them to fire on our aircraft sooner than we could fire on theirs. But for the time being, at least, the fighters kept their distance, probably considering the potency of the 3,000 gun positions in our flotilla.

As we approached Duisburg, we started taking flak. There was a lot of it visible as it exploded, but the puffs were either above or below us. I was throwing out tinsel from a chute that opened just behind the engineer's position. (This was separate from the hatch through which crew members could escape by parachute.) Tinsel consisted of small strips of aluminium foil intended to jam enemy radar frequencies. As thousands of those strips floated downward they would generate false returns to ground radar. This device had first been used over Hamburg in 1943, and it had cut British operational losses to only 12 percent.

Over target, the flak may have only been medium, and we bombed without difficulty, waiting again for the cameras to take a series of photos before turning away and setting a course for home. It was ironic that the accuracy of our navi-gation depended on the Mercator map projection, a system devised by the mathematician and geographer Gerardus Mer-cator, who lived in Duisburg during the 16th century.

Almost unbelievably, after five and a half hours in the air, we returned to base without mishap. As we got out of the aircraft the padre came up to us on a bicycle. "Go to interrogation," he said, "and then hit the sack. You're going out again tonight." Indeed, this was history being made. The thousand-bomber raid was no longer unique, but to have the same crews going out in thousand-bomber sorties on the same target twice in the same day – this certainly was new.

Air Marshall Harris obviously thought Duisburg warrant-ed the treatment it was getting. We were more thrilled by our role in this mind-boggling operation than we were concerned about the degree to which we were tempting fate. It was not likely that the Germans would anticipate another attack so soon, but it was certain that the area around the city would have been strengthened.

We were due on target at midnight. We took off under the moon, made our radar and defence-equipment check as usual, and settled into a numbed silence, each of us thinking private thoughts and trying to avoid thinking of what was ahead. We had been given "wakey-wakey" pills to help ward off drowsiness.

En route, we ran over pockets of ack-ack resistance, which seemed like mere gestures. When we were 100 miles from Duisburg we could see the city burning before us. The incendiaries we had used along with the heavy explosives (HES) had been so devastating that the streets were outlined by fire. The hum of the bombers in our wave was mesmerizing. We were aware of the presence of night fighters, but they kept their distance for a time – then made their play. Howie warned the pilot from the rear turret that an ME-109 was closing in, but it peeled away without attacking. He also saw a Messerschmidt-110, a two-engine fighter, which suggested that this time Duisburg would fight back. The Pathfinders above us had already dropped flares on the railroad marshalling yards, which, according to the photographs taken on the morning raid, had escaped serious damage. As we went into our bombing run the flak from the ground was smothering. Regardless, Wally kept the Halifax – H-How; we had changed aircraft – on a steady keel. On the intercom we heard Pathfinder Leader 2 check in, which meant that Leader 1 was in trouble. The ground fire intensified and we could see aircraft in our stream breaking away with fires burning. This was always unnerving. H-How remained steady as searchlights lit up the sky. They had to be ignored for these crucial few minutes so that our objective could be achieved. Waiting out these moments was the worst part of any operation. Hamish, the bomb-aimer, took over command at this juncture and would retain it until the bomb bay was opened and the bombs released. Then there was the sudden upward lift, and Wally turned on the reciprocal course homeward. I looked back from the navigator's blister and saw Duisburg burning, and wondered how it all had come to this.

We were still over the target area when we were caught by the blue beam of the searchlight battery below. It was tough for a searchlight operator to single out an aircraft like this, but once he did the other lights in the battery would hone in to create a cone, exposing the aircraft to the guns below. This was a fatal circumstance, and we knew it as the powerful beams lit up the interior of the aircraft and blinded us. The flak pounded against our underbelly and sounded like a boat scraping over a reef. The cordite stung in our eyes.

Wally knew what to do, although he had never done it before. The evasive action called for in this situation was a tight corkscrew dive. It was something like parachuting out of an aircraft – you didn't do it unless you had to. Imagine a great flying machine hurtling towards the ground so fast that the wings shuddered against their moorings, so violently that the crew, centrifugal but for their seatbelts, would be hurtling about like tumbleweed in a Kansas tornado. The searchlights persisted, the blue beam holding and the cone guiding the flak guns to the kill.

I didn't know how high we were above the ground when we finally escaped from the cone and the ack-ack fire, and straightened to regain our lost altitude, but I knew that Bruce Wallace had, in those few moments, joined the hall of air force heroes, and won our admiration and gratitude forever. I don't know what other members of the crew were thinking, through this harrowing experience, as we never discussed it, but, in spite of the imminent danger to our lives, I had flashes of H. E. Helliman, the old gentleman on the train who had asked if he could pray for me. Was he praying for me now? The thought was a panacea, and I felt a strange calm, a strange sense of security, which I attributed to forces beyond my understanding. I was completely unafraid. I couldn't rationalize the absence of terror – the kind of terror one would feel if the parachute didn't open when one jumped, or if one woke up in a coffin, having been buried alive.

We didn't get back to Linton. By the time we were over England the weather had closed in and we could not take the chance of stooging around our own airport waiting for it to clear – not with our electrical system doing funny things after its encounter with Henry Shrapnel's diabolical invention. (I thought it ironic that Shrapnel was an Englishman.)

We landed in Ireland, and another interesting adventure began. The Republic of Ireland – as opposed to Northern Ireland, which is part of the United Kingdom – remained neutral during the war. When we got out of the aircraft we were met by Irish policemen and officially interned. The laws of internment were not familiar to us, and we didn't know what was in store. However, being political prisoners in Ireland turned out to give us pleasant insight into how neutrality works in a war zone. We were given an early breakfast of bacon and eggs, and coffee with real cream and sugar – all things that were severely rationed in England. Then we were shown to comfortable beds, and we slept, while someone did the necessary paperwork to release us and our aircraft.

We were in Ireland for two days and were treated with respect. On the night before we were released, we were allowed to visit an Irish pub near the airfield, and there we received the shock of our lives. When we were settled at a table, anticipating some of that excellent Irish dark ale, we noticed at a table near us a group of Germans wearing Nazi arm bands, presumably members of the German diplomatic corps in Ireland. They were living it up, laughing and singing German songs. Our uniforms were not quite so ostentatious as theirs, but they knew who we were and arrogantly ignored our presence – which was just as well. Only short hours before we had risked our lives bombing one of their cities – perhaps one of them was from Duisburg.

The story I am about to relate has to be told in context, and therefore its timeline will be extended beyond the general scope of these memoirs.

When I returned to Linton following the Duisburg raid, one

of the first things I did was to look for H. E. Helliman's card. I wanted to write to him to see if he had really prayed for me, as I was still feeling the effect of my psychic experience. I did not tell him about the Duisburg sortie, but I asked him if he had prayed for me as he said he would, and if he had, I said that it was important for me to know when it was. By return mail I received a letter from him. I will never forget reading it. He said he had indeed offered a prayer for me and told me that he had done it at the exact time the Gen Crew was wrestling with fate over the Ruhr. I don't know how he'd remembered the exact time of his prayer, but I wrote again to him describing what had happened over Duisburg. I never heard from him again.

I guardedly mentioned the incident to the crew, since they were a part of it, but they didn't take it seriously. In fact, no one took it seriously, so I kept it to myself, a private, personal fantasy that warmed me when I thought of it. I did, however, tell my father about it in a letter, thinking that of all people he would have some philosophical insight; but he never mentioned it in subsequent letters to me.

After the war, when I was home again, I decided to pursue the mystery. My father said he had never received a letter from me in which I mentioned the incident, but he made the suggestion that I contact the chief of police in Harrogate, where Helliman lived, and ask him to trace the man. Helliman's card and his letter to me could not be found, but I remembered the address (which I have now long since forgotten) and I wrote to the chief of police. I received a cordial letter in due course advising me that the address I had given him did not exist, and that there was no H. E. Helliman listed on the tax rolls or in the residential directory.

Some time later I chanced to meet a man from Harrogate who was visiting Canada, and I asked him if he would make a try at unravelling the enigma. I heard from him eventually, and he told me he had taken on the challenge, but had been unable to identify anyone by the name of H. E. Helliman in the entire Harrogate area.

Had I dreamed all this? Was it some kind of psychic hallucination? I convinced myself that if Duisburg had happened, so had H. E. Helliman, and I will go to my death believing that more things are wrought by prayer than this world dreams of.

CHAPTER 32

We Hammer the Ruhr
into Submission

Our next target was Hanover, a rubber and aircraft manufacturing centre, with a concentration of oil refineries as well. (There was something ironic about bombing Hanover, as the city's elector had succeeded to the throne of England in 1714, as George I.) But when we reached the enemy coast-in Europe, I received a message from Bomber Command recalling us to base. The mission had been cancelled. Canadian forces were fighting along the Beveland Isthmus at the time, and this may have had something to do with the recall, given the danger of "friendly fire." But they never told us why we were recalled. Again, we were on a need to know basis, and, as usual, we didn't need to know. However, this recall promoted some whispered concerns among the air gunners. Every time an Op was called, George Read, our engineer, hastened to a telephone booth on the outskirts of the station. The gunners might be excused for becoming suspicious, but they were ashamed and embarrassed when it was discovered that George was simply calling his wife in London, to say goodbye.

One could understand George's impulse; still, he shouldn't have been making the calls. It was important that the particulars of the Ops be closely guarded. Loose security could cost human lives. Shortly after this, Command took to disconnecting all public telephones around the air station before operations were called. (The Brits were serious about security, but they also had a sense of humour. Caution signs were posted everywhere: "Don't Talk – there May be a Jerry Under Your Bed," and "Help Dad – Keep Mum.") Alongside the attempts to keep information leaks to a minimum, there were active attempts to give spurious information by radio – just as the English-speaking Lord Haw Haw had been recruited by the Germans.

We usually flew Y-Yolk or Q-Queenie Halifaxes, but when these aircraft were inhibited we would fly others – U-Uncle, L-Love, S-Sugar, O-Oboe.

We were off in Q-Queenie to Düsseldorf on November 11 (Armistice Day at home). We were a bit nerved-up because of the Hanover cancellation. There were 865 aircraft on the mission. Our gunners were tantalized by a single enemy fighter that made several runs on us and then went away. It was a busy target, however, and one 408 aircraft was shot down. Two aircraft from our sister squadron (426) were also lost. One of these bore Pilot Officer Elder's crew, which had previously been Pete Heron's crew. The WAG was Leo Hopper, his death wish fulfilled.

Targets soon to follow were Bochum in the Ruhr – a 5:50-hour flight in heavy cloud, with light defences and no aircraft lost – and Gelsenkirchen, an industrial city in West Germany, of about 400,000 people, and the largest coal-producing centre on the European continent. This was a daylight operation. Other November raids included Julick, where there was a concentration of troops near Aachen; this could be designated an anti-personnel attack. There were a thousand bombers on the raid, comprising 20 squadrons, escorted by fighters. Julick would be virtually destroyed by the war. Next was Munster, a city of 125,000 people, near Osnabruck. There were 800 aircraft on that daylight raid, and we encountered only light flak. My logbook identifies the next target for the Gen Crew as Castrop-Rauxel. We were first in over the target and although we were coned by searchlights and attacked once by fighters, we encountered only light ground defences. Defences were light on Neuss, as well (which must have made the intelligence people happy). It was a diversionary raid, the main stream going to another target (they also experienced only light flak). However, returning to England we were diverted to a United

Ground crew types decorate a bomb destined for Germany

States 8th Army Air Force base at Knettishaw in the south of England, because of bad weather over Linton. This was an experience.

We arrived during the night – 22 aircraft, with 140 men – and though they knew we were coming there had been little advance warning. The Yanks were daylight operators, with little control-tower experience in bringing in aircraft in the darkness. Fortunately, our commanding officer was one of the first to land, and he took over, bringing all aircraft down safely from their stacked positions over the base. Meanwhile, as each crew vacated their aircraft they were whisked to a debriefing session. Each aircraft was anchored down by cables, which amused us, as we never did that. An armed guard was positioned beside each aircraft – another thing we never did. After interrogation we were ushered into a mess hall and fed. The station personnel had already eaten. The Yanks did everything in style. They wouldn't let a war stand in the way of their conveniences. First, we were given a tot of bourbon, which wasn't our drink, but we were grateful. We had to sign for the drink, and doubtless Bomber Command would eventually get a bill for 140 shots of American "rye." We were then served fresh orange juice and real cream and sugar for our coffee (not ersatz). And plenty of butter and jam. The main course was roast pork with pineapple rings, like nothing we had eaten in England. We thought we had gone to heaven.

Meanwhile a ground crew had been busy putting up 140 cots in a hangar. It was done with remarkable efficiency, which gave us new respect for the Americans. At Linton we wouldn't have been able to accommodate a single Yank had he dropped in for dinner on so little notice.

Two nights later our crews were back on Duisburg, this time under different circumstances. Marshalling yards were our specific target and we approached in 10/10ths cloud. There were no fighters, and only slight flak. We were flying at 19,000 feet and the flak was bursting from 16 to 21,000 feet. The searchlights could not penetrate the cloud, and we were able to fly above it in the bright moonlight.

E arly in December, Germany was starting a major offensive, in the Ardennes, which became commonly known as the "Battle of the Bulge." The gathering of information about troops became crucial for both sides. The Nazis had recruited Germans who could speak English, dressed them in captured British uniforms and used them to infiltrate Allied lines, committing sabotage and gaining important operational information.

During the fighting at Bastone, in Belgium, the Germans felt confident enough to invite the Americans fighting there to surrender. Even though the Yanks were being clobbered, the American general, Anthony McAuliffe, replied, "Nuts!"

The Battle of the Bulge was the largest major German offensive of the war. One of the American divisions defending the area was the 106th Infantry Division, which lost more than 8,000 men to the Germans. It must have been strange to be amongst those fighting Allied soldiers – knowing that Germany's defeat was in sight, but that there was still a lot of war to be fought, and that you might lose your life in the process.

The Goose Squadron was kept busy during the month of December. We bombed Hagan using an evasive route which would make the round trip eight hours long. It was like a cross-country exercise.

Karlsruhe was something else again. It wasn't so much because of the flak or the fighters, but because we had taken on a spare bomb-aimer, who did a few trips with us while Hamish was off on a course. Our spare was like Al Capp's little man, always under a dark cloud. If anything could go wrong it would. He couldn't get the bomb doors open and we had to orbit the target. Again, he couldn't release the bombs (we were carrying sixteen 200-pounders and a 2,000 pound cookie), so we orbited again. Finally, I released the bombs manually by pulling a toggle in the instrument panel. We were seven minutes late.

The following night the targets were the rail yards of Soest, a city near Munster, and everything seemed to go wrong again. This time it was my nemesis at work. The radio receiver packed up on the way to the target. Vaughan, the navigator, was demonstrating his skills with nothing to help him but dead reckoning, relying on ground-sightings – and star-shots if they were possible. I had taken the receiver apart, and was trying to remember the fault-finding procedure I had learned in training. Eventually, I was able to improvise a repair, and brought us back on the air again.

On the night of December 9 we were on the battle order for the steel city of Osnabruck. We took off at 1635 hours, and it turned out to be one of the hardest sorties we made on the tour. But we returned safely to base. Wally and I had an operational meal with the new squadron commander, w/c Sharp, from Moosemin, Saskatchewan. And then to bed.

After Osnabruck we bombed Oplagen, a transportation centre in West Germany. We flew on track between Cologne and Düsseldorf and bombed green markers through sketchy cloud. Flak was concentrated from 17,000 to 18,000 feet, but poorly predicted. Our starboard engine cut out over the targets and we returned to Linton on three engines. The worst part of the trip for me was the pain in my ears caused by a cold.

My hearing was completely gone by the time we returned. I went to the MO who advised me not to fly for a few days, but I could not do that. Wally's crew were close to finishing their tour and I wanted to finish it with them. The following night we bombed Trois-Dorf. It was a splendid trip, like flying Trans-Canada Airlines. I experienced excruciating pain from my red-hot eardrums when we descended, however. This would probably be the last trip we would do together. Although Hamish was back with us, sporting a second ring on his sleeve, Al Rothwell, having flown as a spare on several trips before we started our tour, would be screened by the Trois-Dorf do.

My crew ended the last year of the war by bombing the cathedral city of Cologne, on the west bank of the Rhine, on New Year's Eve. The first thousand-bomber raid had been on Cologne in the spring of 1942, and we were making the last raid of the year. There was not much left of Cologne by this time, and we could see the ruins through the coloured flares dropped by our Pathfinders. The cathedral, however, would remain intact. It is often said that Allied bomber crews had instructions not to bomb the 13th-century edifice. We never received any such directions, and it is my opinion that the cathedral survived simply because it didn't get in the way of our bombs.

Cologne was a good prang. We were away from base for six hours and 20 minutes. RAF Mosquitoes livened up the New Year's party at Gestapo headquarters in Oslo during the same night. But on New Year's Day the Germans sent 800 planes against the Allied air bases and ports in France and the Low Countries. They lost 364 planes in that venture, and we lost 125.

The casualty tally for British civilians as a result of German operations in the month of December was 367 dead and almost 900 wounded. For the people of London and other vulnerable locations, the war was not over.

The Cologne sorties brought Wally's crew to within two trips of being screened, the required number of trips being 30. Several of the crews we had trained with had already done their

30 trips and were on their way home or to instructional jobs in the United Kingdom. w/c Jake Eastman had been screened during the month of December and had taken over the Snowy Owl Squadron.

w/c Freddie Sharp was one of the few squadron commanders who still had to complete his first tour. He had graduated from the Royal Military College at Kingston as a flier before the war. Squadron and flight commanders made fewer trips than other types, as Command didn't like to have to replace them too frequently. Heads of sections, like bombing, navigation, gunnery and radio-communication, were similarly restrained, and they conse-

Wing Commander Freddie Sharp, the last CO of the Goose Squadron. He would later become Lieutenant General Sharp, chief of Canada's Defence Staff

quently did not fly with regular crews but only as spares when they were required. I had a feeling that Freddie Sharp would try to make up for his slow start, and as it turned out, I would help him do it.

The Gen Crew, however, would wait a while for its last Op. We were going on leave.

CHAPTER 33

Fun and Games on Leave in Scarborough

B omber crews could go on night after night without relief (although the media liked to dramatize the doghouse aura of fighter squadrons), but when leave came they were ready for it. They played as hard as they fought. There was lots of recreational activity on and about the base, but standbys kept us from going to York or Scarborough. While we were on standby we could be called up at a moment's notice to prepare for an Op.

We often had impromptu parties at the mess – sometimes a dance with girls bussed in from surrounding villages – and often when the evening was just getting started someone on the PA would announce, "All operational aircrew (that meant all aircrew on the battle order) will attend briefing at 0400 hours." You left the party at once and hit the sack. When there was a stand down, all Ops were scrubbed, and you could leave the base.

There was a kind of attic over the mess hall, and we surreptitiously rigged up a "bowling alley" there. Doubtless, the strange noises that emanated from the ceiling of the mess contributed to the notion that the mess was haunted.

We used the mess lounge as a caveman football field at times. The canisters filled with sand for cigarette butts were lined up as goal posts at either end of the room, and 408 and 426 squadrons would go at each other, using a towel tied up into a ball. In due course the canisters would be upturned and the sand strewn over the carpets. Although shooting dice was still taboo, it was tolerated (the winco was in fact often involved) because it helped operational aircrew to relax and forget the war. The non-commissioned aircrew billeted at Beninbrough had their celebrations as well, which is why the paintings on the walls there had been boxed in. The carpets had been taken up, also. Impromptu parties were held in the respective flight rooms (each aircrew trade had digs of their own), a barrel of beer would be ordered from a nearby brewery – this was not difficult to do in England – and unplugged with fervour. These sessions were usually esoteric, with talk of navigation or gunnery, et cetera, and about women. (Politics and religion were not popular subjects.) Much of the beer would be swamping the floor by the time the soiree came to an end.

We all liked pubbing. At the Blacksmith's Arms in Newton, and the Downay Pub, we would play darts and push-ha'penny with the locals. In York we would look for old friends in from other squadrons, and go in search of new pubs, like the Punch Bowl, in the shadow of the "Shambles." And after "Time, Gentlemen, please!" we would stand in queues waiting for taxis to take us back to base. Sometimes, when operational crews were ordered back to their bases, lorries would gather us up and take us home. It was not unusual that a German intruder would come in to strafe, if the lorry's headlamps were not properly masked.

There were serious moments, too, when letters came from home. Reta wrote every day, and I cherished her letters. I received a parcel from my new daughter, Joanie, containing a pair of socks and three licorice suckers. Most of us went to chapel now and then, and occasionally on a Sunday we would cycle to a village church. They all seemed so old. Some of the boys were getting married in these old churches, and even in the minster.

A young WAG from Nova Scotia joined 408 late in the war. Sgt. Doug Havill had been held up at Bournemouth. He missed a number of postings to training stations and when he inquired as to the reason for the delay he was told that, as an American, he was going to be transferred to the US Air Force. Then he remembered that he had been born in the United

States while his parents were temporary residents there. Doug explained that he was a Canadian and didn't want to be transferred to the US Air Force. He was then posted at once, to Linton, but was late in joining a squadron and so unable to complete his tour before the war's end. Doug had lived in Halifax, and later in a community just three miles from my hometown. We became friends, but I didn't see very much of him, as he had met a pretty little lady from Broadway, near Honeybourne, and went there whenever he could. Broadway was an entrancing place, just six miles from historic Evesham. It was known as "the show village of England." It had long broad streets and gracious houses made from honey-coloured Cotswolds stones, with dormer windows. The Broadway Hotel was affable, the 16th-century Lygen Arms picturesque, and the Irish Inn charming – all of which was wasted on Doug, as he didn't drink. But he got his heart's desire and married his girl, and she came home with him to Canada.

There were a number of personnel changes when Freddie Sharp came to Linton. Clare Annis had been succeeded by G/C Pleasance as station commander. New flight commanders replaced others who had been screened. F/L Newt Brydon, DFC, of Berwick, Nova Scotia, had completed his second tour as a bomb-aimer, making way for Hamish to become bomb leader. LaPierre, one of the French Canadians from Guelph Wireless School, arrived at Linton and told me that Warrant Officer Stone, also of Guelph, had been on 426 Squadron and had gotten the chop. I hadn't even known he was at Linton.

Some of my crew and I went to Northallerton hospital to see navigator Jack Rae, who had jumped from Buzz Hopper's aircraft as it was crash landing. He broke his legs and most of his other bones, and lost an eye, but he survived. He was the only one in the crew that did.

Jack and Harold McKinley, the squadron twins, were screened. Although twins could serve on the same squadron they were not allowed to be in the same crew. We also had a new padre, who had just arrived from Canada and was ensconced in a room next to mine in the headquarters mess.

(My move from the tomato can went with my promotion to flight lieutenant.) The day he arrived there was an air-raid warning – "Prepare to take cover!" We could hear the padre moving furniture against the windows, which amused us. (I had never used the station air-raid shelter. On this occasion we heard a bomb explode somewhere in the distance.)

My promotion also obligated me to assume the position of deputy signals leader, and I found myself briefing WAGs before they left on trips. I made up the Battle Order, putting appropriate WAGs up on the chalkboard. They complained to me when I put my name there, saying I did it too often, that they wanted to get home, too. When this happened I would immediately remove my name. I tried to bolster the courage of the WAGs, those who had never faced flak before. I would give them an envelope before they took off and tell them only to open it if they were seriously frightened. If the envelope was unopened it would be returned to me and they would never know what was in it. But it was a source of pride to these young men that they did not have to admit they were afraid. None of the envelopes was ever opened, but this is what was written inside:

> From Psalm 91
> ... He is my refuge and my fortress,
> My God; in him will I trust ...
> He will cover thee with his feathers,
> And under his wings shalt thou trust,
> His truth shall be thy shield and buckler;
> Thou shalt not be afraid for the terror by night;
> Nor for the arrow that flieth by day,
> Nor for the pestilence that walketh in darkness,
> Nor for the destruction that wasteth at noonday;
> A thousand shall fall at thy side
> And ten thousand at thy right hand,
> But it shall not come nigh thee."

On squadron they were trying to decide what to do with P/O Coombs who had waited to join a squadron before announcing that he was a "conscientious objector." Usually, anyone who refused to fly operationally was classified LMF (lacking moral fibre) and a poor view was taken of him by other fliers.

While the Gen Crew was on leave, Hamish and I made a short visit to Edinburgh, he to visit relatives and I to get in more class-time at the university. We visited Tommy's Bar. We always ordered the same drink when we were there – rum and mineral water, and a half-pint of beer as a chaser. This was an unusual drink in Scotland, and every time Hamish and I went there, the barmaid remembered us. Sure enough, this time she came up to us and said, "Will you have the same, Sir?" Al was in Kettering, the shoe capital. Vaughan and George were in London, and Wally and Howie were in Scarborough, where we were all going to meet up, at Doris's. It would probably be our last leave together as a crew.

In Scarborough, we lounged around in the mornings, waiting for the pubs to open, and in the evenings, at 7 o'clock, we converged on the Royal Hotel.

Almost everyone I knew had a girlfriend. Sometimes she was romantic, sometimes she was just a friend, a gentle feminine person to talk to. Vaughan Glover was the exception. We often had a good laugh to see him squirming to avoid a girl who fancied him. My girlfriend was Dorothy, our hostess at Doris's. I saw her almost every time I went to Scarborough. We danced together. We talked and laughed. She tried to refine my lifestyle. I tried to convince her that all colonials did not deserve her harsh stereotyping – "If you meet one you meet them all," she would say. I don't think either of us succeeded, but I did enjoy being with her and I benefited from her womanly tenderness, which was the thing servicemen away from home missed and needed most.

We watched workmen removing the concrete barriers and barbed wire from Scarborough beaches. There was within us a strange intermingling of sadness and triumph at knowing that the great adventure of our lives was soon to end.

F/O Brian Lanktree, Sgt. Fred Ward and F/L Jake Easton examine a Halifax mauled by German fighters on a night raid. Easton later became the commander of 408.

CHAPTER 34

The Gen Crew is Screened

In the first four months of 1945 there were 36 major raids against urban targets in Germany. This was all-out war, not only against industrial targets, but against personnel. This contrasted somewhat with earlier concerns about civilians – "… attacks must be made with reasonable care to avoid undue loss of civil life in the vicinity of the target.…" Crews seriously worried about civilians in the early days, but emphasis was later placed on the operational objective. In addition to the relentless bombing of Berlin by Mosquitoes, there were high-density assaults on cities like Dortmund (to which Bomber Command ordered two night-raids, of 528 and 107 aircraft, respectively), Dresden (805 aircraft), Munich (654) and Bonn (238). The magnitude of these operations is astounding, especially since enemy opposition was becoming more pathetic as time wore on. The Luftwaffe's last raid on Britain was on March 4, and two days later the last rocket fell, on Ditchingfield, Hertshire. Around the North-Sea coastline the defences were being removed. But Goose Squadron Halifaxes were still going out at dawn, and in the dark, to further the damage to cities that were already beyond repair. Much of the air action at this stage was in support of Allied troops still fighting a stubborn war on the continent. Bitsy Grant, the same Bitsy Grant who had been too young to go into the beverage rooms in Prince Rupert, was making a name for himself by destroying trains in the tactical force's operations.

I had already done three 13th trips – Wally's, Al's and my own – and we would now do the two final sorties that would end the Gen Crew's career together. We bombed Ludwigshafen, on the bank of the Rhine, opposite Mannheim, on the second day of January. It was a surprisingly hairy-do, with lots of enemy fighters. This was Howie's last trip. Three days later, using two spare gunners (which made us a bit nervous), we bombed Hanover. It was Wally's last operation, and another "last op" for me. Hanover was not an easy prang, and we were harassed by squadrons of fighters. One of our Hallies was lost – carrying F/L Scheeler as captain and Frank Leithead as WAG.

All of this is remarkable in retrospect. We had done considerable "morale bombing" already, but its value was lost in view of the fact that the Germans had been exhorted successfully by Hitler to fight to the end. Throughout the war, the Führer had prepaid for this last-ditch stand by allowing the continued production of consumer goods: cosmetics, typewriters, electric blankets, refrigerators. In the spring of 1945, the strategic bombing offensive did contribute considerably to the destruction of Germany's ability to continue the war. But Air Marshal Harris had reported as early as 1943 that 19 German cities had been virtually destroyed. (That this assessment was premature was affirmed by the fact that we were still bombing places like Hanover and losing lives in doing so.)

A whole year before our January raid, Flight Lieutenant Charles Owen had noted that the fires of Hanover, from a raid the previous night, could be seen as he approached. Owen was actually returning from a raid on Berlin and passed over Hanover by mistake. He was coned by searchlights for seven minutes, and was lucky to survive. As we approached Hanover on this cold January night we encountered the same searchlights, and bags of fighters. There was still plenty of sting in the Nazi viper, though Germany's utilities – its gas, electric power, water and rail systems – were in chaos. In fact, the weight of the Allied offensive at this time, the dispatching of hundreds of bombers on a single target, seemed to be motivated less by need than by the fact that Bomber Command had the equipment and manpower available to do it.

On the day the Gen Crew broke up, the following item appeared in one of the London papers:

More than 1,100 United States 8th Army Flying Fortresses and Liberators, escorted by more than 300 Mustangs and Thunderbolts yesterday attacked four aerodromes and landing grounds in the vicinity of Bonn, Cologne and Euskirchen road and rail bridges and junctions along the German-Belgian frontier at the mouth of the Ardennes salient, and a large railroad at Karlsruhe.

In the 51 days since Rundstedt launched his offensive the United States 8th Air Force has dropped 185,000 bombs, totalling 40,000 tons. Cologne is now the most bombed city. The total weight of bombs dropped on it amounts to 13,250 tons.

A week later, this item appeared in the same paper:

When the war broke out Canada had six warships and 1,800 naval men. Today Canada has 350 warships – the majority built in Canada – and personnel totalling 95,000. On the North Atlantic route Canadian warships have helped to convey 160,000 tons of supplies.

The paper quoted the Hon. Angus L. Macdonald, Canada's minister for naval affairs, who was in London at the time, and said, "We are going to take part in the Pacific war, but the first great task is to finish the war with Germany."

It was appropriate that Macdonald should mention the war in the Pacific, since all operational members of 408 Squadron had just been canvassed for participation in that campaign once they were free of commitments in Germany. It was on a voluntary basis, of course. We were given a form to sign. I was the only man in my crew to sign up – but I had vowed to stay with it until there was no more fighting to do. Enthusiasm on the squadron in general was something less than spectacular, and we were soon approached again. This time the response was better, and Wally signed up.

I still had nine trips to do to finish my tour. I was becoming more active as a signals leader, but I continued to post my name on the battle order when there was a crew needing

(Top) "Pappy" Snider's crew on the Goose Squadron, at time of screening.
(Bottom) Flight Sergeant gunners Tom Romanchuk and Don Shutka

(Top) LeRoy Pitu (left) and friends. He had planned to team up with Hank for a Pathfinder tour. (Bottom) F/O M.A. Greenbury's crew posing on the rear gun turret of their Halifax

a spare. I realized that this was a chancy way to go, given the number of first, 13th and last trips I might have to do. But I wasn't all that superstitious, and I put myself in the hands of fate.

Wally left Linton for a job at Air Force Headquarters. Hamish was staying on as bombing leader and, like me, would have to finish his tours as a spare. Vaughan, Al and Howie were at Bournemouth Repatriation Centre, waiting to go home. George went back to the Royal Air Force, where he eventually became a squadron leader with the military police in Hong Kong. Hamish and I were in different billets now, so I bought out the shares the others had in the record player, and continued to take inspiration from Addinsell's "Warsaw Concerto."

On February 7 I flew with F/L Sanderson and his crew to Goch, near the Dutch border, where the First Canadian Army was engaged in force fighting. "Friendly fire" was a hazard in this kind of support operation, but it was good to know that we were giving direct help to our fellow Canadians. There were 400 aircraft on this raid, and I think it was the worst Op I was ever on. There was a lot of fighter action, and we picked up some holes from tracer shells. But the real danger on that Op was the crew. It was their first trip, and they were entirely unprepared for it. The intercom discipline was such that I usurped the privilege of the pilot and broke in to get the gunners to concentrate on the enemy instead of their sexual conquests of the night before. We were attacked by JU-88s, and it was only by sheer luck that we weren't shot down. The gunners' procedure was atrocious. Instead of saying something like, "Enemy aircraft approaching from the starboard beam, prepare to corkscrew, go!" the gunners would say, "Look out!" and expect the captain to know what they meant. Three of our aircraft were destroyed, and we saw one of them explode just off our starboard side. Another could be seen spiralling earthward, burning. We saw no parachutes.

I told Sandy when we got back that I would not fly with him again, hoping that this would encourage him to discipline his crew. A few nights later he did not return from an operation over Worms.

I had a lot of leave during this period and went often to Edinburgh and London, but it wasn't the same without the others.

My next Op was in March. Spring had come to England, and it was strange to leave the entrancing smell of roses to bomb strange cities in a country long since stripped of its natural beauty. I outranked the pilot, Warrant Officer Ron Craven, but the rule was that the pilot was always captain of the aircraft, regardless of rank. Craven was something else. A spare, tall man, he had fierce eyes (like Buzz Beurling) and complete confidence. But he was contemptuous of rules and regulations (like Buzz Beurling). When his gunners directed him to "Corkscrew, go!" he would say, "What do you want to do: spoil your aim?"

We went off together into the wild dark yonder on a nine-hour flight to Chemnitz. Chemnitz was just south of Berlin, deep into the enemy's camp, which accounted for the long flight. To make a bomb load worthwhile we had to skimp on fuel. Three of our Hallies ran into icing over the base after takeoff, and crashed. We were all aware of this, but Craven was a great pilot and the crew was well disciplined in the air. The weather had closed in over most of the Midlands when we returned, so we were diverted to Honeybourne. That was G/C Lane's domain, and the following morning as we were all slouched against the control tower, Lane walked by. I jumped to my feet and saluted. The others, all NCOs, held their ground, ignoring the station commander. Lane just shook his head and walked on, an eloquent deference to operational aircrew.

As this was happening, my friend Bill (Gibby) Gibson of Halifax was just being liberated from Stalag Luft III (A), by Russians in a U.S.-built Sherman tank. It was at Stalag Luft III that the "Great Escape" had occurred. Seventy-six airmen had tunnelled out of the camp and fled. Only three of the 76 made it to Britain. Fifty others were shot by the Gestapo.

Bill had joined the air force when he was 17½, and was trained as an air gunner. He joined No. 409 Moose Squadron, located at Middleton-St.-George, and did 10 trips as a tail-gunner in a Lancaster before being shot down. He escaped from his burning aircraft, and encountered the Maquis (the French Underground) before the Germans could reach him. They rigged him out in civilian clothes. This was to be his undoing, as he was eventually captured by the Gestapo and, because he was dressed as a civilian, he was charged as a spy and sent to Buchenwald concentration camp, where he was to be executed. Fortunately, however, the Red Cross identified him as an airman, and he was transported to a prisoner-of-war camp for the duration. His POW number was 8090. Bill would live to go home to Canada on the troopship *Mauretania*, much to the elation of his mother, who had been advised six months before that he was presumed dead.

I flew with F/L Ed Finch to Dorsten on his screening trip. Another last trip. There was a great deal of smoke from the oil installations we bombed. But we only saw six puffs of flak. On the way back we flew in formation with F/L Pitu. Pitu was another devil-may-care pilot whom I got to know. I planned to join his crew so we could offer ourselves to the Pathfinder force for the "Second Phase."

Shortly after this, I was seconded by 426 Squadron. Apparently they had no spares. The crew had only one more trip to do, and they wanted to get it over with, despite being short a WAG. I am vague on the details of this trip, as it is not recorded in my logbook. Obviously, someone at 408 had said to the commander of 426, "We have a spare WAG. Take him."

It started out as a ho-hum trip that left just before sundown. We reached the target, an area in France where Allied armies were clashing with the Germans in heavy tank and artillery warfare. Our target was supply lines. They should have been assigned to the tactical air force, but as the war wound down, smaller numbers of bombers were being dispatched to such objectives. The trip was a piece of cake until after we released the baggage, when an isolated gun-post shot a volley in our direction. There was no more ack-ack action after that, but the one volley had been enough. The starboard engine had been hit. It was not on fire, but the tail unit was damaged, which made it impossible for us to manoeuver. We calculated that we could not make it back to the North Sea, so we decided to find a landing field on our homeward course that could take us. No one wanted to bail out, so the pilot looked in his black book for a station in France to call for an emergency landing. A small landing field in France responded and we made a safe landing.

I was disappointed that this episode in my air force career wasn't more dramatic, like it was in escape movies. It totally lacked the suspense and intrigue one might expect from making a forced landing at night in unidentified territory. The French Underground showed up, but it was only routine. There were no behind-the-lines heroics (although the pilot may well have received the DFC for his efficient handling of the damaged aircraft, as Bomber Command put a lot of emphasis on the safety of the aircraft as well as on the safety of the crew!).

The following day we hitched a ride on a plane going to England.

A few days later I did my last Op. We flew in W-Willie, and Wing Commander Sharp was the pilot. We had flown together on a few cross-countries, more for his benefit than mine, just to practise working together. He had a make-up crew, a motley bunch, including most of the section heads. (Jim Murdock was the bomb-aimer.) It would have been an expensive trip if anything had happened. It was a daylight raid on Munster. Our objective, among other things, was to destroy a ball-bearing factory. We had great fun over that. Imagine the air over the target filled with unrestrained ball bearings. For the first time in our lives we understood how important the ball bearing is in the function of moving mechanical parts. There wasn't much flak, but it was accurate, and we were struck twice in the belly. The sky was cloudless over the target, but the defensive action became less effective under the smoke from the fires below. We could see one of our aircraft falling towards earth, burning and out of control, as it cascaded downward in bits and pieces of burning debris. Then another blew up in our air space. A Lancaster also exploded after being hit, and no parachutes could be seen. No enemy fighters were in evidence. Perhaps they had been shot down by rebellious ball bearings. But we were relieved to observe a Mustang and a Spitfire covering for us. Freddie Sharp had had thousands of flying hours back in Canada, and he was a good pilot. On the west side of the Rhine we could see hundreds of gliders in the fields below, where they had landed after unloading invasion troops. Base was clouded over as we approached England and 408 aircraft were being diverted to other bases. The Winco, however, landed at base, using the beam (the beam was a radar system which allowed a skilled pilot to home in on coordinated aural signals). This performance would win for him the "Immediate Distinguished Flying Cross."

With the Munster sortie, the war ended for me.

CHAPTER 35

The Horror of
Belsen Death Camp

In retrospect it seems curious that servicemen – and I am thinking particularly of airmen, as they rarely had an opportunity to encounter the enemy face to face, as soldiers did – knew very little about the Nazi death camps until very late in the war, when some of these camps were liberated by the Allies. We had heard stories about the Jews being bullied by the Nazis, about their homes and possessions being confiscated, but the reality of the Holocaust just did not sink in, perhaps because it was too inhuman to be believed. We knew that the Jews had been persecuted through all of history, and in particular that the German people had been frightened of their wealth and influence and power. We knew vaguely of the anti-Semitic demonstrations in Central Europe in the early 1930s, when synagogues had been burned, sometimes with the people still inside them. And we knew that Heinrich Himmler, a one-time chicken farmer, was Hitler's hatchetman with respect to the Jewish question, and that he relished the task. We knew that he had ordered the construction of a concentration camp at Auschwitz, in Poland, as early as April 1940. But we thought that it was merely a holding camp for Jews who would then be exchanged for German nationals abroad.

The irony, of course, was that the Jews were not welcome abroad, either. They were not welcome in South America (except, perhaps, in Argentina), in Cuba, or in the United States. By contrast, there were 60,000 Jews in the British armed forces. Thirteen thousand of them, including women, were in the Royal Air Force).

So, while we had some idea that the Nazis were engaging in systematic persecution of the Jews, we had little idea of the full scope of the genocide they had planned – and indeed put into practice. In March 1942 (around the same time that the German U-boat campaign off the American coastline was stepped up), the concentration (read "extermination") camps at Auschwitz, Chelmos, Treblinka and Belsen were converted to death camps. The horrors of these camps, and others, are now well documented.

Auschwitz, in Upper Silestia, Poland, covered 18-square miles, and was originally set up in 1939. Commanded by Rudolph Hess, it became probably the worst and the most brutal of all the death camps. But then, how can it be said that death was more terrifying in one camp than in another? Curiously, the commercial heart of Auschwitz was known as "Canada." It was here that the confiscated valuables of the Jews were sorted, and where their ashes were converted into fertilizer. There was also the infamous Dachau, outside Munich, which had been established as early as 1933. (Thirty-two thousand prisoners would be released from Dachau in April of 1945.) There was Theresien, commanded by the sadistic Dr. Sigfried Seidl, which went by the chilling euphemism "State Old People's Home." This sadist, who was later commandant at Belsen, was executed after the war. There were other camps, too: Chelmo, Flossenburg, Ravensbruck, Natzviller. There was Trablinka, in Poland, where more than 700,000 Jews were sent; only 40 would survive. The Nazis operated a mass-murder site in the woods at Borki, where Soviet prisoners of war and Italian soldiers, among them Jewish children, were killed and then buried in lime. At Cracow ghetto, in Poland, the walls were designed in the shape of Jewish tombstones; the Nazis, it seems, were making no secret of their intentions. And yet, they did go to some lengths to try to conceal the atrocities being committed at the death camps. Civilians who lived in the areas of these camps always claimed they knew nothing of the goings-on there.

In fact, the camps – which were usually isolated from large

Boxcar that brought Jews to the Belsen death camp

centres and somewhat remote from the nearby villages – were cottage industries. Local farmers grew the produce and raised the chickens that would feed camp personnel. (Little food went to the inmates.) Tradesmen – cobblers, plumbers, carpenters – did maintenance work at the camps. The villagers, directly or indirectly, profited from the agony of the Jews. It is hard to imagine that they would have seen the smoke coming from the chimneys, or smelled the sweet smell of burning bodies, without knowing what was happening.

The only thing saving the German people from eternal guilt is that it is difficult to see what they could have done to stop what was happening. The pattern of hate had been established centuries before. In 1543 Martin Luther, the German leader of the Protestant Reformation, said, "All Jews in the town should be put under one roof or in the stables, like Gypsies." He continued: "... if they were too dangerous, these poisonous bitter worms, should be stripped of their belongings which they have usuriously extorted from us, and driven out of the country...." More than four centuries later, Adolph Eichmann, the overseer of the extermination plan, would declare that he could go to his grave happy that he had helped kill six million Jews. (He was executed by the Jews in Israel in 1960.)

Belsen concentration camp was infamous for its zeal in contributing to the "Final Solution," continuing the murder right up to the end of the war. It never let up. Even when the officials there knew the war was lost they continued to fuel the ovens with human bodies.

Belsen was near the village of Belsec, just 10 miles from the Ukraine border. The Ukranians had no love for the Jews, and many of them collaborated in the killing. During the first three months of 1945, tens of thousands of Jews from slave-labour camps throughout central and eastern Germany were literally dumped at Belsen. Forty-five rail cars stinking with excrement and decomposing bodies arrived bearing 6,000 people still living. (Some of the Jews never made the trip in the first place. If they were too old or too sick to get on the boxcars they were shot. That they were not all shot can be attributed to the fact that the Nazis wouldn't have known what to do with the bodies.)

When they arrived at Belsen the Jews were driven with whips and ordered to strip and give up their valuables, including artificial limbs and eyeglasses, virtually the last possessions they had. The women had their hair cut off, as it could be made useful in the operation of submarines. And then they all stood naked, still believing that the men were to be employed in street-work projects and that the women would do housework. Over the loudspeaker, a voice told them: "Nothing is going to hurt you. Just breathe deep. It's a good disinfectant." Then they were marched, without resistance, to the gas chamber. As the camp commandant flailed his whip over them they were packed so tightly into the bare rooms that they could not fall down.

When the bodies were taken from the chambers there were dentists waiting to open the dead mouths with iron hooks and to knock the teeth out if they contained gold. The bodies were then thrown into ditches where they bloated in the sun until they could be disposed of in lime pits.

At the Natzviller concentration camp, the prisoners were systematically separated by sex, age, race and profession. The professors gathered in one group. The homosexuals in another; soldiers, priests, anarchists, socialists, criminals and Gypsies clustered in conglomerates of their own. The Germans had a use for all of them – even unto death – for medical and psychological experimentation, for slave labour, for sadistic pleasure.

The victims travelling to the death camps, on the so-called resettlement transports, carried with them a bizarre collection of possessions they valued. When they arrived, other Jews, who were told they would survive if they helped, stacked the prams in one pile and the pots and pans in another, shoes in another, photographs and paintings, and even plants, in others still. The prisoners' overcoats, with the yellow arm bands of identification, ended up in the clothing pile – no longer of use to their owners, these garments could still be recycled for the profit of others. Toothpaste tubes were squeezed out on the spot, because the Jews tried to hide jewels in them. The Jews had retained all of these items, of course, in the hope that they might still have a later life in which to enjoy them.

The British army liberated Belsen on 13 April 1945. They found 10,000 dead bodies still unburned and still unburied. By coincidence, the man who had looked forward so passionately to seeing the camps liberated had died the day before. President Roosevelt's death cast a pall of sorrow and regret over Great Britain and over the armies fighting the final battles on the continent.

My role in the Belsen epic came about unexpectedly. Although I had been on the squadron longer than any other crew member, except for Hamish, I had only done my last Op on March 25, and received the coveted operational wings (with a bar). I was still the only spare WAG on the squadron, however, and apparently on the station. On April 15 I was seconded by the Thunderbird Squadron again to make up a crew going on a special assignment. The special assignment was to transport a group of VIPs, representing a cross-section of British officialdom, to Belsen concentration camp. It was quick thinking on the part of those who were running the Allied war efforts (and those who would be running the peace after the war) to show government, social and community leaders that the Holocaust had indeed happened. There were about a dozen people in the group, men and women, who had been selected and gathered together for this purpose. I knew none of them, but most, if not all, were from the United Kingdom. A Lancaster had been hurriedly rigged out to accommodate seats for the unusual passengers, and they silently climbed up the ladder and settled themselves inside the aircraft. They were the only payload. We carried no bombs, though we had gunners. The last stages of the war were still being fought.

The Lanc landed at an airfield some distance from the village of Belsec and the group was loaded into a bus and driven to the prison camp. Someone had thought of making up box lunches, which was a practical but un-useful idea, under the circumstances. Since I was not part of the special coterie, I assumed that my presence on the bus was to take care of the box lunches.

We were discharged in the village and then transferred to automobiles and driven to Belsen camp itself. We entered the camp proper through gates now being monitored by British soldiers.

The camp straddled the railroad tracks (a spur line of the regular tracks that ran through the village), which led directly to the square in which the prisoners had answered their names at roll call. The Nazis were curiously meticulous in keeping records of their victims. Flanking the square was the shed in which the belongings of the Jews were collected. Near this were separate undressing barracks for males and females. This fastidious respect for modesty seemed grossly at odds with the indignity to which the prisoners were otherwise exposed. In this area there was another shed in which the women were shorn of their hair, in much the same way as sheep are shorn of their wool. Just beyond this were the gas chambers. Down a dirt road from the gas chambers were five large areas designated as mass graves.

There was a barracks near the gate leading to the gravesites which housed Jewish slave labourers. Removed somewhat from all this was a compound for Ukrainian guards. Surrounding the entire camp was a high barbed-wire fence with watch towers at three of its corners. There was a fourth tower located in the centre of the compound.

The Germans must have operated this killing field right up to the time the British army tore down the gates. The extermination plan was an utter failure. Not only was the evidence of the massacre unconcealed, but it was clear that the crematorium ovens had not been able to handle more than a fraction of the accumulated corpses.

The inspection group was formally recognized by a British general (and, I seem to recall, by a representative of the Red Cross) and was escorted around the camp. The ovens, overshadowed by the sinister, towering chimney, still held bodies, only partially cremated. The open burial pit contained thousands more, their identities lost forever, their dignity destroyed. Germans from Belsec had been commandeered to do some of the grisly disposal work. We felt strangely sorry for them as they picked up bodies and placed them in carts, for removal to a burial plot. In lieu of gloves, they used paper and bits of fabric to grasp the wrists of the dead, lest the decomposed flesh strip off in their bare hands. The employment of the villagers in this manner was a kind of punishment for their having denied the crimes taking place at Belsen and elsewhere.

The citizens of Belsec would never again deny the crimes of their fellow men, however. The stench was almost too much to bear, and people working at the pits vomited in their masks. The reek of rotting human flesh permeated the entire camp and many of the officials succumbed to it and became ill. It would be a smell that would recur to them psychologically for the rest of their lives.

Six-hundred thousand human beings had been murdered at this place. Among them was Anne Frank, a German Jewish girl who, with her family, had lived for two years above a Dutch warehouse in Amsterdam. The family was discovered after a local informed on them in August 1944. Anne was sent to this ghoulish place, where she died of typhus at the age of 15, just two months before the camp was liberated. In her diary she had the grace to say she believed "in spite of everything, that people are truly good at heart."

As my eyes surveyed this devastation – and as my mind came to realize the full scope of the wickedness explicit here – I wondered how this had been allowed to happen by literate people, people who could build bridges and compose beautiful music, who loved their children, and who could pray to a God they recognized. The horror of seeing the victims, their nondescript bodies – or what was left of their bodies – entwined in lime pits with the bones of their friends, their parents, their children; of those dead eyes – if they had not yet rotted from the sockets – without a fire left in them; the horror of that remains with me to this day. The validity of war could never again be denied, it seemed to me, insofar as that war was fought to prevent or avenge a human tragedy such as this one.

It made me ashamed of the human race.

CHAPTER 36

Last Days of the War

S o much was happening in Europe in April 1945 that the significance of my experience at Belsen did not register in my mind then as it would later. With Belsen liberated, there seemed no point in Germany's resisting; this was further reinforced by the announcement of Hitler's death on April 12. Yet at Linton-on-Ouse there was business as usual. We couldn't understand why the war was being prolonged. On April 3 the squadron was briefed for an early-morning raid on Erfurt, but it was scrubbed because the Allies had already taken the manufacturing and cultural centre. There was a lot of that happening. We would be alerted for a mission to assist the ground troops, but before we could get airborne, the target would be captured by our armies. On April 18, the Goosers bombed Heligoland Island, a submarine and naval centre in northwest Germany. Pilot Officer Hull's aircraft exploded over the target. It took 94 minutes for all the aircraft to pass over the bombing flares.

British guns were shelling Hamburg, and Berlin was being bombed by the RAF every night, even as the 1st French Army occupied Stuttgart. The Canadian army advancing towards Amsterdam was under heavy fire.

On the 22nd we went to Bremen, but again did not bomb because of the presence of our own troops. On April 25, both squadrons at Linton did their final run, on Wangerooge Island, in the East Frisian Chain. The aircraft flown by Warrant Officer J. C. Tuplin collided in mid-air with another aircraft (W-William), flown by F/L Ely. Three days later Himmler made his peace offer, but it was rejected. Munich was captured by the Allies on April 29, the same day Mussolini was executed in

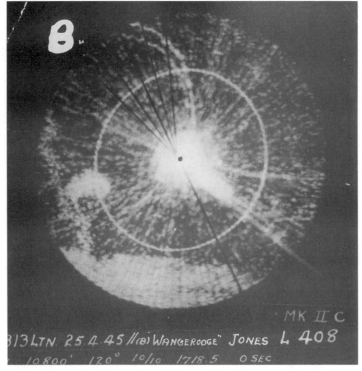

Radar picture of 408's last bombing raid, on Wangerooge, April 25, 1945

Italy. On the following day 408 Squadron had a muster parade
(we hadn't had one in all the time I was on the squadron), and
we were told that for us the German war was over. We were on
permanent stand down.

At about that time, I attended a conference at No. 6 Group
Headquarters, and learned for the first time of the plans
that were being made for the Second Phase in the Pacific. I
had never been to Group Headquarters before, and I was
impressed by the conglomeration of machinery and personnel
that had been employed in telling us what to do on dark nights
in flak-filled skies. When I appeared in the group signals section, and they saw the double stripes on my sleeve, I had an
instant job and instant promotion to squadron leader. I hadn't
realized it happened that way. A flight lieutenant WAG, still

involved in operations, indicated experience, and the officer in charge of the signals groups was aching to get home after having done two tours. I was his chance. I didn't even know what a group signals head did, but it didn't matter. I would have to wait for the Pacific to find out, in any case, as it looked like the shop at Group had closed down.

These were the plans for the reorientation of the Goose Squadron. All but two of 6 Group's squadrons would be flying home in Canadian-made Lancaster Mark Xs. The crews flying home would all be experienced, but with no more than 20 trips. Those with more than 20 trips would be screened and credited with a tour. They would not be sent to the East unless they volunteered. New crews would have no choice. They had volunteered for duty in the air force, had been trained for operations and still had to do a tour of duty to complete their obligations. All would be given a month's leave in Canada.

Those who had volunteered for the Second Phase would train at Canadian operational schools for seven weeks. Then they would return to England, by ship, where they would convert to Lincolns (a development of the Lancaster). Then they would return to Canada, en route to the Pacific. The "Tiger Force" was to be made up of eight RCAF bomber squadrons: 408, 419, 420, 425, 428, 431, 434 and 495.

Those of us who had signed up for the Second Phase were fascinated that so much had been put into planning our futures.

My own situation had become more complicated. I would fly home and then report to Greenwood Air Station for my Group signals duties. But earlier I had discussed with F/L Leroy Pitu the possibility of making up a crew and applying to the Pathfinders. This seemed even more plausible now, as the Thunderbirds had left Linton in April and had been replaced at Linton by No. 405 Pathfinder squadron. (Of course, in view of the new circumstances it was not certain what role 405 would play in the new operational set-up.) To further complicate things, Wing Commander Sharp also wanted a Pathfinder squadron, and he had prevailed on me to slow down the rate of trips I was taking to finish my tour so I could join his crew. This appealed to me, and I even started going on cross-country exercises with him, training for the flight back to Canada.

Hamish Murdock and I made one last trip to Edinburgh together. We went to another party at the Renton's, Hamish's Scottish relatives. This time they brought out the bottle of Scotch they had been saving for the defeat of the Germans. It was a little premature, but not unwarranted. Dusty bottles of Scotland's favourite stimulant, that were almost impossible to get during the war, were being brought out of hiding places all over Britain and shared with the uniformed men and women who had made the victory possible. Edinburgh was overflowing with servicemen, many of them up from Italy, where the Germans had surrendered to General Alexander.

The dance halls in Edinburgh were packed, and it seemed there were more civilian young people attending them, as though the approaching end to the war was their cue to take back their pleasure palaces from the colonial armies. Hamish and I went to a dance at the Palais. We were frisked at the door, apparently in an attempt to suppress rowdiness. Now that strong alcohol could sometimes be obtained for four pounds and 10 pence a quart, some of the dance halls were becoming rough. The Palais was as big as a hockey rink, and the music was continuous. One of the bands played "I'll Never Smile Again," which served to remind some of us from Overseas that we had made vows before we left home long years before. The song was written by a Torontonian named Ruth Lowe and was a smash hit when Tommy Dorsey and Frank Sinatra released it in 1940.

I walked a pretty lass home after the dance and she said to me, "You're the first man who iver said gie nicht to me by shakin my hand." I've never forgotten her.

We stayed at the Dominion Officers Club for five shillings a night. And we went back to Tommy's Bar for the last time. While we were in Edinburgh the English-language German propaganda program, "Germany Calls" (over Radio Hamburg), broadcast as usual. But now the announcer was an Englishman, or perhaps an American. We learned that German forces in Northwest Germany, and in Holland and Denmark, had surrendered, but that Norway was still in enemy hands.

We met a navy officer at the Dominion Club who had been involved in an attempt to sink the Tirpitz. Although it was No. 617 RAF Squadron that had eventually succeeded in sinking the Tirpitz on 12 November 1944, the officer's account made us realize that the air force wasn't alone in the war.

When Hamish and I returned to Linton we were struck by the inactivity. It was May 7 and all the German armies had surrendered. The quietness stretched over the entire aerodrome. All aircraft engines were silent, and the entire area looked like the backstage of a theatre that had closed for the season. The people who lived in the surrounding farming communities had waited patiently for five years for peace, and now that it was here they could not comprehend it. They could hardly believe that this "Last Post" meant quiet skies and rest. They had looked forward to this day for so long that they had forgotten what things had been like before the Blitz.

The powers that were did a commendable thing to compensate those proud people. Open House at Linton had been declared. People from the area were invited to visit the airfield and see close-up the aircraft they had only ever seen before in flight over their homes. Thousands of people thronged to Linton. They climbed into the standing Lancasters and Halifaxes and examined the positions where crew members had done their thing. They were shown the bomb dumps and were taken through the operational room, and they had explained to them how bombing sorties were organized. It was a marvellous public-relations project. Linton personnel were available everywhere to talk with the visitors, and felt proud to do so.

Aircrew at Linton, not on leave, were as confused as the civilians. We were seized by an ennui, and a feeling of uneasiness. For a long time we had known nothing but regimentation. This new thing we were experiencing would take some getting used to.

On the evening of May 7 some of us took the bus into York City. We had planned to go dancing at the deGrey Rooms, but had arrived a bit early, so we milled around with others, starting conversations and leaving them hanging, waiting for the doors to open. Everybody was talking about the German surrender. Suddenly a man appeared from the building and positioned himself on the stone steps in full view of everyone. He wore a white collar of the clergy. I couldn't tell whether he was a Catholic or a Protestant, and it didn't matter. Like Moses on the Mount, he raised his hand in supplication and started to pray. Instinctively, the onlookers all fell to their knees on the cobblestones. It was what they wanted to do, as though they had only been waiting for someone to lead them in expressing their spiritual gratitude.

I went down to London, where Great Britain was staging the greatest celebration of its history. For three days the city was crowded with revellers. Uniformed personnel from all three services, on leave from ships and army camps and air stations, streamed into the old capital. I wrote in my diary:

> Come with me among the cosmopolitan peoples who are rejoicing in this England. See with me the many splendoured expressions of elation and joy. Look into the hearts of these people, and read their thoughts. These people – service and civilian alike – who in allied effort have won the victory. It is three o'clock in the afternoon. There is standing-room only at Trafalgar Square, the pigeons have found roosts elsewhere. Piccadilly Circus has a sold-out performance, and I stand near Swan and Edgars, the meeting place of the world, and join in the spirited hurrahs. The Mall is shoulder to shoulder with people, laughing, waving flags and banners, and shouting, nothing intelligible, just the noise of happiness. There are thousands – nay millions – of people here. Suddenly, the shouting stops and like a seaside squall the silence drifts through the crowds as the voice of the Prime Minister can be heard from public announcement speak-

ers located everywhere. He speaks with fire, reminding us that the job is only half done. We still have enemies in the East. Then he ends with a typical Churchillian quote: "Long live the Allied unity; long live the cause of Freedom; God save the King." The applause is an unabated roar that lasts for minutes. A father has lifted his young son to his shoulders so that he may talk about this day when he is a man. A dog barks. Some prankish boys throw some fire crackers in the street and one of them explodes under a girl's skirt and burns the silk stockings she has saved for the occasion. A Sally Ann passes among the multitudes, holding a tambourine into which coins clatter generously, marking recognition of the Salvation Army's considerable part in the victory. A lady wears a formal gown and a feathered hat she has closeted for the duration, cherishing this opportunity to wear them.

In the evening I stood at Victoria's monument, facing the palace. The floodlights splashed against the balconies where the king and royal family had assembled. London had removed its blackout curtains and turned on the lights. The king spoke, but no one heard what he was saying because of the cheering that resounded along the Thames. It didn't matter. The crowds knew what he was saying: he was speaking for them. Among the gathered, however, the tragedy of the war could be seen in the faces of those who had lost their homes to the Hun, whose sons and daughters, mothers and fathers, wives and husbands, had paid the supreme price. It was not a hollow victory for them, but it was a sad one.

I left London, its restaurants serving real beefsteaks so soon, Lily Ann Carol still singing "I Walk Alone" on the Forces Radio, and the London side streets having parties they would never forget. I would not see this city again for a long time.

CHAPTER 37

Going Home

When the war ended, it was difficult back at Linton to read the faces in the mess, what thoughts might be behind them. Slowly the airmen began to realize that they had survived the war, that they had lives to live. Those who had not finished their tours were willing to trade the lost recognition for the privilege of going home safely. Still, the operational bods had become accustomed to the world of excitement they had lived in, and would be returning to a world they did not know. It was a letdown not to be doing Ops, not to feel the adrenaline coursing through your veins as you stretched your neck to see the destination for the night.

We started to train in earnest for the flight back to Canada. I was assigned to S/L Alex Bossenberry's crew, and started doing training flights and a lot of dinghy drill with him. Dinghy drill would pay off if we had to land somewhere on that great expanse of water that separated England from Canada. Bossenberry was from Grand Bend, Ontario, and all the members of his crew were commissioned.

Warrant Officer Cameron crashed his aircraft on one of those training flights. The ironic sadness did not escape the rest of us – that he had survived the war and succumbed to the peace.

We were getting used to the Lancasters, and a team-psychology was beginning to work through the crew. The radio equipment in the Lanc was Bendix, which I had used on 5 (BR) Squadron, so it was not a difficult adjustment. Bad weather plagued us during these days, however, and we had lots of time to visit breweries in Hull, York and Leeds. These were called "Sports Days."

My old friend Roy Cook, from the University of Toronto, had just been posted to the base as signals officer. Everyone was trying to get rid of the things they had been hoarding from their parcels from home, and Roy made a sandwich that helped the effort along. He started with a slice of cake and then a layer of dates, honey and peanut butter, from Ray Jones's grocery supplies. Then he added, from one of Reta's parcels, a fat Pilchard's sardine and a colourful layer of canned apricots, topped by several pieces of licorice, and then another slice of cake. It was a mundane happening, but the bizarre culinary creation took the place of Op-talk all over the station. How our priorities had changed since May 8.

The Goose Squadron was scheduled to fly home on June 16, and there was a great celebration in the mess the night before, a sad-happy event. It was my duty to rouse the NCOs at Beninbrough at 0400 hours, which I did. The NCOs had been celebrating, too, but, alas, with less restraint than the officers. As I entered the old mansion there was an ominous quiet. Not an NCO was about, but water from the firehoses was still cascading down the winding stairs. They had wrecked the place.

We left Linton-on-Ouse on schedule at 0810 hours, each of us carrying the allowable 80 pounds of luggage, and no heavy souvenirs. Both sides of the runway were lined with people to see us off, ground-crew types who had kept our aircraft in safe operation, the people who worked in the kitchen and the motor transport section, the people who looked after the parachutes, the post- office staff and so many others who had been part of that ten-to-one ratio of ground crew to aircrew. They were there to say goodbye. As we lifted off, I looked down to see them waving. We were thrilled, and sad.

> And now our task is done, I shake
> your hand and sigh,
> And wonder why it is so hard
> to simply say "Goodbye"

Our real departure point was at Land's End, the southern-

Jim Fitzsimmons's crew. Keith Hickey, Fitzsimmons, Ray Jones, Milton Knight, Bill Hepper, Fred Pratt and Frank Charlton

most tip of England, where palm trees mocked the chill of Yorkshire. We landed at St. Mawgan's, Cornwall, but were detained there for 24 hours while the Air Ministry determined what to do about the damage the NCOs had done to Beninbrough Hall. It was a time of embarrassment for us, as well as making us a day late in getting home.

Ray Jones, a bomb-aimer, his skipper Jim Fitzsimmons and I hitchhiked to a small community called Newquay, where we had a steak in a restaurant. On the way back we were picked up by a man in a long black limousine. The driver explained that he managed the Royal Estate at Newquay, and that the car in which we were driving belonged to the king. We were impressed.

When finally the squadron was released, we took off, losing one aircraft which crashed into the sea at the end of the runway. It was a tragic incident none of us was prepared for. We landed again at Lagen's in the Azores, the group of islands belonging to Portugal, on which air and naval bases had been granted to Great Britain. The flight had taken 6.25 hours, over

The entire 408 Squadron in front of a Halifax at Linton, before returning to Canada

water. I kept constant radio contact, sending messages to base (MTBs) and taking bearings on continental stations. I was fascinated by the extent to which communication had been perfected since I had become a WAG.

Lagen's was a Transport Command station. Hundreds of aircraft, of all stripes and designs, were parked there, and others were coming and going constantly from and to all points of the globe. Long lines of Liberator bombers flanked the runways. The climate, of course, was tropical, a contrast to the miserable weather we had been experiencing in England. The food we were given was excellent, à la stateside, and the beer, though sudsy and weak and in tins, was cold. English beer was never cold.

Goose Squadron aircraft left the Azores early in the morning of June 17, and set course due west. There were no enemy fighters, no flak. For the 165 airmen involved it would be the longest time they had ever been airborne.

I would report to base every hour on the hour (no security required). We would land at Gander, Newfoundland, to refuel, and have steaks and ice cream for lunch. Then we would complete the last lap home to our wives, sweethearts and families – only to leave them again to fight in another war. This was a time for old emotions to sharpen, for the recalling of last adieus and last kisses, memories which had been so long suppressed by time and distance. I felt a gnawing guilt that my plans involved another tour of duty, instead of strengthening a marriage just begun. Reta could never have suspected that the separation caused by the German war would continue with me in yet another foreign land.

Epilogue: Per Ardua ad Astra

As it turned out, there was to be no "Tiger Force," no Second Phase. The Americans dropped A-bombs on Hiroshima and Nagasaki, forcing the Japanese to surrender. August 15, 1945, was Victory in Japan Day. The Goose Squadron was disbanded – but it had fought a good fight, and had more than 210 Distinguished Flying Crosses, Distinguished Flying Medals, Distinguished Service Orders and other honours. The Royal Canadian Air Force had put 232,632 men and 17,030 women in blue uniforms. More than 17,000 had lost their lives in the fight for freedom. The peace challenged the world to make those sacrifices meaningful.

The cessation of hostilities had some immediate effects. Thousands of veteran airmen, who had lived so long on the edge, suddenly found themselves responsible for making decisions on their own and for preparing themselves to manage their leftover lives. Many of them were not up to it. They had stood up to the confrontation of death, but they could not meet the challenges of life. They had felt important when they were pranging cities and tasting cordite. Now they were back to where they started, prepared for nothing.

Most airmen succeeded in adapting to their new environment, however. In some ways, the war was good for Canada. It provided the nation with a new generation of leaders. Thousands of veterans were able to go to college. They trained, as they never would have done had there been no war, to be doctors, teachers, engineers and geologists. They took positions in high places, in science, in government, in business and industry. They embraced the opportunities they had fought for.

Those who failed to make the transition became a different kind of war casualty. Their marriages failed, their dreams evaporated. But they shared with their comrades the conviction that they had fought a just war for a grateful country. And there would never be anything in their lives that would eclipse that greatest adventure of all.

I can hear the sound of engines warming up at daybreak. I can hear the sound of glasses clinking in a thousand British pubs and the enchanting laughter of pretty girls. I can hear the enrapturing sounds of the Warsaw Concerto coming from our old record player. I can taste those operational bacon-and-egg meals. I can see the boyish faces of my crew, my dearest friends. They are all gone now. Wally and Vaughan were both awarded Distinguished Flying Crosses, so much deserved. Now they belong to the ages. I can hear the symbolic "Last Post," acknowledging all the magnificent young men on my squadron who missed the chance to grow up.

> Life to be sure, is nothing much to lose,
> but young men think it is, and we were young.

Gaspereau Press acknowledges the support of the Canada Council
for the Arts and the Nova Scotia Department of Tourism & Culture.

Typeset in Quadraat & Quadraat Sans by Andrew Steeves and
printed offset, Smyth-sewn and bound at Gaspereau Press,
Kentville, Nova Scotia.

Quadraat & Quadraat Sans were designed by Fred Smeijers,
Netherlands.

9 8 7 6 5 4 3 2 1

Library and Archives Canada Cataloguing in Publication

Hancock, Glen, 1919–
Charley goes to war : a memoir / Glen Hancock.

ISBN 1-894031-95-4
1. Hancock, Glen, 1919–   2. Canada. Royal Canadian Air
Force – Biography.   3. World War, 1939–1945 – Personal
narratives, Canadian.   I. Title.

D811.D297 2004   940.54'8171   C2004-905480-5

GASPEREAU PRESS   PRINTERS & PUBLISHERS
47 CHURCH AVENUE, KENTVILLE, NOVA SCOTIA
CANADA B4N 2M7